Endorsements for *Equipping*

Dr. Bob Kellemen knows that God has called all Christians to be active participants in the ministry community he designed the church to be. Bob also knows that it is not enough to give people a vision and call them to commitment—they must also be biblically trained. Equipping the body of Christ for personal ministry has been Bob's life work. This practical, step-by-step equipping manual is the mature fruit of that lifelong commitment.

—**Paul Tripp,** Founder and President of Paul Tripp Ministries,
Author of *Instruments in the Redeemer's Hand*

This is a must-read book for everyone who longs to see their church be more effective at helping people grow and handle the issues of everyday life. It is intensely biblical with a model that flows right out of the pages of Scripture. And it's equally practical. You'll be encouraged and equipped to be a person who…encourages and equips. My friend Bob Kellemen has done a masterful job at helping us strategize how to be truly effective in the culture in which Christ has placed us.

—**Steve Viars,** Senior Pastor, Faith Church, Lafayette, Indiana;
Author of *Loving Your Community*

Equipping Biblical Counselors is an excellent resource both for individual leaders and group discussion. The insights gained from years of experience by Dr. Kellemen and by the twenty-four best-practice churches is evident throughout the book. This is the book for you if you want to launch a biblical counseling ministry or want your church's current counseling ministry to move to a place of increased effectiveness.

—**Randy Patten,** Founder and Executive Director,
TEAM Focus Ministries

Bob Kellemen—trainer and coach extraordinaire—has a focused goal: He wants to see your church's one-on-one ministry transformed. The way he does that is by giving clear, practical instruction along with a full package of supplies and tools. And when you follow his coaching, you'll be surprised to find that the result is not so much Bob's system as it is an equipping model that is specific to your church.

—**Ed Welch,** Faculty and Counselor, CCEF,
Author of *Created to Draw Near*

So many of us long to see our churches equipped to minister the blessings of God's Word to one another. Yet somehow it seems all too easy to get bogged down in the *how*. Bob Kellemen has given the church a tremendous resource—outlining not only the *how* but also the *why* and most importantly the *who*. This is a resource that will revolutionize the way your church does ministry and will give you the resources you need to offer practical help from a many-membered body serving one another and their community.

—**Elyse Fitzpatrick,** Author of *Counsel from the Cross*

Do you ever wish someone would help you better envision, understand, organize, and implement personal ministry in your church? If so, this book is for you. After interacting with twenty-four ministry leaders, Dr. Kellemen serves as your personal coach, giving you insight on how to better serve the body of Christ. As you seek to serve those God has called you to help grow and maneuver through the challenges of life, this book will help you understand, plan, develop, and implement authentic and lasting personal ministry in your church.

—**Kevin Carson,** Pastor, Sonrise Baptist Church, Ozark, Missouri

Has your church come to the realization that your personal ministry of the Word needs to be more robust? So often we can see the destination that would better unleash God's glory, but we can't see the pathway that will take us there. Intimate knowledge of God's Word, decades of experience, and countless conversations have equipped Bob well to speak to you on this very point. He understands the gap and has invested his life in learning how to close it. *Equipping Biblical Counselors* is not a one-size-fits-all how-to manual. Rather it's a user-friendly workbook to guide you to God—your Guide who already knows the pathway laid out for your church for his glory.

—**Betty-Anne Van Rees,** Adjunct Faculty and Counsellor,
Heritage College and Seminary

Bob Kellemen's *Equipping Biblical Counselors* is a desperately needed gift to church leaders for helping the church to envision, enlist, equip, and empower the saints for the work of ministry. Bob's seasoned, insightful, and humble experience emerges in each chapter. I highly recommend this work whether you are just starting out or have been in the trenches for years. I was personally encouraged and challenged in addition to coming away with many ideas that I will use in my own ministry.

—**Robert Cheong,** Pastor of Care,
Sojourn Church Midtown, Louisville, Kentucky

There are people sitting in your church who don't realize the potential they have to impact lives. There are police officers, psychologists, physicians, teachers, nurses, and moms who are now biblical counselor/disciple-makers who would never have imagined that they could be used by the Lord to save marriages, help others deal with unruly emotions, and grow to be Christlike worshipers. Bob skillfully provides a user-friendly biblical strategy for how to train more like them by unleashing the potential of your church through training disciple-makers. Personal, impactful ministry is not just for the professionals, and Bob shows you why and how.

—**Ernie Baker,** Pastor of Counseling and Discipleship,
First Baptist Church of Jacksonville and Chair of the online
BA in Biblical Counseling, The Master's University

Dr. Kellemen has produced a landmark book that fills a significant vacuum in the biblical counseling literature. This is a comprehensive work that not only offers an exceptional overview of biblical counseling, but also provides a wise, strategic, and thoughtful guide outlining the essentials of developing a robust counseling ministry within the local church. *Equipping Biblical Counselors* has the potential to influence a massive paradigm shift in how ministry is exercised in the body of Christ both now and in future generations.

—**Jeremy Lelek,** President, Association of Biblical Counselors

Bob Kellemen knows equipping biblical counselors from A to Z. He has done a tremendous job of structuring a stepwise strategy to develop the lay counselors in your church. In his humble style, Bob has gathered the best leaders of local church counseling ministries and done the work of benchmarking for you. This is a book that you will reference often as you help the hurting and equip the saints for the work of soul care in your church.

—**Garrett Higbee,** Pastor of Biblical Soul Care,
Harvest Church North, Indianapolis, Indiana;
Leader Care Specialist for the Great Commission Collective

Dr. Kellemen's book fills a long-standing gap in biblical counseling and church-based ministry literature. It's an excellent resource for church leaders and counselors who are looking for practical biblical guidance, which includes instructions and all the necessary nuts and bolts for developing the one-on-one personal ministry component in their church's spectrum of care. It is marvelously comprehensive and systematic, while at the same time flexible enough to apply to a variety of church personalities.

—**Sam Williams,** Professor of Counseling,
Southeastern Baptist Theological Seminary

Equipping Biblical Counselors is invaluable for ministry leaders and for all one-another ministers. It paints a compelling biblical vision for the heart of church leadership—equipping God's people for ministry. When I had lost sight of this, Dr. Kellemen not only reminded me of this but rekindled my passion for this important calling. Bob also gives us practical coaching on how to actually do this. He does this not by giving us a prepackaged formula, but by giving us practical principles and tools that we can adapt to our own context.

—**Jeff Ballard,** Pastor of Soul Care,
College Park Church, Indianapolis, Indiana

Equipping Biblical Counselors fills a gaping void. Bob lays out a thorough theology and an adaptable strategy for training congregations in soul care that has been honed over his twenty-five years of ministry as a pastor, counselor, trainer, and consultant. Bob also shares insights from two dozen best-practices churches that have been guided by the New Testament's vision of soul care. As a result, *Equipping Biblical Counselors* provides a practical framework that has both the breadth and depth needed by a congregation to make an impact for Christ in today's world.

—**Jeff Forrey,** Senior Writer/Content Developer for Church Initiative

If you are considering growing or establishing a biblical counseling ministry in your local church, *Equipping Biblical Counselors* is the *first* book I recommend. It has been personally helpful as well as incredibly practical for the churches I do consulting and training for. Bob Kellemen provides a compelling vision and road map for creating a biblical counseling culture that fits your particular church. I hope this new, revised, and updated version will equip many more pastors, leaders, and churches for years to come!

—**Jason Kovacs,** Executive Director, The Gospel Care Collective

EQUIPPING

BIBLICAL

COUNSELORS

Bob Kellemen, PhD

HARVEST HOUSE PUBLISHERS
EUGENE, OREGON

Italics within Scripture quotations indicate emphasis added by the author

Cover design by Studio Gearbox, David Carlson

Cover photos © HANNA KUBLITSKAYA, T30 Gallery, Mr Twister, TWINS DESIGN STUDIO / Shutterstock

Interior design by KUHN Design Group

For bulk, special sales, or ministry purchases, please call 1-800-547-8979.
Email: Customerservice@hhpbooks.com

For confidentiality purposes, counseling scenarios in this book have been revised and collated from multiple counselees, and the names of those involved have been changed.

Equipping Biblical Counselors
Copyright © 2022 by Bob Kellemen
Published by Harvest House Publishers
Eugene, Oregon 97408
www.harvesthousepublishers.com

ISBN 978-0-7369-8567-3 (pbk)
ISBN 978-0-7369-8568-0 (eBook)

Library of Congress Control Number: 2021949299

Acknowledgments

The year was 1973 and I was fourteen. My older brother, Rick, began dating a Baptist girl, and if you date a Baptist girl, you attend a Baptist church. Rick, being the *older* brother, informed me that if he had to go to church each week, then so did I. That, from the human side of the equation, was how God sovereignly arranged for me to begin attending Grace Baptist Church in Gary, Indiana. Within a year, I surrendered my life to Christ as my Savior.

During my high school years at Grace Baptist, my life intertwined with four individuals, without whom this book would never have been written. The first was Senior Pastor Bill Goode (who is now home with Christ). Though I didn't know it at the time, it was during these very years that Pastor Goode was instrumental in the launch and early development of what now has become known as the modern biblical counseling movement. Pastor Goode's commitment to equipping counselors has stayed with me these fifty years.

At Grace Baptist, I also met and was discipled by our Youth Pastor, Ron Allchin, and his wife, Sherry. Pastor Ron and Sherry not only ministered to me; they also reached out to my family in many ways. Though the Lord led the Allchins to another church during my high school years, we always stayed in contact. Today, Dr. Ron Allchin and Sherry equip biblical counselors around the nation and the world. They were a model for me as a youth; they remain an example for me now.

A fourth influential person from Grace Baptist was Steve Viars. Steve and I had met years earlier in the neighborhood when I was in second grade and he was in first grade. So our paths go way back. Steve is now the Senior Pastor at Faith Church in Lafayette, Indiana—one of the premier biblical counseling equipping churches in the world. Steve's real-life, best-practice approach to equipping counselors has richly influenced my ministry.

Who, other than God, would have thought that Rick dating a Baptist girl would lead to Bob writing *Equipping Biblical Counselors*? All I know is that this book would not be in your hands without the shaping influence of Bill Goode, Ron and Sherry Allchin, and Steve Viars. It is with gratefulness to Christ that I dedicate *Equipping Biblical Counselors* to Bill, Ron, Sherry, and Steve.

Contents

Foreword

Dr. Ron Allchin, Sherry Allchin, and Dr. Tim Allchin

As leaders in the biblical counseling movement, we have been amazed at increasing opportunities to care for more people in more places than ever before. Effective discipleship in churches is shifting from discipleship systems to discipleship conversations and personal care. Yet many churches feel uneasy about how to equip their church members to engage in effective discipleship conversations and personal care. Bob Kellemen's *Equipping Biblical Counselors* addresses this gap as it helps church leaders care with competence, confidence, and compassion.

We are honored to write this foreword as a family because of the special friendship and ministry partnership between the Allchin family and the Kellemen family. Our relationship began when the teenage Bob started attending church youth meetings under the ministry of Pastor Ron and Sherry Allchin. While he was part of the youth group, Bob came to Christ and was discipled, then encouraged in his decision to pursue ministry leadership. Throughout the years, Ron and Sherry and Bob and his wife, Shirley, have enjoyed a friendship that has strengthened both couples. In recent years, Bob and Tim Allchin (Ron and Sherry's son) have worked together on a number of projects to increase resources for churches looking to better equip leaders and to develop a culture of compassionate care. Both the Kellemens and the Allchins have devoted their ministries to equipping church leaders to effectively care and then to disciple others who will also care.

Equipping Biblical Counselors imparts a practical, biblical, user-friendly approach to our shared passion that church leaders should intentionally equip lay leaders to engage in conversations that reflect the wisdom and heart of Christ. More and more churches are realizing they must be effective in counseling if they are to be effective in discipleship. In the years since Bob wrote the first edition of his book, much has rapidly changed in our world and and the church, with greater needs and thus greater opportunities. A pandemic, political unrest, and changing worldviews challenge the church to have different discipleship conversations and to personalize the care offered. The message of the gospel hasn't changed, nor has the need for redemption and reconciliation, but our conversations do change as we use Scripture to bring specific hope, comfort, and confrontation to a hurting world.

What makes this book unique is that it isn't just another book about the merits or methodology of biblical counseling. Instead, this book equips leaders with an intentional process, developing counseling teams that will care for others with competence, confidence, and compassion. Dr. Kellemen has modeled each of these traits in the counseling conversations that have taken place in evangelical circles over the past few decades. He has networked with all the best leaders, learned from them, and compiled this volume that reflects the best practices of scores of biblical counseling ministries.

COMPETENT COUNSELING MINISTRY

More than just another doctrine that the church should embrace, Dr. Kellemen has modeled a plan to develop competent counselors who succeed in helping others gain godly perspectives and personal care. Biblical counseling needs to be more than just an idea. It must become a culture of care leading to carefully developed opportunities for the gospel to meet people in their moments of greatest need. Poor planning and execution will undermine a gospel witness. However, Bob's book helps to avoid the most common mistakes that a church can make. Within this volume you will learn best practices from a leader who has developed teams, and who is sought after as a speaker and writer in helping churches increase their quality of care.

CONFIDENT COUNSELING MINISTRY

In recent years, there has been remarkable growth in the desire for churches to reclaim responsibility to offer Christ-centered counseling. However, we still are often asked the same questions about where to start. Reader, if you want to start equipping your people to counsel and care for one another effectively, *then this book is for you.* Most seminaries provide little practical counseling training and even less training on how to equip leaders and people to provide competent care. *Equipping Biblical Counselors* guides you with a practical "how-to" that produces confidence in a biblical strategy that works. Each church is a body with unique gifts and experiences that were given by God to serve one another. However, many church members lack confidence in how to share their story and to walk with others through trials. This book equips you with the confidence to equip others in how to counsel those in need.

COMPASSIONATE COUNSELING MINISTRY

Bob's growing influence among church leaders flows from his personal compassion and his desire to demonstrate the love needed for counselors to be most effective. While expertise is important, it falls on deaf ears without love, and facts alone rarely motivate others to act on the counsel they receive. Dr. Kellemen demonstrates from both a biblical and research perspective why love and compassion make a major difference in the outcomes a counselor should expect. There are two extremes in counseling: 1) compassion without a commitment to the gospel and biblical wisdom, and 2) a so-called Christian commitment that treats those in need of help with little or no compassion. Bob's writing and ministry both model how counseling the truth must be done with love and compassion.

Nearly four decades ago, Ron and Sherry Allchin made an investment in the life of a young Bob Kellemen. In recent years, the mature Bob has encouraged and collaborated with Tim Allchin in developing resources for biblical counseling leaders through the ministry of Biblical Counseling Center, where Tim is Executive Director. Bob has personally encouraged Tim and his family. As we all grow older, we often think about our life's work and the impact we will leave behind for God's glory. This book challenges leaders and their churches to be a community where disciple-makers are equipped to impact future generations. In a complex, chaotic, and hurting world, the opportunities for those who counsel with competence, confidence, and compassion are greater than ever before. *Equipping Biblical Counselors* will empower you to leave a legacy of impacting others for Christ by equipping future generations to do the same.

—**Ron Allchin, DMin,** Founder and Associate Director,
Biblical Counseling Center, ACBC Fellow

—**Sherry Allchin, MABC,** Director of the Online School,
Biblical Counseling Center

—**Tim Allchin, DMin,** Executive Director, Biblical Counseling Center

Want to Change Lives?

During the early days of television, two shows dominated the airwaves. One aired on Tuesday nights and the other on Sunday evenings. Initially the more popular of the two shows was *The Texaco Star Theatre* hosted by Milton Berle. It was originally designed along the lines of an old-fashion vaudeville variety hour with a host highlighting half-a-dozen guests each week. However, little by little, Milton Berle became the star. As the format changed, the accent gradually focused increasingly on Berle himself. There were fewer guest acts, and Berle began to dominate each show. In just eight years, the show ran out of steam. *No one person is talented enough to carry any show, or any ministry, for more than a short time.*

The other show, *The Ed Sullivan Show*, experienced a very different fate. If any show in the history of television could be called an institution, it would be *The Ed Sullivan Show*. Every Sunday night for more than two decades this show brought an incredible variety of entertainers into homes. Sullivan's show continued as a major hit for fifteen years longer than Berle's.

Unlike Milton Berle, Ed Sullivan never wavered from his original format. *He was the host who called other people to center stage.* Numerous performers made their television debut on his show: Walt Disney, the Beatles, Elvis Presley, Bob Hope, Dean Martin, and hundreds more. Though Ed Sullivan died soon after his show ended, his legacy outlives him.

ARE YOU LIKE MILTON BERLE OR ED SULLIVAN?

God calls Christian leaders to be like Ed Sullivan, not like Milton Berle. If we're like Milton Berle, and the spotlight increasingly focuses on us and our individual ministry, then biblically, we're missing God's mark as equippers. If we fail to focus on equipping, then we selfishly treat God's people like children who have never grown up spiritually.

God wants us to be like Ed Sullivan—a host who calls others to center stage by equipping them to fulfill their calling. When we focus on equipping, we leave an other-centered legacy of loving leaders. Allow me to introduce you to several modern-day Ed Sullivan-like leaders. I've provided discipleship consulting for each of these leaders, and they represent well the readers I picture as I write this book.

Pastor Eric is planting a church. He and the eight families ministering with him are passionate about launching a church where every member is equipped to speak the truth in love. They want biblical counseling to be the DNA of their congregation.

Jan has been a volunteer women's ministry director in her church for more than a decade. She wants to train a dozen women in biblical counseling. She envisions some of them using their training to be more effective small-group leaders—relating truth to life. Others she foresees providing biblical counseling to the growing number of women who seek her help.

Randy and Monica serve together on a ministry launch team that's so new they don't have a ministry name yet. Randy is an elder, seminary student, and youth pastor; Monica is a volunteer ministry leader. The leadership team in their church of two hundred wants them to launch a counseling ministry. As Monica put it when she emailed me, "We don't want another *program*. We want a *ministry* that saturates our whole church with equipped one-another ministers."

John is the Senior Pastor of a large church, and his wife Rachel has two degrees in counseling. They called me to ask, "Bob, do you help churches to do course corrections and relaunches? Five years ago we tried to launch a biblical counseling ministry, but it was too program-focused. Could you help us figure out how to do it more relationally this time?"

I've written this book for people like Eric, Jan, Randy, Monica, John, and Rachel. People like *you*—pastors, ministry leaders, women's ministry directors, elders, deacons, church planters, and students. I've written this book because I'm convinced that you want to be an Ed Sullivan, not a Milton Berle. I know that you are passionate about equipping God's people for every-member ministry as disciple-makers—as biblical counselors. I want to be part of the process of equipping you to equip others (2 Timothy 2:2).

THE 4E MINISTRY TRAINING STRATEGY

The people I consult with are hungry for a comprehensive, real-world approach to equipping God's people for one-another ministry. Like you, they want to empower others for the personal ministry of the Word—as biblical counselors, caregivers, spiritual friends, elders, deacons, small-group leaders, disciplers, and mentors. *Leaders want to change lives.* However, for most leaders, the training process can seem overwhelming—vision casting confusion, change management struggles, recruiting headaches, quality of care matters, training material questions, supervisory difficulties, legal issues, and other legitimate, complex concerns often derail the equipping process.

My purpose in writing *Equipping Biblical Counselors* is to assist leaders like you in equipping people confidently, wisely, lovingly, and biblically. I want this book to be like a personal conversation with your private consultant—coming alongside you, walking step by step to equip you to fulfill your Ephesians 4:11–16 calling to empower the body of Christ to change lives with Christ's changeless truth.

As I speak about one-another ministry, people share with me their rejection of the old model, where the pastoral staff hoarded the ministry. They're clamoring to be unleashed and mobilized for the personal ministry of the Word. *God's people want to change lives.* They care, but they feel ill-equipped to care like Christ. They know the Bible says they are competent to counsel (Romans 15:14), but they also know that the Bible calls them to be equipped to speak the truth in love (Ephesians 4:11–16).

So my second purpose in writing is to launch a revolution in every-member ministry. That's why the subtitle of the book is *A Guide to Discipling Believers for One-Another Ministry.* I call this four-part discipleship process "The 4E Ministry Training Strategy" (see Figure I:1).

FIGURE I:1

The 4E Ministry Training Strategy

- Disciple-Making Strategy #1: Envisioning God's Ministry

- Disciple-Making Strategy #2: Enlisting God's Ministers for Ministry

- Disciple-Making Strategy #3: Equipping Godly Ministers for Ministry

- Disciple-Making Strategy #4: Empowering Godly Ministers for Ministry

These four disciple-making strategies offer you a twenty-first-century, best-practice guide for Christ-centered, church-based, comprehensive, and compassionate mobilization of the priesthood of all believers. They equip churches to become a congregation not simply *with* biblical counseling ministries, but *of* biblical counseling. My goal is not the production of yet another program. My goal is to promote a congregation-saturated mindset of every-member ministry—resulting in a congregation passionate about and equipped to make disciples.

Passing the Baton of Ministry

It's a nice goal, right? But I know that you've "been there, done that." You've heard the promises before. Lots of theoretical talk, but little practical, real-world, biblical help. You're tired of equipping approaches that promise much but deliver little. If you're like the people I consult with, then you're ready for an approach to equipping that is comprehensive, simple to implement, and relationship-oriented rather than program-focused.

Some equipping approaches are like straitjackets with a one-size-fits-all model. The 4E Ministry Training Strategy provides practical principles that you can personally, relationally, and uniquely apply in your specific ministry setting. I've drawn these strategies not only from my experience in four churches, but also from two dozen best-practice churches with a wide diversity of ethnic, demographic, and denominational backgrounds. My goal is for you to be empowered to design a practical process for *your* ministry.

Some equipping approaches offer piecemeal advice that address aspects of equipping but lack a comprehensive strategy to move from launch to leaving a legacy of loving leaders. The 4E Ministry Training Strategy moves you through the four stages that every ministry launch must tackle to establish ministries built to last—envisioning, enlisting, equipping, and empowering.

Like you, I dread seeing effort expended on programs that don't launch or don't last. This is why I've focused the past half century on answering questions such as, How do we pass the baton of ministry? How do we effectively disciple the body of Christ for one-another ministry? How do we equip disciple-makers and biblical counselors?

After launching biblical counseling ministries in four significantly different churches, after three decades of training hundreds of pastors, counselors, and ministry leaders in the seminary setting, and after two decades of consulting with churches, I'm answering those questions in writing. To paint for you the big picture of the disciple-making skills this book will help you to hone, imagine with me passing the ministry baton in a four-lap relay.

Lap One: Envisioning God's Ministry—Core Values

I understand that some of you have spent countless hours in relatively unproductive vision catching/casting training. We'll see why such sessions often fall short of producing lasting change. Chapter 1 shows how to saturate an entire congregation with a passion for equipping in one-another ministry. Chapters 2 through 4 model how to facilitate relationship-building gatherings that excite people about mutually developing a powerful *Mission, Vision, Passion,* and Commission Statement (MVP-C Statement) that results in a practical ministry action plan.

Here's what you'll learn in lap one:

* *How to jointly create church-wide and ministry-specific MVP-C Statements that nourish the compassion, conviction, and connection needed to launch flourishing training ministries.*

You'll learn to discern if you're running in the right direction—core values. It does no good to equip people for the wrong purposes for your church and community. That's why we need to learn the ministry mindset shift that changes everything. It's why we need clarity about God's calling.

Lap Two: Enlisting God's Ministers for Ministry— Connected People

I understand that some of you have launched ministries with great expectations, but then experienced crushing resistance. Even the best-laid plans can face bumps in the road, and even the best prepared runners can stumble when jostled by other participants. Chapter 5 addresses this reality with strategies that many training curriculums omit—relational change management (consensus building) and biblical conflict resolution. I also understand that some of you have spent countless hours in relatively nonrelational recruiting. Chapter 6 describes how to move from "panicked recruiting of warm bodies to a program," to relational enlisting of like-minded, committed servant-leaders connected to a captivating vision.

Here's what you'll learn in lap two:

- *How to mobilize ministers by nurturing a family and building a team prepared for change, skilled in conflict resolution, and connected to the MVP-C Statement.*

You'll learn how to assure that the right people are running the right lap in the relay race—connected people. It does no good to launch a ministry if the congregation is not passionately involved. That's why we need a connected congregation.

Lap Three: Equipping Godly Ministers for Ministry— Coached People

I understand that some of you have spent wasted hours in somewhat disorganized training. Chapters 7 through 10 demonstrate how to unite the "4Cs" of biblical equipping. These four chapters explain how to equip the head (content/truth), the heart (character/love), and the hands (competence/skills) in the context of the home (community/relationship).

Here's what you'll learn in lap three:

- *How to apply transformational training strategies that comprehensively address the 4Cs of biblical content, Christlike character, counseling competence, and Christian community.*

You'll learn to ensure that every race participant is a skilled runner—coached people. It does no good, and potentially much harm, to send ill-equipped people into the personal ministry of the Word. That's why we need clear biblical counseling equipping goals, objectives, curriculum, materials, strategies, and methods.

Lap Four: Empowering Godly Ministers for Ministry—Comprehensive Strategy

I understand that some of you experience a negative reaction to words like "organizing," "administrating," and "programs." It all sounds—and often is—so nonrelational. I get it. That's why chapters 11 and 12 map out organizing the organism and administrating the ministry. These chapters equip you for *relational* leadership that leaves a legacy of loving leaders.

Here's what you'll learn in lap four:

- *How to oversee the ongoing organizing of the organism for God's glory by leading ministries that are built to last, that grow from good to great, and that leave a legacy of loving leaders.*

You'll learn to discern if the runners are running on all cylinders—comprehensive strategy. It does no good and wastes valuable time to envision, enlist, and equip, only to stop short of the ongoing administering of the ministry. You have these trained folks, now what do you do with them? How do you equip people in a caring way that builds community? How do you become a community as you impact your community?

"THESE ARE YOUR GRANDBABIES!"

Sister Ellen Barney is the First Lady (Senior Pastor's wife) of a large, predominantly African American church near Baltimore, Maryland. She has implemented the 4E Ministry Training Strategy for two decades to equip over a thousand women in her LEAD (Life Encouragers And Disciplers) Ministry.

They do it up big! Their graduation ceremonies are better than those of many colleges. I remember the first time Sister Ellen invited me to be their commencement speaker. As she introduced me, she looked over the crowd of more than fifty graduates and said, "These are your grandbabies, Dr. Kellemen! You trained me and I trained them!" Now, years later, as Sister Ellen has trained trainers who train others, she tells me, "Dr. Kellemen, these are your great-great-grandbabies!"

Do you want to be a spiritual grandparent—discipling disciple-makers? Do you want to pass the baton of ministry? Do you want to change lives? Keep reading.

PART 1

ENVISIONING GOD'S MINISTRY

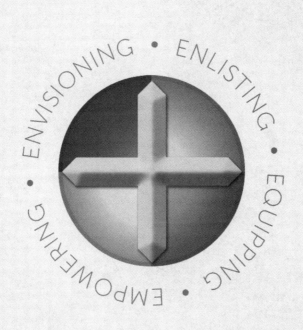

Envisioning

When our daughter, Marie, was young, we played *How Much Do I Love You?* I'd say, "I love you as big as this room." Marie would respond, "I love you as big as this house." I'd answer back, "I love you as big as this city!" Marie would counter, "I love you as big as the world!" Not to be topped, I'd reply, "I love you as big as the solar system!" Marie would top even that with "I love you as big as the universe!"

When most people think about vision, they think too small. They focus on church-specific or ministry-specific vision. Those are vital areas of focus, and we'll learn together how to develop them biblically. But we're going to start bigger than that—much bigger—*universal*. Before you can catch God's vision for a church or ministry area, you have to be caught by God's grand vision for *the* church. So we'll launch Part One with the ministry mindset shift that changes everything: *More Than Counseling: Catching God's Vision for the Entire Church*.

Then you're ready to do envisioning work, right? Close, but not quite. Before you can catch God's vision for your specific church or ministry area, you need to know where you've been and where you are now. Vision points to the future, but to pursue a better future, you have to know your history and your current culture. So chapter 2 focuses on *Examining Heart Health: Diagnosing Congregational and Community Fitness*.

Once you have caught God's vision for the church and examined the past and current state of your church and community, then you're ready to catch God's vision for your specific congregation. Thus, chapter 3 explores *Dreaming God's Dream: Becoming an MVP-C Congregation*. Here you'll learn *what* and *why*: what a *M*ission, *V*ision, *P*assion, and *C*ommission Statement (MVP-C) is, and why it is so vital to develop one.

Biblical principles must lead to practical plans that work in the real world of church life. This is why chapter 4 guides you step by step through the how to of *Living God's Calling: Jointly Crafting Your Biblical Counseling MVP-C Statement.*

I'm a coach and teacher at heart. Coaches and teachers love concrete, measurable objectives. In the classroom, I call them SOLOs: Student-Oriented Learning Objectives. For this book I label them ROLOs: Reader-Oriented Learning Objectives. Through your active reading and application of these first four chapters, you'll be equipped to

- Be a catalyst for a congregation-saturated shift to the ministry mindset that changes everything—every member a disciple-maker (chapter 1).

- Be a spiritual cardiologist who diagnoses the heart health of your congregation and community, to establish a baseline for envisioning God's future dream (chapter 2).

- Champion the biblical meaning of and necessity for jointly crafting congregation-wide and ministry-specific MVP-C Statements (chapter 3).

- Guide your biblical counseling ministry team collaboratively in crafting a ministry-specific MVP-C Statement (chapter 4).

How big does God love you in Christ? Bigger than the universe! Because he does, he has given you his Word so you can be captivated by his universal vision for his church. Join me in chapter 1 as we learn about Christ's grand vision for his Bride.

1

More Than Counseling

Catching God's Vision for the Entire Church

With our attendance of 275 people, ours was an average-size church, at least in the megachurch culture of the day. But because our church served an infinite God and tenaciously pursued a giant vision for every-member ministry, we were significant in God's eyes. Perhaps that's why, in his affectionate sovereignty, he called us to face a significant situation.

At first glance, Steve and Alexis were the all-American couple living the American dream. Married more than two decades, three teen children who would make any parent proud, great jobs, beautiful home, active in their previous church…

But look beneath the surface and you would see another story, as I did the day that their oldest son, Eric, knocked on my office door. Hesitantly, he unfolded a family narrative that shared how their American dream had become a family nightmare. The dad was angry, controlling, verbally abusive to the children, and intimidating to his wife. The mom was fearful, in denial, and struggling with anxiety. One child was struggling with depression. Infidelity had previously rocked the family.

BECOMING A CHURCH THAT CARES

An average-size congregation, surely we did not have the resources to meet such an immense and complicated crisis, right? A church our size should immediately refer them to an outside counselor, right?

There was nothing small or average about this problem. If most churches and Christians are honest, there is nothing that unusual about the problem either. Filled with sin and suffering, yes; out of the norm, no. By God's grace, there was nothing small or average about our response because there had been nothing small or average about our *proactive, congregation-wide preparation* for such messy, real-life issues.

From the day I first candidated to be Senior Pastor, I asked God to help us change the ministry mindset from small church, pastor-centered (the Milton Berle church) to big God, equipping-focused (the Ed Sullivan church). To communicate this shift in perspective, I declined the title Senior Pastor, choosing instead the clunky but more descriptive title Congregational Discipleship Pastor. That didn't mean that I would disciple everyone. It did mean my main calling was to oversee that *we* discipled every member.

This was the reason that two short but intense and active years later, an entire congregation was prepared to unite as a team, a family, and as the body of Christ to minister to this young man, his parents, and siblings. Even before Eric walked out of my office, biblical, relational, relevant plans were in place to begin addressing not only the immediate crisis, but also the ongoing heart issues. Our "average" church had learned the awesome lesson about how to change lives with Christ's changeless truth. Together, we caught and cast the vision of the priesthood of every believer—not as some academic idea, but as our biblical calling.

We understood that pastoral care is not just what the pastor does, but what every member is equipped to offer. With my education—ThM in Biblical Counseling and PhD in Counselor Education—I could have (unwisely) tried to handle this on my own. Instead, we responded as a united family to minister Christ-centered help to this family.

Because there were accusations of verbal abuse and threatening behavior, we contacted the proper authorities, worked through the proper channels, and worked out a plan for the father to stay for a period of time in the home of a family in our church—a family equipped to minister biblically and lovingly. Our Iron Sharpeners men's ministry provided Steve with love—tough love. Our women's ministry became a haven for Alexis.

Steve met with me for formal biblical counseling (while a trainee participated in our sessions). One female biblical counselor met with Eric's younger sister in a mentoring relationship, and another met for formal biblical counseling with Alexis. One of our elders began an informal but intensive mentoring relationship with Eric. One of our deacons began the same with Eric's younger brother. After Steve began to evidence repentance and ongoing changed behavior, I met with him and Alexis for formal biblical marriage counseling (again with a trainee present). Still later, our Women's Ministry Director and I met with the entire family for counseling.

We understood that biblical counseling is not simply a ministry of a few in one corner of the church, but a mindset of an entire congregation that the Bible is sufficient for every life issue. With our active LEAD (Life Encouragers And Disciplers) group of trained biblical counselors, we could have (unwisely) tried to handle this within the confines of the biblical counseling ministry. Instead, we responded as an equipped congregation to minister to this family.

It took a congregation. It took both formal biblical counseling and informal one-another ministry. Both emphasized the personal ministry of the Word where members spoke and lived God's truth into the lives of this family. We understood that one-another ministry is not just shallow chitchat reserved for the "easy stuff," but a biblical vision for the entire church for all of life. With our connections with licensed Christian counselors in the community, we could have referred this family to outside professionals and assumed that our only roles were to pray and hug (both essential callings). Instead, we ministered comprehensively to this family as the unified body of Christ. (Of course, we communicated with outside authorities about abuse, conferred with experts on abuse-related issues, and we consulted with medical personnel about depression and anxiety.)

The ongoing, intensive, intimate, biblical response of our church exemplifies the purpose of this book. I want to help your church become a place not simply *with* a biblical counseling ministry, but *of* biblical counseling. You don't need another program. You want a congregation saturated by the vision of every-member ministry and equipped to offer one-another ministry. Even more, you want a congregation where *every member is a disciple-maker.*

EVERY MEMBER A DISCIPLE-MAKER

It's *in* to talk about every member being a minister. I agree. However, I don't think the language of every member a minister goes far enough. My passion, and most importantly, God's passion, focuses on every member becoming a disciple-maker. That ministry mindset shift changes everything.

Every member a disciple-maker explains the title of this chapter: *More Than Counseling.* Biblical counseling is vital—it's my life calling. Launching biblical counseling ministries is important—you'll learn how to do that in this book. You won't learn less than that; however, you will learn more than that—much more.

The 4E Ministry Training Strategy is an application of Paul's admonition in 2 Timothy 2:2 to pass the baton of ministry. "The things you have heard me say in the presence of many witnesses entrust to reliable people who will also be qualified to teach others." It's the Ed Sullivan church.

"Teach" is the same Greek word Jesus chose to use in the Great Commission in Matthew 28:20. The word implies much more than academic knowledge. Instead, it embodies the 4Cs of disciple-making that we'll learn throughout this book:

- Biblical *C*ontent/*C*onviction

- *C*hristlike *C*haracter

- *C*ounseling *C*ompetence

- *C*hristian *C*ommunity

In order to help Steve, Alexis, and their family—especially to help them not only in a reactive crisis mode but also in a proactive discipleship mode—our congregation needed 4E equipping for 4C ministry. That's exactly what you are about to learn in this book—how to *make disciple-makers*. This chapter equips you to become a catalyst who spurs your congregation to catch God's vision for every-member disciple-making.

The Big Picture: The End Goal—Transformed People

The end goal of this book and of all church ministry is not to launch a biblical counseling ministry. The end goal is transformed people—people transformed into the image of Christ. Remember this core theme:

- A relationship with *the* transforming Person (Christ)

- produces transforming leaders (you and your team)

- who relationally lead a transforming process (the 4Es)

- that the Spirit uses in transforming your church
  (the body of Christ)

- so others (the congregation and community) are also
  transformed into disciple-makers.

My vision is to equip you to build an equipping culture. God's fundamental vision for church growth focuses on every member speaking the truth in love to one another in every situation. That's it. Get that and you get this chapter—you get God's purpose for his body today.

It's everywhere. It's in Ephesians 4:11–16; Ephesians 5:19; Colossians 3:16; Romans 15:14; Hebrews 3:12–13; Hebrews 10:24–25; Philippians 1:9–11; 1 Thessalonians 2:8; 2 Timothy 2:2; Matthew 22:34–40 with Matthew 28:16–20. God's end goal is for every member to be a disciple-maker who speaks and lives gospel truth in love to help every member grow in content, character, competence, and community.

We have wrongly defined biblical counseling so that it's about solving problems. We've made it a subset of discipleship focused on reactive work with persons struggling with sin. Instead, we should think of biblical counseling as another word for comprehensive personal discipleship. Biblical counseling is focused one-another ministry designed to fulfill the Great Commandment and the Great Commission.

We don't want to create the ministry mindset where the only way people can relate to one another is by discussing their problems. The goal is to move people forward in Christlikeness whether or not they are facing specific crisis problems. We need a definition of biblical counseling that encompasses all of life:

> Christ-centered, church-based, comprehensive, and compassionate biblical counseling depends upon the Holy Spirit to relate God's Word to suffering and sin by speaking and living God's truth in love to equip people to love God and one another (Matthew 22:35–40). It cultivates conformity to Christ and communion with Christ and the body of Christ leading to a community of one-another disciple-makers (Matthew 28:18–20).

I love biblical counseling, but we can't see it as a ministry of a few people to a few "unhealthy" people. Biblical counseling is the calling of all God's people all the time because we are all striving to grow in Christ all the time.

Does that mean we shouldn't launch local church counseling ministries? Not at all. There is nothing unbiblical about people with a special gifting and a special passion wanting to focus their ministry energy on biblical counseling. Just like there is nothing unbiblical about some folks in a church taking extensive training in evangelism. Does that mean that only the "evangelism folks" are called to share their faith? Of course not. We want a church *of* evangelists where everyone is passionate about and equipped to share their faith, even if we have members who focus more time on evangelism. In the same way, we want a church *of* biblical counseling where everyone is passionate about and equipped to speak the truth in love, even if we have some within the church who focus more time on biblical counseling. This book helps you with *both* goals.

In my ministry as a pastor in four churches and in my consulting ministry, I try to use simple language to identify this both/and idea of equipping every member for one-another disciple-making *and* equipping some members for biblical counseling. I call every-member ministry the *Informal Model.* Throughout this chapter and book you'll gain practical insight into how to saturate your congregation with passion for and equipping in every-member disciple-making through the informal model. You will also be trained to envision, enlist, equip, and empower biblical counselors—the *Formal Model.*

Disciple-Making Champions

As part of my best-practice research, I surveyed two dozen cutting-edge churches that equip their people to speak the truth in love. Throughout each chapter we'll hear from these Disciple-Making Champions. First up, two pastors from Faith Church who model a church *of* biblical counseling.

DISCIPLE-MAKING CHAMPIONS

Steve Viars, Senior Pastor; Rob Green,
Counseling Pastor, Faith Church

Steve Viars and Rob Green are just two of the many leaders of the biblical counseling ministry at Faith Church in Lafayette, Indiana. At Faith, you find no discrepancy between what happens in the pulpit, what occurs in formal biblical counseling sessions, and what transpires in informal spiritual conversations. Steve and Rob observe,

> "Our goal is to be a church of biblical counseling—we want these truths to permeate everything we do. Call it counseling; call it specialized discipleship. We want to be a progressive sanctification machine, a discipleship factory. We want people growing and

changing where God's Word and Spirit make each of us more like Christ through careful attention to the inner person. The goal of our biblical counseling training, just like the goal of all our ministries, is to glorify God by winning people to Christ (for unsaved counselees) and equipping them to be more faithful disciples (for saved counselees)."

Pastor Bill Goode, the senior pastor who preceded Pastor Viars and who launched Faith's Biblical Counseling Ministry, clung to the same vision. He says,

"The local church *is* a counseling ministry. The question is not, Should Christians counsel each other? because they already are. Most Christians are ministering to one another on a personal basis. So the questions are, What kind of counseling is offered? How *effective* is the ministry? Do people have *confidence* that God's Word has answers to daily life problems?"

The Big Question: The End Game—Disciple-Makers

When we understand the big picture, then we're prepared to ask the big questions—the right questions:

- How do we make disciple-makers?

- How do we leave a legacy of loving leaders?

- How do we encourage our congregation to catch God's vision for every member a disciple-maker?

It's when we ask and answer these big-picture questions that we're best prepared to ask the more specific questions related to equipping biblical counselors for one-another ministry:

- How do we effectively disciple the body of Christ for one-another ministry in the church and community?

- How do we prepare people for the personal ministry of the Word?

- What is God's strategy for preparing a congregation to speak the truth in love to one another?

I asked you the biggest of big questions in the introduction: *Want to change lives?* There's nothing more life-changing than discipling disciple-makers, passing the baton of ministry, and leaving a legacy of loving leaders.

This was our goal in ministering to Steve and Alexis. Not only is their marriage united and glorifying Christ, not only is their parenting (of their now-young-adult children) vibrant, they are discipling other disciple-makers. They not only made it through their family crisis, but they became disciple-makers as a result of moving through their crisis with Christ and the body of Christ.

THE PERSONAL MINISTRY OF THE WORD: SEVEN CHURCH STYLES

Sometimes when I train pastors I receive some pushback. It typically goes something like this: "I do my counseling from the pulpit. People don't need anything but the preached Word."

Having been a Senior Pastor, and rarely having given up the pulpit, I don't take issue with any pastor who is passionate about the pulpit ministry of the Word. I do take issue with anyone who pits the pulpit ministry of the Word against the personal ministry of the Word.

All biblical ministry should involve speaking the truth in love. That should be done from the pulpit to the crowd through an equipped person fully focused and prepared to relate God's truth to people's lives—*the pulpit ministry of the Word.* Speaking the truth in love also should be done one-to-one and in small groups, both formally and informally, as members of the body of Christ change lives with Christ's changeless truth—*the personal ministry of the Word.*

If we want a church *of* biblical counseling where everything is saturated with the conviction that God's Word is sufficient for all of life, then pulpit ministry and personal ministry must remain in harmony. Knowing how personal needs are met in typical churches helps us to compare and contrast these models with God's vision for his church.

1. The Staff Model

When a church member has a "problem," many churches respond to that person through the *staff model,* where the main caregiver is one of the pastors. This approach uses the classic pastoral care model where the pastor marries and buries, ministering from cradle to casket, in the home and in the hospital. The pastor typically focuses in a reactive way on crisis needs.

A potential strength of this model is that theoretically, you have well-trained caregivers. Unfortunately, very few pastors believe they have received effective training in the personal ministry of the Word. There are major weaknesses in this approach, including pastoral burnout and the pastor monopolizing the ministry (the Milton Berle church). Also, the majority of members are not ministered to because the focus is on the unhealthy person in crisis. People learn that if they want the pastor's attention, they had better have a problem. As a church grows, there is no way for one person (or even a staff of people) to minister to the entire congregation.

2. The Shepherding Model

Because the staff model can't work as churches grow, other churches implement the *shepherding model*. In this approach, the primary caregivers are deacons, deaconesses, elders, ministry of mercy team members, shut-in teams, and visitation teams. Typically the ministry occurs on a regular but infrequent basis as the focus is on "touching base" so no one "falls through the cracks."

Strengths of this method include many members having a ministry, every member having a minister, and no one being isolated. Weaknesses include resistance to being assigned to a group, since this model is often based on geography rather than natural relationships. Additionally, the team members may burn out, drop out, or drop the ball. At times, training is inadequate and nonexistent.

3. The Small-Group Model

Since intimacy and frequency are often missing in the shepherding model, many churches use the *small-group model* as their primary vehicle for meeting personal needs. Here, the caregiver is the small-group leader and hopefully each small-group member. Methods vary since small group ministries have a myriad of philosophies. The frequency of care typically involves weekly to monthly connection on an ongoing basis, sometimes being time-limited.

There are numerous strengths to this model when it is run well. Many members are ministered to and many members can have a ministry. Close relationships can develop and spontaneous need-meeting often occurs. There are, however, weaknesses in this model. Those not in small groups (in many churches at least 50 percent of the congregation) fall through the cracks. Unfortunately, many churches provide little equipping in small-group leadership—especially in the personal ministry of the Word of speaking the truth in love.

4. The Sunday School Model

Larger churches often institute adult Sunday school classes frequently known as Adult Bible Fellowships (ABFs). These ABFs become mini-congregations within the congregation. The caregiver in this *Sunday school model* is the ABF teacher, or the ABF care-group leader(s). The focus is on crisis need-meeting, plus semiregular touching base, as well as periodic social/fellowship gatherings.

There are several strengths in this approach. Many members have a ministry and many are ministered to. No one in the ABFs falls through the cracks. Weaknesses include the tendency of those *not* in ABFs to fall through the cracks, along with the possibility of untrained caregivers, few counseling needs being met, and ministers burning out and dropping out.

5. The Specialist Model

Some churches, especially with "hard cases," select the *specialist model.* In this method the caregiver, if inside the church, is the pastoral counselor or lay counselor. If outside the church, the caregiver is the parachurch biblical counselor, licensed Christian counselor, or Christian psychologist. The focus is on crisis need-meeting and ongoing counseling with scheduled appointments for primary care.

Theoretically, the strengths include well-trained caregivers offering intensive help for intense life issues. If inside the church, weaknesses include a professionalized and specialized model of ministry, counselors who are not fully equipped, and few members ministering. If referred out, weaknesses include the potential that the care is secular, or Christian care that is not biblically based. Also, the role of the church as a discipling community is minimized. At best, this model results in a church *with* biblical counseling, but it is not a church *of* biblical counseling.

6. The Spontaneous Model

In reaction to the professionalized approach, many churches follow the *spontaneous model.* In this method, theoretically, every member cares intimately for a few other members. The methods include an Acts 2 spontaneous combustion model aided by a passion for connection built into the preaching, the vision statement, and the hearts of members. The focus is on the holistic care of members as found in Acts 2:42–47. Ideally, the frequency of one-another care is daily as needs are perceived and shared.

The strengths are obvious: the model is biblically based and involves Holy Spirit-empowered reciprocal one-another ministry of every member. However, in actuality, often only the deeply connected are cared for. Additionally, this model often minimizes training because it lacks a focus on "organizing the organism." At best, this model results in a church *of* one-another ministry, but it is not always a church *with* biblical enlisting, equipping, and empowering.

7. The Scripture-Only Model

Other churches react against a therapeutic culture and decide to follow a *Scripture-only model*. Picture this as the pulpit ministry of the Word minus the personal ministry of the Word. The method involves little structured means for caregiving and need-meeting, with the assumption that the truth preached from the pulpit provides all the biblical counseling necessary, and motivates the body equipped by the pulpit to minister to one another. The focus typically is upon doctrinal correctness and depth.

There are obvious strengths to this model. Truth is preached. Doctrine is learned. There are also weaknesses. The personal ministry of the Word is de-emphasized, and if it happens at all, the caregivers are often ill-equipped to translate truth to life. They know truth, but they don't know how to bridge the truth-life gap. At times, the staunch preaching of doctrine can lead to a mood of truth trumping love, of head over heart.

The Biblical Plumb Line

As you reflect on these seven styles of meeting congregational needs, which do you value? As you ponder your church, which methods does it blend together? How well do the people function?

My objective in presenting this overview is not to dissuade you from implementing any of these models. Many have real value. My purpose is to encourage you to evaluate each model using Ephesians 4:11–16 as your biblical plumb line.

My goal is to urge you to use a 4E strategy when you implement any of these models. In my ministry experience, research, and consulting, very few of these models apply a comprehensive *envisioning, enlisting, equipping, and empowering* philosophy to ensure that the model is biblically sound and practically effective.

My aim is to highlight how most of these ministry models fail the "both/ and" test. They rarely include both the pulpit ministry of the Word *and* the personal ministry of the Word; both truth *and* love; both the formal *and* informal modes of speaking the truth in love; both pastors-teachers equipping the body *and* the body doing works of service; and they rarely include the vision of a church *of* and a church *with* biblical counseling. They lack a comprehensive approach to training God's people.

Most importantly, none of these models highlight or effectively result in making disciple-makers. Most focus on meeting personal needs—not a bad aim, but not God's ultimate vision. Others focus on caregiving and some on every member a minister—but not on *every member a disciple-maker*. Even the Scripture model, which seeks to prioritize making deep disciples, follows a model that will not result in equipped disciple-makers. Telling truth does not produce 4C disciple-makers. Part 3 on equipping describes the type of training that best produces disciple-makers who are complete in knowledge (content/conviction), full of goodness (character), and competent to counsel (competence) one another (community).

GOD'S GRAND VISION FOR HIS CHURCH: EPHESIANS 4:11–16

In Ephesians 4:11–16, Paul highlights the Bible's most powerful, focused vision statement for the church. This passage offers God's ministry description for church leaders and for every member. By distilling the essence of God's call, his vision captures our imagination and motivates the shift in ministry mindset that changes everything.

The Résumé of Pastors

Most pastoral search committees would be thrilled to read a candidate's résumé that demonstrated the ability to preach, counsel, and administrate. Most seminaries would be delighted if graduate exit interviews indicated that pastoral ministry students perceived that their seminary training had equipped them for preaching, counseling, and administrating. Being equipped to *do* the work of the ministry seems to be everyone's ideal goal for church leaders.

Everyone but Christ. His pastoral ministry description demands the ability to *equip* others to do the work of the ministry. If seminaries followed Christ's vision for pastoral ministry, they would focus on *training trainers*. If pastoral search committees desired in a pastor what Christ desires, they would throw out every résumé that failed to emphasize experience in and passion for equipping the saints.

You would think we would listen to the head of the church. Paul spends the chapters and verses leading up to Ephesians 4:11–16 showing why Christ has the right to write the pastor-teacher's ministry description.

- He is our Redeemer in whom our full salvation is complete (1:1–14). We should surrender to his will for his redeemed people.

- He is seated at God's right hand ruling over everything with all authority, appointed the Head over everything for the church (1:15–23). We should follow his directives for the church.

- We are his workmanship, created in Christ to do the beautiful work prepared for us from all eternity (2:1–10). We should want to know what he prepared pastors and people for.

- He is the chief cornerstone upon whom the whole building (the church) is being built (2:11–22). We should follow his architectural drawings for the church.

- He is the revelation of God's grace toward which all time and eternity have been moving (3:1–14). We should yield to his infinite wisdom for his people.

- His love for us surpasses all knowledge (3:15–21). We should submit to his calling on our lives.

- He ascended higher than all the heavens in order to fill the whole universe (4:1–10). We should listen to the Creator, Sustainer, and Ruler of the universe.

Pastoral Ministry Mindset Shift That Changes Everything: Every Pastor an Equipper of Equippers

Instead, we listen to modern church culture that screams, "The pastor is the preacher, caregiver, and CEO!" It's time for us to listen to the head of the church. "So Christ himself gave the apostles, the prophets, the evangelists, the pastors and teachers, to equip his people for works of service" (Ephesians 4:11–12). *Christ's grand plan for his church is for pastors/teachers to focus on equipping every member to do the work of the ministry.*

Under the Spirit's inspiration, Paul launches verse 12 with a tiny Greek word (*pros*) translated by an even smaller English word ("to") with giant meaning: with the conscious purpose of, in order for, for the sake of, with a view to. The word indicates the future aim and ultimate goal of a current action. That is, by definition, a vision statement—Christ's grand vision statement for every pastor/teacher.

What is the future view, the future vision for which Christ sovereignly gave his church pastors and teachers? Paul says it succinctly: "*To equip his people for works of service.*" These eight words must be every church leader's reason for existence.

One central word—"equip"—must capture every leader's passion for ministry. "Equip" comes from the word for artist or craftsman. Local church leader, your special craft, your opus, is people, prepared people, disciple-makers. Your spiritual craft or gift is to help others scout out their spiritual gift, identify that area of ministry, and empower them to use that gift.

In Paul's day, people used "equip" in the context of conditioning an athlete. Local church leader, you are a spiritual conditioning coach. Your job is not to play all the positions on the team, but to coach every player on the team, to strengthen their spiritual condition so they are able to do works of service. This fits perfectly with how Paul uses the word "equip"—to train someone so they are fully fit and mature enough to complete their calling. *The leader's calling is to help God's people fulfill their calling.*

These weren't just words for Paul. He made producing disciple-makers his personal ministry description—Colossians 1:28–29. He made equipping equippers his personal ministry practice—Acts 20:13–38. Christ's grand vision so captured Paul's ministry mindset that at the end of his life he passed onto Timothy the vision of equipping equippers of equippers—2 Timothy 2:2. The baton of equipping passed from Christ's hands, to Paul's hands, to Timothy's hands, to the hands of reliable disciple-makers who passed it on yet again.

Let's not drop the baton. Let's keep Christ's grand vision alive and moving into the future.

Yes, But

Some may ask, "Are you saying that pastors should not preach the Word, counsel, and administrate?" Not at all. Christ, the head of the church, has written the primary ministry description for all pastors. Pastors should equip equippers for the work of the ministry. Within this overriding calling, pastors can preach, counsel, and administrate.

When I was a Senior Pastor, when I preached, I asked myself, *How does this message further my calling to be a catalyst for equipping the saints for the work of ministry?* As a player-coach, when I counseled, I had trainees in the room with me. When I visited the hospital, I took apprentices with me. My goal wasn't to be the church's primary caregiver, but to equip a church of caregivers. In my administrative role, I sought to oversee the equipping of every member. Yes, I preached, counseled, and administrated—always within the context of Christ's grand vision for the church, which is the pastor as the equipper of equippers.

You may be thinking, *I'm with you 100 percent. I'm not an ordained pastor, although I am a recognized, active ministry leader in my church. How should I apply these truths?* Ephesians 4:11–12 provides the ministry description for all those raised up for church leadership. If you are the small-group director, ask, "How can I orchestrate all our small-group leaders and members to be discipled to speak the truth in love?" If you are the women's ministry director, ask, "How can I fulfill Christ's call for me to equip women to equip others?"

The Résumé of the People of God

Sadly, in too many churches, the people of God are second-class citizens when it comes to the work of ministry. If a layperson makes a hospital visit, that's okay, but the patient will ask, "Where's my pastor?" Christ's vision is so different. *Pastors and teachers serve the people so God's people can serve the congregation and community.* Far too many laypeople are recruited to fill a position and fill a need, but not to fulfill a calling.

Paul's phrase "works of service" elevates the ministry of God's people. "Works" has a sense of divine calling and meaningful purpose. We could translate it as vocation and mission. The Bible uses it to describe God's creative work. God the Creator commissions us for creative, zealous, purposeful work—work that glorifies him as we serve one another.

Paul's word for "service" highlights personal service rather than serving for wages, serving as a slave. It involves love in action through sacrificial ministry modeled after Christ's sacrifice. Christ calls his people to creative, purposeful, meaningful, sacrificial, personal ministry to one another in his name. In the context of Ephesians 4:11–16, that work is nothing less than producing disciple-makers through the personal ministry of the Word.

Member Ministry Mindset Shift That Changes Everything: Every Member a Disciple-Maker

When leaders and members fulfill their purposes together, the body of Christ builds itself up in two specific, cohesive ways: doctrinal unity and spiritual maturity (Ephesians 4:12–13). When a congregation knows the truth not just academically but personally, their love abounds in knowledge and depth of insight (Philippians 1:9–11).

We often miss the vital real-life, how-to application of every-member disciple-making that Paul embeds in this text. How does the church come to unity and maturity? Exactly what are pastors equipping people to do? Specifically how do members do the work of the ministry?

Paul answers in this way: by "speaking the truth in love" we grow up in Christ (Ephesians 4:15). Every word in this passage funnels toward this remarkable phrase "speaking the truth in love." *Christ's grand plan for his church is for every member to be a disciple-maker by speaking and living gospel truth to one another in love.*

Paul selects an unusual Greek word that we often translate as "speaking the truth." We should translate it as *living* the truth. We might even coin the term "truthing." Paul likely had in mind Psalm 15, where the psalmist asks, "Who may dwell in your sacred tent?" (verse 1). He answers, "The one whose walk is blameless, who does what is righteous, *who speaks the truth from their heart*" (verse 2). Who can serve in God's sanctuary, the church? The one who embodies truth in relationships.

The word for "truthing" that Paul uses means transparent, truthful, genuine, authentic, reliable, sincere. It describes the person who ministers from a heart of integrity and Christlike, grace-oriented love. It pictures the person whose relational style is transparent and trustworthy. The tense and context indicates that the body of Christ should continually, actively, and collectively embody truth in love as it walks together in intimate, vulnerable connection. In one word, Paul combines content, character, and competence shared in community!

While the word for "truthing" means more than speaking, it does not mean *less* than speaking. While it means more than sheer factual content, it does not mean *less* than the gospel fully applied. Paul uses the same word in Galatians 4:16. There he is speaking of preaching, teaching, and communicating the truth of the gospel of Christ's grace (salvation) applied to daily growth in Christ (progressive sanctification).

The Personal Ministry of the Word

Combine Galatians 4:16 with Ephesians 4:16, both in context, and we find an amazing description of gospel-centered biblical counseling—of the personal ministry of the Word. Speaking the truth involves the following:

> Communicating gospel truth about grace-focused sanctification in word, thought, and action through one-another relationships that have integrity, genuineness, authenticity, transparency, and reliability,

done in love to promote the unity and maturity of the body of Christ for the ultimate purpose of displaying the glory of Christ's grace.

The normal agenda and priority of every Christian is to make disciple-makers. Christ's training strategy for disciple-making is pastors and teachers equipping every member to embody the truth in love through the personal ministry of the Word—biblical counseling.

What happens when leaders focus on equipping God's people to make disciple-makers through the personal ministry of the Word by speaking and living the truth in love? Paul shows us in Ephesians 4:16. The body in robust health grows and builds itself up in love as each part does its work.

DISCIPLE-MAKING CHAMPION

Pastor Robert Cheong,
Pastor of Care, Sojourn Church Midtown

Dr. Robert Cheong, Pastor of Care for Sojourn Church Midtown in Louisville, Kentucky, is passionate about equipping God's people for gospel-centered counseling. His definition of church-based counseling harmonizes beautifully with Paul's Ephesians 4:11–16 vision. Dr. Cheong says,

"Gospel counseling is a way of loving one another by understanding the struggles of unbelief in the midst of sin and suffering through listening to and exploring the heart, while proclaiming how Christ and his gospel truths apply in deeply personal and particular ways, so we can live out and grow in the gospel by faith in community, enabled by the Spirit's grace and power."

Pastor Cheong unites counseling and the personal ministry of the Word.

"Gospel counseling is an aspect of gospel ministry that represents the relational ministry of the Word in which every Christian is called to participate. The essence of counseling is helping one another understand and apply the gospel to the details of life so we can live the gospel by faith in community."

Pastor Cheong's connection between the church and counseling is an apt exclamation point on Christ's grand vision.

> "Counseling that flows from the gospel reflects the essence of gospel ministry and must be done by the church—the people of God. God calls every member to the relational ministry of the Word where people labor to help those in the church family to grow in maturity in Christ (Colossians 1:28–29) and to help those outside the church family to see their need for Christ. The renewal of counseling is not to have such a ministry done *in* the church, but *by* the church, so the church can *be* the church."

COMMENCEMENT: IT TAKES A CONGREGATION

I call my final biblical counseling meeting "commencement" because I want to communicate positive progress on an ongoing journey with Christ. For the same reason, I'm calling the end of each chapter in this book the "Commencement." Let's commence.

When I started my ministry as Congregational Discipleship Pastor, I didn't begin by launching a biblical counseling program. That never would have been sufficient to minister effectively to Steve, Alexis, Eric, and the others in their family. Instead, I invited our congregation to join me on a journey of catching God's vision for every-member disciple-making. Because of that focus, this family received both formal biblical counseling and informal one-another ministry.

As our congregation engaged in the vision-catching process, we joined together to assess and diagnose the heart health of our congregation and community. We knew that we couldn't understand where to go until we knew where we had been and where we currently were. Join me in chapter 2 as we learn about that process: "Examining Heart Health: Diagnosing Congregational and Community Fitness."

GROWING TOGETHER: QUESTIONS FOR REFLECTION, DISCUSSION, AND APPLICATION

1. If the all-American family entered your congregation, how prepared would your church be to minister to them in their current crisis and in their ongoing Christian lives? What do you think your congregation might need to do in order to be better prepared?

2. Would you say your church is a church *with* biblical counseling or a church *of* biblical counseling (a congregation saturated with equipped one-another ministers)? Why?

3. In your life and in your church, how much of a transition would it be to shift from doing the work of the ministry to producing disciple-makers? What might that shift involve?

4. Of the seven styles of church ministry, which do you value? Which methods does your church use? How well do the styles function in your church?

5. Reflect on the résumé and the ministry description of the biblical pastor/teacher/leader.

   a. Who has equipped you to equip others? How did they do it?

b. Who have you equipped to equip others? How did you do it?

Ponder the definition of speaking the truth in love:

> Communicating gospel truth about grace-focused sanctification in word, thought, and action through one-another relationships that have integrity, genuineness, authenticity, transparency, and reliability, done in love to promote the unity and maturity of the body of Christ for the ultimate purpose of displaying the glory of Christ's grace.

1. Based on this definition, how would you evaluate your personal ministry of the Word?

2. Based on this definition, how would you assess your congregation's personal ministry of the Word?

Examining Heart Health

*Diagnosing Congregational
and Community Fitness*

In my first church, I served as Counseling and Discipleship Pastor at an urban-suburban church with three thousand members. The church had a long history of extensive equipping ministries. In my second church, I served as Congregational Discipleship Pastor (Senior Pastor) at a rural, blue-collar church of one hundred (which God grew to three hundred). This church had a long history of a pastor-centered mindset. Looking back, I should have realized how different these two churches were.

It took me just two days to learn. A senior saint and longtime member asked to speak with me about a counseling issue. After an initial response of empathy and listening, I instinctively reached into my files for a four-page Personal Information Form for her to complete.

To me, this was natural and caring—her responses would help me to understand her current issues, past history, and future goals. For her, this was unusual and uncaring. Thankfully, she told me so in no uncertain terms. "I'm here to talk to my pastor, not to fill out paperwork. I don't know how they did things where you came from, but we're not like that around here."

Although I graduated from a fine Bible college and an excellent seminary, not one professor ever told me that two churches, especially with predominantly the same ethnicity, could be so drastically different. I was never taught to understand the culture of my church and community—the way things are done, the way people think, the expectations people have, a congregation's history, and a community's values. I was culturally tone deaf.

If not for this encounter with this senior saint, I would have launched the biblical counseling ministry in my new church the same way I had successfully done so in my first church. Since my former church already had a vision for disciple-making, I started there with a formal two-year training program complete with extensive interviews, the selection of a limited number of trainees, homework assignments, and supervision.

As I began to understand how vastly different my new church was, I decided to spend my first six months getting to know my congregation and community. As a result, I started my training there with an informal spiritual friendship model of one-another ministry—helping the entire congregation grow in their ability to speak truth in love. I waited until my second year before I launched a more formal biblical counseling training ministry.

A CHURCH CARDIOLOGIST

Much of what I teach arises from mistakes I made and from my desire to save you from making those same mistakes. No one taught me how to become a spiritual cardiologist. That's what you're going to learn in this chapter:

> *How to diagnose the heart health of your congregation and community to establish a present baseline for envisioning God's future dream.*

From Ephesians 4, we know the *eternal baseline* for a robustly healthy church. Christ's grand plan for his church is for church leaders to equip every member to make disciple-makers by speaking and living God's truth to one another in love. Before launching Ephesians 4 ministry, we need to learn *how to diagnose and assess our congregation and community's current readiness, health, and fitness compared to Christ's vision for his church.*

The church is the body of Christ, and each individual congregation, like each individual human body, has a body type. Christ makes this plain in his unique interactions with the seven churches in Revelation 2—3. Christ has a distinctive purpose, calling, gift-mix, and method of ministry for every local congregation in its specific community.

Biblical counselors are soul physicians who understand people, diagnose problems, and prescribe solutions—biblically. We also need to be church cardiologists who understand our church and community, diagnose the heart condition of the culture where we minister, and prescribe God's cures—biblically. Church cardiology equips us to understand how to move wisely from Christ's universal calling to unique congregation and community-specific applications.

DON'T JUST DO IT; DO IT RELATIONALLY

I'm a Nike type of person—"Just do it!" I don't like to waste time. Many church leaders think similarly. "Let's just get on with it—launch this ministry already. Enough preparation!" I empathize. However, we must balance the extreme of planning so long that nothing ever happens against the extreme of moving so quickly that we endure a haphazard launch that alienates people and results in ineffective ministries.

The wisest way to avoid these two ditches is to follow an unhurried but steady pace, focused on *organizing the organism*. We have to *be* a community before we can reach our community. We have to minister to one another *during* the launch process if we want to create a culture of one-another ministry *after* the launch. In ministry, speed kills. Shortcuts are often dead ends. This is especially true when *organizing* is emphasized above the *organism*.

Our starting point is listening to Christ—his vision for his church. Then we listen carefully to one another.

Assessment is a personal discovery process involving intentional one-another spiritual conversations that emphasize other-centered listening and understanding. Assessment isn't marketing. People want to be cared for in community, not targeted as customers.

The relational launch process fans into flame the individual and congregational passion that carries forward the entire ministry. Remember our end goal: a relationship with *the* transforming Person (Christ) leads to transforming leaders (you and your team) relationally leading a transforming process (The 4E Ministry Training Strategy) that the Spirit uses to transform your church (the body of Christ) so others (the congregation and community) are also transformed into disciple-makers.

JESUS AND PAUL: SPIRITUAL CARDIOLOGISTS

That dear saint walked out of my office after an hour of gospel conversations during which I never lifted another finger to touch another counseling form!

Then I prayed. "Lord, what have I gotten myself into? Why did you send me *here?*" After praying, I took the next logical step: I began a biblical study that, thirty years later, became this chapter. I examined how Jesus and Paul wisely moved into new cultures, into new ministry terrain. Through that study I came to the conviction that *before we catch God's future vision, we must first diagnose the past history and current condition of our congregation and community.*

Jesus: Culturally Informed Ministry—John 2:23—4:42

Jesus' interaction with Nicodemus in John 3 is one of the most familiar stories in the Bible. His spiritual conversation with the woman at the well in John 4 is another well-known biblical narrative. Unfortunately, we often fail to connect these two passages because we fail to detect the textual marker John provides. John informs us that Jesus is the ultimate Soul Physician who "knew all people. He did not need any testimony about mankind, for he knew what was in each person" (John 2:24–25).

John's introduction is like a flashing neon light shouting, "Pay attention to what lies ahead! I'm going to demonstrate to you how Jesus understands people, diagnoses problems, and prescribes solutions through knowing the human heart universally, internally, and culturally."

Could any two people be more different than Nicodemus and the Samaritan woman? Nicodemus is a well-known Jewish male Pharisee—a hyper-moral religious leader. The woman at the well is a nameless Samaritan female—an immoral, irreligious follower.

From vastly different cultures, Jesus understands them both personally. He diagnoses that each has the same problem (sin) and prescribes the same solution—a personal relationship with God through personal faith in Christ. Yet he gets there in markedly different ways.

Nicodemus came purposefully to Jesus at night. Jesus came purposefully to the Samaritan woman in broad daylight. Jesus replies to Nicodemus's overture with a direct declaration of the truth—you must be born again. Jesus initiates a conversation with the Samaritan woman about his own physical thirst. He illustrates spiritual truth with Nicodemus by focusing on the wind, Spirit, flesh, and birth. He illustrates spiritual truth with the Samaritan woman by focusing on thirst, drinking, and water.

Neither individual got it at first, each thinking too much about physical reality and missing Jesus' spiritual meaning. To penetrate Nicodemus's dense spiritual blindness, Jesus turns his attention to Moses lifting up a snake in the desert and then declares that God so loved the world that he gave his only Son. To penetrate the Samaritan woman's dense spiritual blindness, Jesus turns her attention to her immorality and to worshipping in spirit and truth. To Nicodemus, he starts as a rabbi, becomes Israel's teacher, and ends as the Son of God. To the Samaritan woman, he starts as a thirsty traveler, becomes a prophet, and ends as the Messiah.

Christ's understanding, diagnosis, and prescription are the same. The people he engages, however, are incredibly different. This is why Jesus' interactions—his personal ministry of the Word, his way of speaking and living gospel truth in love—are unique to each. He models for us that the *message* is the same, but the *methods and means of communication* vary because of the personal and cultural differences of the specific audience.

Paul: Study Scripture; Study Society—Acts 17

Jesus didn't need to do cultural assessment because he is the God-man. Paul, you, and I must do cultural assessment—congregational and community diagnosis.

As Paul arrives in Thessalonica, he enters the synagogue three consecutive Sabbath days to reason from the Scriptures, explaining and proving who Christ is. Chased out of town, Paul follows a similar ministry strategy in Berea. Agitators arrive again, so Paul heads for Athens.

While in Athens, Paul is "greatly distressed to see that the city was full of idols" (Acts 17:16). Paul allows himself to experience and understand the new cultural context in which he is ministering.

After he opens his heart and eyes, he opens his mouth and the Word. He reasons with the people where they are—in the marketplace and in the Areopagus. He feels compassion for their lost culture, understands their unique culture, but doesn't give in to their culture. He offers their culture a biblical message in a culture-specific manner.

Paul interacts with the Epicurean and Stoic philosophers, sharing Christ's truth in language they can understand. He starts where they are. "People of Athens! I *see* that in every way you are very religious. For as I *walked around* and *looked carefully* at your objects of worship…" (Acts 17:22–23a).

Do we feel? See? Do we walk among and look carefully at the people in our congregation and community? We fear doing this because we fear capitulating to the culture and becoming need-focused and humanity-centered, instead of remaining God-focused and gospel-centered.

Instead, we need to follow Paul's model. *He is not culturally influenced; he is culturally informed so he can be a culture influencer for Christ.* He preaches the good news about Christ's resurrection in a way that connects eternal truth to their temporal situation. "So you are ignorant of the very thing you worship— and this is what I am going to proclaim to you" (Acts 17:23b). He opens his eyes, then he opens his mouth to open Scripture in a culturally understandable manner. Paul quotes one of their poets, but he doesn't integrate their philosophy into his theology. He *builds bridges between the two worlds* of God's truth and their lives, boldly and lovingly calling for repentance before the risen Christ.

Like Paul, God calls us to speak the truth in love in a Christ-centered, culturally informed manner.

- We open our hearts to experience the pain of the hopelessness of our society.

- We open our eyes to know our society, listening to their earthly story.

- We open our mouths to share Christ as society's only hope.

- We open the Word to explain Scripture, sharing God's eternal story.

Through diagnosing the spiritual condition of our congregation and community, we learn to communicate Christ's changeless truth to our changing times.

Church Cardiology: Diagnosing Congregational Readiness for Making Disciple-Makers

I'm thankful that my four pastoral ministries were in dissimilar churches: an urban megachurch, a suburban church with five hundred members, a rural church that went from one to three hundred members, and a suburban/urban church with five campuses. Otherwise, I might advocate a prescriptive strategy that communicates "Do X, and then Y will happen." Ministry with real people doesn't work like that. Churches, even with seemingly similar demographics, are each one of a kind.

So, consider the following how-to section on diagnosing your church not as a straitjacket, but as a GPS: *God's Positioning Strategy.* The approach I'm suggesting is grounded in biblical principles and presented as a guide with directional markers you can alter and apply to fit your ministry setting. No how-to is one-size-fits-all because we're not franchising a McDonald's restaurant; we're ministering to people.

DISCIPLE-MAKING CHAMPION

Dr. Kevin Carson, Senior Pastor, Sonrise Baptist Church

Dr. Kevin Carson, Senior Pastor at Sonrise Baptist Church in Ozark, Missouri, supplies a church-planting perspective on biblical counseling. Pastor Carson balances the necessity of a biblical theology of ministry with the practical reality of an effective ministry development process built upon that theological foundation. He says,

> "As part of the church plant *philosophy* and subsequent *methodology*, biblical counseling ministry (one-another ministry built upon a biblical theology of sovereignty, sufficiency, sin, suffering, Savior, salvation, and sanctification) was fundamental to the church plant foundation. The church through *various means* exists together in authentic life to become more like Jesus practicing one-another commands as part of everyday life."

Pastor Carson's ministry includes equipping members to understand people in their context. He believes that "out-of-context ministry" is a frequent problem.

> "The tendency is for new churches to copy what is heard in a conference or read in a book. The methods of ministry the church planter is copying were all developed inside a local context. That context includes a regionally based people. To take, for example, the purpose-driven model and try to remake Saddleback Church in Ozark, Missouri, would be unwise."

Structure not only must be contextually applied, it must be scripturally derived. Building upon his exegesis of Ephesians 4:11–16, Pastor Carson explains:

> "The church's structure must consistently engender the work of progressive sanctification in the life of believers, recognizing

> the importance of ministry that is vertically integrated (Christ-centered) and horizontally mutual (speaking the truth in love)."
>
> Scripture provides the structure that we wisely develop in our specific situation.
>
> "The Scripture pushes the faithful pastor-teacher to equip every believer in the church, ensuring the congregation's ability to engage in the process of change by speaking the truth in love to each other. To facilitate each member's personal ministry to the body, the church planter must anticipate *forms and structure* necessary to complement the process."

Self-Cardiology: Watch Your Life and Doctrine Closely

Applying biblical principles in congregation-specific ways takes more than IQ. It takes SQ—a high spirituality quotient. In the midst of Paul's instructions to Timothy about "how people ought to conduct themselves in God's household, which is the church of the living God" (1 Timothy 3:15), Paul exhorts Timothy to "watch your life and doctrine closely" (1 Timothy 4:16).

Life and doctrine are the same themes Paul highlighted in Ephesians: unity in the faith (doctrinal intelligence, biblical wisdom) and maturity in Christ (relational intelligence, Christlike character). We can't attempt to examine the heart health of others if we are not turning first to the ultimate Soul Physician (Christ) and to mutual spiritual friends (the body of Christ) to examine our own heart condition. Self-cardiology is the prerequisite for doing the work of a church cardiologist.

As you read this chapter, ask yourself, *How ready and fit am I to live out Ephesians 4 ministry? What is the spiritual condition of my heart? What prescriptions does God's Word recommend for my heart condition?*

Congregational Cardiology: The Geography of the Heart—Diagnosis, Not Demographics

As God's Word diagnoses our hearts, we become ready to begin congregational cardiology. But what is it and how do we do it *relationally*?

Most churches, if they perform a cultural analysis of their congregation and community, tend only to collect biographical (age, gender, marital status, education, socioeconomic status) and geographical information. In diagnosing congregational fitness, you want to examine the *geography of the heart*. If you're going to assess how ready your church is for the relational ministry of speaking the truth in love, then your mindset must be *relational connection, not data collection.*

As the Bible does, think of your congregation as one body, as one corporate personality. Assess your congregation's readiness for one-another disciple-making by examining the current spiritual fitness of your church according to the Ephesians 4 ministry model. (Throughout this chapter I use "Ephesians 4 ministry" as shorthand for the robustly healthy church we examined in chapter 1.)

A survey can receive out-of-the-blue results in out-of-context responses and low return rates. Before you use a survey, precede it with sermons, lessons, and congregational gatherings to explain the Ephesians 4 ministry focus and the purpose of the survey. Use pulpit and bulletin announcements, e-newsletters, your website, social media pages, and personal contact to encourage participation by a scheduled date.

It's typically wise to avoid anonymous surveys. If we're going to relate maturely in Christ, then we should be able to put our names behind our loving feedback.

Your launch team should ask at least 10 percent of those who complete the survey if they would agree to a follow-up face-to-face interview. Select people who are representative of the congregation. For effective interviews, use the material from this chapter and from Appendix 2.1 (available free online at https://rpmministries.org/ebc-resources/) to guide your team in creating congregational and community surveys. In this way, your launch team owns the questions and understands them.

Train your team in basic listening skills so they can use the survey questions as a springboard for relational interviewing. Equip your team to draw people out by using follow-up questions to probe deeper.

Use the survey interview method in conjunction with other means for becoming culturally informed about your congregation's heart health. Conduct congregational input nights to provide opportunities for members to communicate their sense of where they've been, who they are, and where they're headed. Host leadership community nights with a similar purpose but a more focused audience—those active in church ministry leadership. Participate with your leadership team (pastoral staff, elders, deacons) in similar conversations. Read your church constitution, mission statement, doctrinal statements, and written historical documents. With every method, your goal is to define the gap between God's grand vision for a healthy church, where you are as a congregation, and where you see God calling your church.

Some leaders are nervous about the survey interview process because they fear "the pooling of ignorance." However, because you have crafted your survey based upon the Ephesians 4 ministry model, the process is not a pooling of ignorance but a pulling out of insight. Using your trained interviewers who lead spiritual conversations about heart health means that conversations are facilitated. Once you've collated the results, your equipped launch team directs the diagnosis of the congregation's spiritual condition and leads the process of prescribing God's spiritual cure.

Designing Congregation-Specific Diagnostic Tools: The Congregational SWORD Heart Exam

If I only provide you with sample survey questions and conversation starters, then you'll have a fish, but you won't know how to fish. And your fish will fit my ministry setting, but not yours. Instead, you *first* need transferrable principles for creating your own congregation-specific diagnostic tools. I provide those principles for you in the SWORD Heart Exam. With those principles in hand, *then* you can effectively use the sample questions provided later in this chapter and the sample Congregational SWORD Heart Exam contained in Appendix 2.1.

Many people use a SWOT Analysis (Strengths, Weaknesses, Opportunities, Threats) as their diagnostic grid. I use a SWORD Heart Exam (Strengths, Weaknesses, Opportunities, Risks, Diagnosis) because God's Word is sharper than any two-edged sword, able to discern the thoughts and intents of the heart (Hebrews 4:12–13). The SWORD examination focuses your attention on responding proactively as you grow in understanding your congregation's past, present, and future heart fitness for Ephesians 4 ministry.

- **S: Strengths**—Identifying Strengths: What have we done and are we doing well in Ephesians 4 ministry?

- **W: Weaknesses**—Recognizing Weaknesses: Where and why do we need to improve in Ephesians 4 ministry?

- **O: Opportunities**—Picturing Opportunities: How can we move toward robust Ephesians 4 ministry?

- **R: Risks**—Evaluating Risks: What obstacles stand in the way of healthy Ephesians 4 ministry?

- **D: Diagnosis**—Diagnosing Heart Fitness: What prescriptions does God's Word suggest, given the state of our congregation's Ephesians 4 heart health?

Identifying Strengths: What Have We Done and Are We Doing Well in Ephesians 4 Ministry?

Identifying strengths is biblical. When Jesus addressed the seven churches in Revelation 2—3, in most cases he began with a positive presentation of their present spiritual strengths. The Spirit promises to sovereignly assemble spiritually gifted believers to form a unified, empowered body (1 Corinthians 12). Starting your SWORD exam by assessing past and present health builds on the positive work God has done and is doing among your congregation.

This is particularly important if you're new to your church. Your perception may be, "I have to fix this place." The people's perception may be, "Why does it have to be his way or the highway? Is everything going to have to change? Haven't we been doing anything right in God's eyes?" We should appreciate what has gone before rather than assuming we are the answer person who knows exactly what the church needs. We create trust by communicating that some things should not change, but rather be valued, maximized, and amplified.

As a spiritual conditioning coach, do what many sports trainers do—view videos of success. Don't only observe the times when your congregation struck out. Spot the times when they hit a home run. Applaud them. Cheer them on. Affirm the good work God has accomplished and is accomplishing in them. Ponder together how to keep the good things going and growing.

Recognizing Weaknesses: Where and Why Do We Need to Improve in Ephesians 4 Ministry?

Engaging in spiritual conversations about spiritual weakness is never easy. However, it is necessary. When Jesus addressed the seven churches of Asia Minor, he pulled no punches in exposing their sin.

The objective is to isolate specific samples from the past and present where the congregation lacks Ephesians 4 heart health. Seek to discern heart motivations by looking for longstanding, underlying patterns. What in the corporate system—the congregation's mindset about ministry—is causing heart blockage?

How do you respond to what you see? First, realize that in the assessment process you don't have to solve everything. You are learning the heart of your people. Second, the eventual response may be similar to what Jesus called for in Revelation 2—3—individual and corporate repentance. There are spiritual reasons for unhealthy churches that we must address by speaking the truth in love. Third, chapter 5 addresses further responses under the headings of relational change management and biblical conflict resolution.

Picturing Opportunities: How Can We Move Toward Robust Ephesians 4 Ministry?

Here you look forward to an even brighter future. You prime the congregational pump so members begin envisioning future opportunities. As you talk to people who are excited about this future vision, recruit these change agents as part of your pilot team.

Even in negatives, emphasize positive possibilities. Ask, "What dormant gifts for Ephesians 4 ministry can we fan into flame? What will our ministry look like when we turn this around? What resources are going untapped? How can we tap into them?"

Evaluate linkage. Ask, "Where is Ephesians 4 ministry taking place, but in disjointed ways? How can we organize the organism so these natural, informal gatherings become a supernatural, normal part of our congregational life?"

Seek to determine priorities moving forward. You can't do everything all at once, so ask, "Where do we move in the Ephesians 4 ministry process? How? Where should we start? What's our next step?"

Evaluating Risks: What Obstacles Stand in the Way of Healthy Ephesians 4 Ministry?

Now you look toward the future, but not with naïve eyes. You survey the current landscape and scout the potential roadblocks in the congregation's path toward church health.

Jesus teaches how foolish it is to attempt to build something new without first counting the costs (Luke 14:28–33). The context for that passage is discipleship. In explaining how costly it is to commit to producing disciple-makers, Jesus is encouraging disciples to gain a realistic perspective on potential hindrances to ministry. Who and what may stand against us? What apple carts might we upset? What cherished, longstanding ministries may need to die an honorable death because they no longer serve a disciple-making purpose?

We know we are called to Ephesians 4 ministry, but how committed are we? Are we committed enough to work through the change management process? To wade into conflict resolution situations? To reach into our pockets, purses, and bank accounts to provide the necessary resources?

Diagnosing Heart Fitness: What Prescriptions Does God's Word Suggest, Given the State of Our Congregation's Ephesians 4 Heart Health?

We should not expend our time or ask for others to give their time in the assessment process unless we have a plan for how we'll use the insights we glean. Congregations are tired of surveys and questionnaires that accomplish nothing. Diagnosing your congregational heart fitness communicates that you value your people, what they're doing, and the wisdom they have shared with you.

Practically speaking, this begins with the tedious task of collating the responses—written responses, responses from the in-person interviews, and responses from various congregational gatherings. After someone has organized that collation, your team's primary task is to assess the assessment by *identifying themes*. What comes up repeatedly? What messages are you hearing?

As you identify themes, keep your goal in view. Use God's eternal vision for his church as a spiritual EKG to diagnose the heart health of your congregation in order to establish a present baseline for envisioning God's future dream. Pray for a big-picture understanding of who you are as a church family. Ask, "What are the past and present strengths and weaknesses, as measured by the Ephesians 4 portrait of God's healthy family? What future opportunities and risks do we face as we move toward growth as Christ's healthy body?"

Ask your team, "If Christ were speaking to us as he spoke to the seven churches in Revelation 2—3, what would he say?" Lead your team in using the results of the SWORD Heart Exam to write an extensive paraphrase of Revelation 2—3 as if it were addressed to your church. The letters to the seven churches lend themselves well to this. In each letter we read Christ's *understanding* of the congregation, his *diagnoses* of their spiritual strengths and sins, his *prescription* of spiritual remedies, and his *prognosis* depending upon their responsiveness.

Report your summary to the church leadership and work with them to craft your next steps. Your final task is to communicate back to your congregation. Your people will be greatly encouraged when they realize that what they shared has played a significant role in shaping your decisions about your ministry launch.

Congregational Survey Samplers

You can find a sample Congregational SWORD Heart Exam in Appendix 2.1 (available free online at https://rpmministries.org/ebc-resources/). You'll note that the questions on the following pages are worded for *your team*—these are the types of issues that you want to raise. You'll then note that the questions in Appendix 2.1 are worded for *a specific congregation*. The following sample questions are intended to spark your imagination so you can create *your own congregation-specific* interactions—using wording that your congregation will understand and that fits your ministry focus.

Identifying Past and Present Strengths: Informal Congregational One-Another Ministry

- What powerful stories does our church tell about amazing times of being together?

- Which people do you point to and say, "That's an encourager! That's a spiritual leader!" What stands out about those people?

- Share examples of ways our church (past/present) has provided equipping for mutual encouragement and one-another care. What methods were used? How long did the training last?

- How confident are you in your ability to provide biblical encouragement to a friend who is suffering or struggling with a sin issue?

Identifying Past and Present Strengths: Formal Biblical Counseling Equipping

- What compelling stories does our church tell about times when lives have been changed through biblical counseling?

- Share examples of ways our church (past/present) has provided equipping for formal biblical counseling and disciple-making. What methods were used? How long did the training last?

- As you look around our congregation, which people are discipling others? Who would you go to for discipleship?

- How confident are you in your ability to equip disciple-makers? To counsel biblically?

Recognizing Past and Present Weaknesses: Informal Congregational One-Another Ministry

- What patterns or mindsets might make it difficult for our church to become a place where we speak the truth in love to one another?

- What training ministries for one-another care have we launched that "fell flat"? Why do you think this happened?

- Have you or someone you know ever needed care from our congregation but been unable to receive it? What happened?

- What are specific ways our church could improve the provision of one-another care?

Recognizing Past and Present Weaknesses: Formal Biblical Counseling Equipping

- When biblical counseling is needed, how long does it take to receive it? Have you or someone you know ever requested biblical counseling but been unable to receive it?

- Are there any weaknesses in our discipleship ministry that you would like to see us address? How?

- Compared to Ephesians 4:11–16, what priority does our congregation give to discipling disciple-makers? How could we become more effective?

- How would you assess our congregation's ability to provide biblical premarital counseling? Marital counseling? Family/parental counseling? Individual counseling? How could we improve?

Picturing Future Opportunities: Informal Congregational One-Another Ministry

- What would a mission/vision statement look like that helps our church meet the challenge of one-another ministry?

- How can we move forward toward a more robust Ephesians 4 one-another ministry of speaking the truth in love?

- What dormant gifts for Ephesians 4 ministry can we fan into flame?

- What level of interest would you have in being further trained as a spiritual friend who could help others in an informal, friend-to-friend manner through speaking the truth in love?

Picturing Future Opportunities: Formal Biblical Counseling Equipping

- What would a mission/vision statement look like that helps our church meet the challenge of equipping one another to make disciple-makers?

- Who is God calling us to be as a unique disciple-making church within the larger body of Christ in our particular community?

- Where is Ephesians 4 ministry taking place, but in disjointed ways? How can we organize the organism so these natural, informal gatherings become a supernatural, normal part of our congregational life?

- What level of interest do you have in being further trained as a biblical counselor who relates Christ's truth to people's lives?

Evaluating Future Risks: Informal Congregational One-Another Ministry

- In the past, how has our church responded to change and to the launch of new ministries? How might similar responses hinder a renewed focus on every member disciple-making?

- What obstacles might stand in the way of healthy one-another ministry in our church?

- Where do we need to grow or change if we are to move forward as a church in which every member speaks the truth in love?

- What potential hindrances and limitations might we face as we move toward Ephesians 4 ministry?

Evaluating Future Risks: Formal Biblical Counseling Equipping

- Rate how large the gap is between where we are now and where you think we need to be in order to build a healthy equipping church.

- If we launched a biblical counseling training ministry, who and what might stand in the way? What apple carts might we upset? What objections might people raise?

- What would you add, subtract, or reprioritize in our church for us to become a more effective disciple-making church?

- What people, time, and financial limitations might we face as we move toward launching a biblical counseling training ministry?

Community Cardiology: Diagnosing Community Readiness for Gospel-Centered Ministry

God calls us to be a church *of* biblical counseling *to* the community *for* his glory. Paul's request should be our prayer: "Pray also for me, that whenever I speak, words may be given me so that I will fearlessly make known the mystery of the gospel" (Ephesians 6:19).

Community cardiology follows the gospel-centered biblical counseling passion of equipping every member to speak and live gospel truth in love to fulfill the Great Commission of going and making disciples. The 4E Ministry Training Strategy prepares God's people not only for ministry *in* the body but also *to* the community.

Community cardiology asks, "Who is God calling us to be as a unique church within the larger body of Christ in our particular community?" It seeks to understand how to build gospel-centered bridges of connection between the congregation and community to relate Christ's changeless truth to our changing times. In a culturally informed manner, we influence our culture for Christ.

DISCIPLE-MAKING CHAMPIONS

*Steve Viars, Senior Pastor; Rob Green,
Counseling Pastor, Faith Church*

We met Pastors Viars and Green of Faith Church in chapter 1. A church *of* biblical counseling, their counseling ministry is not only *within* their congregation, it is also *to* their community. Every week, nearly one hundred community members receive free biblical counseling. Their mission explains why: "Faith Church is a family of followers of Jesus Christ who desire to honor God by applying his sufficient Word *to all areas of life and ministry.*" They are reclaiming biblical counseling for the community. Pastor Viars explains:

> "To fulfill our vision, we built a community center, not for our congregation, but for our community. We also built a state-of-the-art outdoor skateboard park. Many skaters end up in church every Sunday with their skateboards, torn jeans, body piercings, and tattoos to hear the pulpit ministry of the Word. Equipped members hang out at the skate park to engage skaters through the personal ministry of the Word."

Pastor Green notes:

> "Faith's Vision of Hope residential treatment center offers biblical counseling for women who are struggling with unplanned pregnancy, alcohol or drug abuse, eating disorders, or self-harm. State agencies and the court system regularly refer girls to Vision of Hope with the full knowledge that the program is based upon biblical counseling." (To learn more about the Faith Church model, see Pastor Viars' book *Loving Your Community.*)

Reclaiming Biblical Counseling for the Community: Diagnosing Your Community's Heart

Consider three primary ways to understand the heartbeat of your unique community:

- Be in your community to understand your community.

- Ask your congregation about your community.

- Ask your community about your church.

Be in Your Community to Understand Your Community:
Incarnational Cultural Awareness

Like Paul, we have to be in our community to understand our community. For a quarter century I coached youth and high school wrestling in public schools. I've learned a great deal about how people in my community think, what their passions are, where they struggle, and what they think of Christ and the church.

Take advantage of natural connections—yours and those of your members. Discover who is already serving in nonchurch volunteer agencies and learn about your community from them. Actively teach your people to view their lives beyond the walls of the church as places that hold opportunities for the personal ministry of the Word. Celebrate the ministries of your people in your community. Establish relationships with nonprofit organizations, local agencies, and the school system.

Ask Your Congregation about Your Community:
Intentional Cultural Awareness

In the Congregational SWORD Heart Exam in Appendix 2.1, you'll find questions for your congregation about your community. Here are some sample probes that you can word to match your congregation and adjust to fit your ministry context.

- How can we support you in your connections with our community?

- What community activities/agencies are you involved in, and what are you learning about the people of our community?

- Tell us about the history of our community.

- List five words that come to mind when you think of the folks in our community.

- What are some unique characteristics of the residents of our community?

- What are people in our community passionate about?

- How do the people of our community spend their time?

- What are the five greatest concerns of the residents of our community? Five greatest struggles? Five greatest counseling needs? How could we address these issues biblically?

- What is the typical resident of our community looking for in a church?

- What type of person is attracted to our church? Who feels at home in our church? Why?

- What would the average community member consider to be the five greatest strengths of our church? The five greatest weaknesses?

- How would community members describe our church in one sentence or word?

- How can we minister biblically to our community?

- What impact might a more intentional, structured approach to biblical counseling have on our community?

- How responsive do you think our community would be if we offered biblical counseling?

- Who is God calling us to be as a unique disciple-making church within the larger body of Christ in our community?

- Ephesians 3:20 says that God will do more than we could ever think or imagine in our church for his glory. What do you think God wants to do through our church in this community?

Ask Your Community About Your Church: Invitational Cultural Awareness

Only the brave ask their community about their church. Be brave and train your pilot team to enter into probing conversations with community members, asking questions such as,

- What first comes to mind when you think about our church?

- How would people you know describe our church in one sentence or one word? How would you? What impressions do you have about our church?

- How can our church make a positive contribution to this community?

- What are the five greatest concerns of the residents of our community? Five greatest struggles? Five greatest needs? How well or poorly has our church been addressing these issues? What more could we do moving forward?

- What would you consider the five greatest strengths of our church? The five greatest weaknesses?

- What is the typical resident of our community looking for in a church? What would you look for?

- Who do you think would feel at home in our church? Why?

- What questions do you have about our church?

- What counseling needs do people in our community have?

- Would the people of our community be open to receiving biblical counseling from our church?

COMMENCEMENT: GOSPEL TRUTH FITLY SPOKEN

"I don't know how they did things where you came from, but we're not like that around here." Those blunt words encapsulate why we must diagnose our congregation's and community's readiness, health, and fitness compared to Christ's vision for his church. If we don't, then our application of God's truth will sound more like us than like Christ communicating his timeless truth through us. There's nothing Christ-centered about communicating truth with a my-way-or-the-highway mentality.

We need to follow Paul's specific application of speaking the truth in love. He insists that our conversations must be "helpful for building others up according to their needs, that it may benefit those who listen. And do not grieve the Holy Spirit" (Ephesians 4:29–30). We grieve the Spirit when we stubbornly refuse to be culturally informed spiritual cardiologists. Grace-oriented gospel conversations build up others when our personal ministry of the Word suits the present time and the present person in their present context.

As we begin to understand Christ's eternal vision for his church *in the context of* our current congregation and community, then we have a present baseline for envisioning God's future dream for our church. It's to that dream that we next turn our attention as we learn how to lead God's people in jointly crafting a congregation-wide MVP-C Statement (Mission, Vision, Passion, Commission). Be prepared to be captured by what captures the heart of God—bringing Christ glory in the church by showing his people his vision for them, which is immeasurably more than all we could ask or imagine (Ephesians 3:20–21).

GROWING TOGETHER: QUESTIONS FOR REFLECTION, DISCUSSION, AND APPLICATION

1. Reflecting on Jesus and Paul:

   a. What can you apply to your ministry from Jesus' culturally informed ministry?

   b. What can you apply to your ministry from Paul's focus on studying Scripture and society?

2. What self-cardiology processes are you regularly involved in? How often do you turn to Christ, your Soul Physician, for a spiritual heart exam? What spiritual friends help you watch your life and doctrine?

3. How could you take the Congregational SWORD Heart Exam sampler questions and make them congregation-specific for your ministry?

4. How could you take the questions that ask your church about your community and make them specific for your ministry in your particular community?

5. How could you take the questions that ask your community about your church and make them specific for your community?

Dreaming God's Dream

Becoming an MVP-C Congregation

vividly recall the responses I received when I introduced the idea of vision casting to my church. Naively, I was excited. Just looking at the body language of my elders, however, I quickly discerned that they failed to share my enthusiasm.

Their skepticism about vision follows similar doubts that others—perhaps you—share. One elder explained, "Pastor Bob, we tried this before you came, and it seemed like a major waste of time—lots of work and little lasting benefit."

Another elder stated, "I work in industry and we do vision stuff all the time. So what makes this anything more than secular marketing strategies?"

A third elder added, "Well, when we did this in another church, it felt like it came down from Moses on high. It was more dictatorial than congregation-based."

Still a fourth elder countered, "My experience was the opposite. I've been involved in the process twice. Both times it felt like pooling ignorance because it was so democratic."

MEN WANTED FOR A HAZARDOUS JOURNEY

Not one to be easily deterred, I responded to their less-than-enthusiastic reactions by telling them the story of Sir Ernest Shackleton (1874–1922). The British Antarctic explorer placed the following advertisement in London newspapers in preparation for the National Antarctic Expedition—which subsequently failed to reach the South Pole.

MEN WANTED FOR HAZARDOUS JOURNEY. Small wages, bitter cold, long months of complete darkness, safe return doubtful. Honor and recognition in case of success.

—Ernest Shackleton[1]

Shackleton later said of his call for volunteers, "It seemed as though all the men in Great Britain were determined to accompany me, the response was so overwhelming."[2]

I then told my elders, "I'm convinced that we ask too little of God's people. Gone are the days when, without apology, we summoned God's people to an arduous journey like Ernest Shackleton. *The ways we typically invite people to do church and be the church are not compelling enough. We cater to consumers with eye candy instead of challenging Christians to live courageously for Christ.*"

I continued, "What if, together as a congregation, we searched God's Word for his compelling mission, vision, passion, and commission (MVP-C) for our church in our community? What if we did it in a Christ-focused, other-centered, biblically based manner that rallied people like Shackleton did?" I then wondered if such a calling might sound like this:

GOD'S PEOPLE WANTED FOR ARDUOUS JOURNEY. No human wages, but the internal reward of joy and the eternal reward of hearing, "Well done!" Bitter cold and long months of complete darkness because servanthood is lonely. Safe return of your spirit guaranteed. Complete safety doubtful because in this world we will have tribulation, and all who attempt to lead a godly life will be persecuted. Honor and recognition guaranteed from God. Henceforth there is laid up for you the crown of righteousness.

—Your Elders

NOT YOUR FATHER'S VISION CASTING

When these godly elders glimpsed the concept of vision catching and casting, they became as excited as I was. We became champions for the MVP-C

---

1. Roland Huntford, *Shackleton* (London: Hodder & Stoughton, 1985), 362.

2. Huntford, *Shackleton*, 365.

(Mission, Vision, Passion, Commission) process. Together, we helped our congregation see what envisioning was and was not about.

- Vision catching and casting is *not* about catering to consumers; rather, it challenges committed Christians to follow Christ for God's glory. Envisioning involves a biblically based, Christ-centered, God-focused process of determining God's will for our congregation in our community.

- Vision catching and casting is *not* dictatorial or a Moses-like handing down of a vision from on high; it is *not* so democratic that it becomes a pooling of ignorance. Rather, it requires humble leaders facilitating a congregation-wide dialogue. Envisioning involves leaders and members together searching God's Word for his wisdom for their ministry.

- Vision catching and casting is *not* secular marketing strategies or worldly business principles; rather, it follows a biblical theology and methodology of discerning God's will congregationally. Envisioning involves searching the Scriptures to become captivated by God's specific calling for our church in our community for God's glory.

- Vision catching and casting is *not* a waste of time; rather, the envisioning process produces further unity and maturity as the body grows together into Christ, the Head. Envisioning results in an increasingly clear picture of God's mission, vision, passion, and commission for our church in our community.

I don't know your past experiences related to the envisioning process. Nor can I guess your visceral gut reaction to "vision talk." I do know that I've experienced the joy of an entire congregation, like the men of Great Britain, determined to accompany their leaders in an overwhelming response to catching God's vision. This is why I long to see you equipped to lead God's people in jointly crafting a compelling MVP-C Statement.

Now that you have caught God's vision for the entire church (chapter 1) and examined the current state of your church and community (chapter 2), you're ready to catch and cast God's dream for your specific church in your unique community. To accomplish that, we need to understand *what* an MVP-C

Statement is and *why* it's so vital (chapter 3). Then we need to learn *how to* jointly craft a biblical counseling ministry MVP-C Statement (chapter 4).

CAPTURING YOUR BIBLICAL CALLING

Church ministry can be filled with activities that seem disjointed and disconnected. We sometimes wonder, *What's the big picture? Where are we headed? What's our biblical purpose?* The MVP-C process addresses this confusion by bringing focus to our ministries.

People who write and speak on envisioning use different terms in various ways. I'll be the first to acknowledge that MVP-C is *not* inspired. What follows is *one* way to organize and communicate a practical theology that assists God's people to catch and cast God's plan for ministry.

Through the congregational process of envisioning God's ministry, we discover why we do what we do. Envisioning involves the following:

- *M*ission: Determining our biblical reason for existence

- *V*ision: Detecting our unique future focus

- *P*assion: Depicting the essence of who God calls us to be

- *C*ommission: Mapping out how to move from here to there

Congregational and community diagnosis shows us where we are today.

- *M*ission tells us where we should be according to God's Word.

- *V*ision pictures where God is leading us.

- *P*assion tells us who we are on our journey.

- *C*ommission provides the road map to travel from the present to the future.

Mission: Your Universal God-Given Calling and Purpose— God's Compass

One of the legitimate concerns that some Christians express about the envisioning process is that there is typically little or no Bible or theology involved.

To counter that problem, before we launch any ministry, we should examine a biblical theology of that ministry. That is true whether we are planting a church or launching a biblical counseling ministry.

The mission statement process examines what God calls *every* biblical counseling ministry to be. It clarifies God's timeless purpose. Picture how this revolutionizes the mission process. You invite everyone who is interested in your biblical counseling ministry to explore together *what the Bible says about biblical counseling*.

A pastor I was consulting with described the benefit. "It's a no-brainer. How can it be a bad thing to bring your team together to study the Scriptures!" He reported later,

> Even if we had never launched a biblical counseling ministry, just our time of joint exploration of God's Word would have made the whole process worthwhile. We *became* a team, a family, a group *of* biblical counselors as we studied what the Word says *about* biblical counseling!

Mission is a Word-saturated, Bible-focused process of answering these questions: Why do we exist? What is our purpose? What does the Bible say about how we should minister in this area? Mission answers are *universal*, timeless, and clearly revealed in God's Word—they are always true for everyone.

A biblical mission provides a theological foundation for ministry. It's God's compass pointing true north. To use God's compass, mission statements seek to finish these sentences:

- According to the Bible, we exist to…

- According to the Bible, the mission of our church is to…

To help you to understand the MVP-C process, I'll provide two sample MVP-C Statements from my pastoral ministry.[3] One is a church-wide statement and the other is a biblical counseling ministry-specific statement. These are simply illustrative; not statements you must use.

After several months of congregational interaction about God's Word, our congregation united around the following church-wide mission.

---

3. To view the complete MVP-C Statements, see Appendices 3.1 and 3.2 (available free online at https://rpmministries.org/ebc-resources/)

OUR UNIONTOWN BIBLE CHURCH
MISSION STATEMENT

According to the Bible, the mission of Uniontown Bible Church is to:

make disciples who love Christ, love the body of Christ, and love the world on behalf of Christ. Therefore, the fivefold purpose of our church is to fulfill the Great Commandment and the Great Commission through:

- Discipleship: Equipping God's People

- Worship: Exalting and Enjoying God

- Fellowship: Encouraging God's People

- Stewardship: Empowering God's People

- Ambassadorship: Evangelizing the Unsaved

Building upon the congregation-wide mission statement, two years later we developed a biblical counseling mission statement. We called our ministry LEAD (Life Encouragers And Disciplers).

OUR LEAD BIBLICAL COUNSELING MINISTRY
MISSION STATEMENT

According to the Bible, LEAD exists to:

equip encouragers and disciplers who lovingly, wisely, and powerfully relate God's truth to human relationships. We will apply Christ's grace to the evils we have suffered and to the sins we have committed. Through the personal ministry of the Word, we will empower one another to grasp these truths:

- It's normal to hurt (Romans 12:15; 2 Corinthians 1:3–9);

- it's possible to hope (Romans 8:28; 2 Corinthians 1:8–11);

- it's horrible to sin, but wonderful to be forgiven (Romans 1—6);

- it's supernatural to mature (Romans 7—15).

Vision: Your Unique Ministry Dream and DNA— Your Fingerprint

In the envisioning process, you travel from the present (mission) to the future (vision). You move from the universal and biblical (mission) to the unique and contextual (vision). Your mission focuses on the purpose of your church or ministry, while your vision focuses on the projected future state of your church or ministry. You ask, "How do we move forward as we advance Christ's mission? How has God shaped us to complete his mission?"

It's helpful to picture vision as a future dream that seeks to glimpse a better future. To focus on this better future, vision statements seek to finish the sentence:

- *It is our dream to…*

It also helps to see vision as a church's DNA or fingerprint. No two are alike. That's why in the vision process we ask, "How does our *unique* congregation use its *distinctive* gift-mix to fulfill our *special* calling in our *specific* community?" It's also why I have launched four very different biblical counseling ministries in four very different congregations.

Vision answers are idiosyncratic—they apply uniquely to your congregational ministry team in your setting. Vision orients your congregation to your sovereign gifting and to the profound thirst of your community. You determine your ministry vision by prayerfully and jointly pondering your congregational SWORD Heart Exam, your community diagnosis, and your biblical mission. At Uniontown Bible Church, as we walked through this process, we co-created a vision statement that united our congregation around the following jointly pursued future dream.

OUR UNIONTOWN BIBLE CHURCH
VISION STATEMENT

It is our DREAM to be:

a dynamic family, creatively and relevantly sharing Christ's grace with our neighbors in Carroll County and beyond.

We will skillfully equip one another through small-group and one-another discipleship ministries that empower us to build loving relationships that last through all the storms of life.

We built our biblical counseling vision statement upon our congregational vision.

OUR LEAD BIBLICAL COUNSELING MINISTRY
VISION STATEMENT

It is our DREAM to be:

a dynamic family of soul caregivers and spiritual directors who encourage one another through the personal ministry of the Word to turn upward in worship of our Father to find grace to help in our suffering and sin, and to turn outward in fellowship with our brothers and sisters to give and receive Christ's grace.

Passion: Your Captivating Ministry Identity and Imprint—Your Heartbeat

Mission is our universal calling—where God wants us. Vision is our unique future—where God is leading us. Passion is our captivating identity—*who* we are as we serve Christ together. We can picture passion as a pithy phrase capturing and communicating the essence of who we are as we fulfill God's calling and our ministry dream.

Passion communicates what we will die for and therefore what we will live for. Passion is our ultimate purpose statement. For my ministry, RPM

Ministries, I've captured it as *Changing Lives with Christ's Changeless Truth*. For my life, I have pictured it with one word: *Coach*. I'm writing this book because the passion of my life is to coach people to coach others. Passion statements answer the question,

- How do we convey our mission and vision in a compelling way?

Passion answers are creative, imaginative, and memorable. Passion statements typically develop out of prayerful, joint pondering where someone has something of an "Aha!" experience.

At our church, after three months of studying our biblical mission and catching God's vision, one of our deacons had just such an experience. He reported, "We've been praying and thinking about this. Last night it hit me. What do you think of this? *A Loving Place to Grow in Grace*." We didn't have to think much more. That caught the essence of who we wanted to be as we moved into the future for God's glory. As one of our elders said, "That's it! That's us!"

**OUR UNIONTOWN BIBLE CHURCH
PASSION STATEMENT**

A Loving Place to Grow in Grace

In a similar way, our LEAD biblical counseling ministry united around the following passion statement.

**OUR LEAD BIBLICAL COUNSELING MINISTRY
PASSION STATEMENT**

Sharing Christ's Grace Face to Face

Commission: Your Strategic Ministry Action Plan—Your MAP

In my consulting ministry, I've found that few people start with a mission process focused on biblical theology. I've also discovered that most churches end the process before the commission statement. The lack of a biblical foundation is a major reason some churches hesitate to start an envisioning process. The lack of a strategic plan (commission statement) causes some churches to believe that the envisioning process was wasted time.

The commission statement addresses how, *in practice*, you fulfill the mission, vision, and passion. That explains why I place the hyphen after the MVP and before the C. A well-crafted commission statement maps out how we become an MVP ministry.

A commission statement provides the strategy for getting from here to there, how you will "pull it off" and keep your ministry going and growing. Picture the commission statement as a signpost, directional markers, or a GPS. It is your MAP—*M*inistry *A*ction *P*lan.

Jesus provided such a map for his disciples. Jesus fulfilled his mission by preaching and teaching the good news (Matthew 9:35). He pursued his vision as he saw the crowds and had compassion on them because they were like sheep without a shepherd (Matthew 9:36). He followed his passion of being the Chief Shepherd by calling his disciples to become under-shepherds (Matthew 9:37–38).

Then Jesus did something that we sometimes miss. "These twelve Jesus sent out with the following instructions" (Matthew 10:5a). For the next thirty-seven verses, Christ drew his disciples a map—a ministry action plan. He organized the organism. He ad-ministrated the ministry. To his relational and spontaneous compassion, Jesus added a relational and specific commission. (While perhaps grammatically incorrect, I sometimes hyphenate the words "ad-ministrating" and "ad-ministering." In doing so, I'm indicating that there is nothing inherently nonministerial or nonrelational about administration.)

Our commission, like his, should answer questions such as, What's our strategy? What's our action plan? How will we work cooperatively to fulfill God's call? Commission answers are practical while including the big picture. They don't describe every step (that's more tactical than strategic). Instead, they outline the journey by providing signposts. To convey this practical-yet-broad perspective, commission statements strive to complete this sentence:

- *We will seek to fulfill our mission, vision, and passion through...*

**OUR UNIONTOWN BIBLE CHURCH
COMMISSION STATEMENT**

We will seek to fulfill our MVP through:

mutually overseeing the equipping of God's family as servant leaders, modeling maturity, mentoring disciple-makers, managing ministers and ministries, and mending the flock.

We will mutually equip one another to lovingly evangelize the community for Christ, we will encourage the congregation toward vital connection with Christ and the body of Christ, and we will empower one another to become makers of disciple-makers.

Two years later we stated our LEAD Biblical Counseling Ministry commission as follows:

**OUR LEAD BIBLICAL COUNSELING
MINISTRY COMMISSION STATEMENT**

We will seek to fulfill our LEAD MVP through:

the 4Es of *e*nvisioning, *e*nlisting, *e*quipping, and *e*mpowering a congregation of spiritual friends, biblical counselors, and small group ministers.

We will comprehensively equip soul caregivers and spiritual directors in the 4Cs of biblical *c*ontent, Christlike *c*haracter, counseling *c*ompetence, and Christian *c*ommunity so they can sustain, heal, reconcile, and guide individuals, couples, and families in our congregation and community to know Christ, grow in Christ, and become Christlike disciple-makers.

Each of the components of our commission statement contained operational definitions that we then used to chart our journey forward. For example, envisioning, enlisting, equipping, and empowering suggested for us the tactical plans you are learning in this book. They became our map throughout each step of our journey to help us plan and assess our progress.

DISCIPLE-MAKING CHAMPION

Pastor Greg Cook, Soul Care Pastor,
Christ Chapel Bible Church

Pastor Greg Cook oversees the Soul Care ministry at Christ Chapel Bible Church in Fort Worth, Texas. In his doctorate dissertation, Pastor Cook assessed how his congregation and staff viewed the Soul Care ministry and perceived the need for biblical counseling. Their Soul Care team used that information, their biblical studies, and their joint reflection to develop their purpose statements. Their mission statement affirms this as follows:

> Soul Care exists to glorify God by
> caring for sufferers, restoring sinners,
> and equipping the saints.

They explain, "Our fundamental purpose is to create disciples. We exist to equip the body of Christ to care for others within the church and in the community so that they will, in turn, take the comfort they have received from Christ and help and train others how to do the same."

They stated their vision this way:

> To stretch *every* involved person from the threshold
> of their spiritual pilgrimage toward becoming
> a fully developing follower of Christ.

Though they do not list a passion statement per se, they clearly have a passion. When asked to describe their biblical counseling training ministry in one brief phrase, they choose one word. When asked to define biblical counseling, they choose the same word:

> Discipleship

Their version of a commission statement revolves around a sequence of caring, restoring, and equipping.

"We make sure that people are initially cared for, work toward having them restored to God and to others, and then train them so that they can, in turn, care for others. Our ultimate goal in the supervision of our lay counselors is that we have experienced lay counselors leading the supervision groups and then the staff oversees those key leaders."

They map out their ministry training commission in detail. They include five core components (training of soul care ministers, ministry and staff support, personal ministry, specialized small groups, and marriage mentoring), each with underlying stages and process plans.

THINKING BIBLICALLY ABOUT MINISTRY

It's not enough to know what *M, V, P,* and *C* mean. More importantly, we need a biblical answer to the question, Why is an MVP-C Statement so vital?

Everyone Has an MVP-C, Some Let the Bible Shape It

We commit the time and energy to develop an MVP-C Statement because *something* always guides our choices about how we do church and ministry. Some develop their MVP-C purposefully and biblically; others don't realize or understand what guides them. In my consulting, I've detected at least seven factors that influence church decision-making: tradition, the world, negative people, the neighboring church, finances, consensus, and the pastor's opinion.

Some churches allow *tradition* to lead them, rather than letting the Bible shape their direction. We've all heard the seven last words of the church: "We've never done it that way before." When assessing a congregation-wide or ministry-specific direction, we would be wise to ask, How did that tradition develop? Is it biblical? Is what we're doing and where we're heading what God wants for us?

Some churches allow the *world* to guide them rather than letting the Bible shape their purpose. This can be fad-oriented: "What's the latest fad, trend, or bandwagon we can jump on?" Others are felt-need oriented: "What do people want that we can give them?" Still others are relevance oriented: "What's relevant to our culture?" I've already indicated that we need to be good students of our congregation, community, and culture. However, in following Jesus' and Paul's examples, we must let the Bible direct how we communicate God's changeless message to our changing times.

Some churches seem to run more on the fuel of *negative people* than on guidance learned from God's Word. The squeaky wheel gets the grease. Anyone who has been a church leader has faced the temptation to say, "We can't upset _____." Will we make church decisions in reaction to negativity, or will we determine direction based upon wisdom from the Word? This doesn't imply that we should become defensive about criticism or close our ears to negative feedback. It means we develop our ministry focus through what we learn from God in his Word and not based upon what we hear from the vocal minority.

Others model their church off the *neighboring church*. We can become shaped by the big-church orientation. We are tempted to say, "We have to do it the way the best-selling Christian author does it." Or, "That church is growing. Let's do church the way they're doing church." While there's nothing wrong with learning from others, there's plenty wrong with plopping someone else's MVP-C focus on your church without doing your own biblical work.

Still others decide how to do church based upon *finances*. The mentality becomes, "We do this because it's all we can afford." A past orientation develops. "Last year's income becomes this year's budget, which becomes this year's vision." Obviously, any MVP-C must be realistic. It must set priorities. However, tight times provide more reason to be sure that every penny spent is directed toward God-shaped ministry.

Some let *consensus* or "secular democracy" shape the envisioning process. Majority rules. I understand congregational government—I was saved and discipled in a Baptist church. I'm not disputing that style of church decision-making. Rather, I'm raising the issues of pooled ignorance and of decisions guided by human opinions instead of God's Word. Even in churches governed by congregational rule, God still calls spiritual leaders to guide people to use biblical principles to make wise church decisions.

The opposite of consensus is the *pastor's opinion* or "secular dictatorship." This method reflects a problem that many people have with the way vision casting has frequently been practiced. It's top-down, Moses-like. The pastor sees himself as uniquely and directly receiving God's vision for the entire church. Although some popular Christian authors and church leaders teach and practice this method of envisioning, it's not the model I'm presenting. The authority does not lie in a person; the authority lies in God and his Word. The model we follow suggests facilitative leadership in which mature, equipped, and called church leaders guide the congregation through the process of *jointly* catching and casting God's vision.

But Is It Biblical?

After I shared with my elders these seven factors that influence church direction, they all wholeheartedly agreed that the Bible must shape our purposes. However, some still wondered whether these mission, vision, passion, and commission ideas were biblical. I explained that while we do not find one specific passage that unites these four concepts, we do find systematic biblical support for the envisioning process. Because we were committed to building our ministry on the sufficiency of Scripture, we explored the following biblical theology of envisioning.

Facilitative Envisioning Leadership

First, we studied what the Bible teaches about how God makes his people aware of his purposes. Our understanding of mission focused on a biblical theology of God's calling. We believed in the equipping of the saints (Ephesians 4:11–16), we believed in a team of equipped equippers (2 Timothy 2:2), and we believed in the priesthood of all believers (1 Peter 2:5; 1 Timothy 2:5). So one elder spoke for us all: "God works through his Word to his people, not just through one individual, no matter how godly or learned."

Another elder thumbed to Proverbs 15:22. "Plans fail for lack of counsel, but with many advisers they succeed," he read for us all. "We need the combined wisdom of God's people to discern jointly his will for our church," he summarized.

Another elder read portions of the vital decision made by the church in Acts 15, including verse 22: "Then the apostles and elders, with the whole church, decided to choose some of their own men and send them to Antioch." "Clearly," this elder stated, "the leaders facilitated a process that actively engaged the people of God."

Yet another elder said, in his typical to-the-point style, "We don't get to make this stuff up. God's Word tells us how to function as a church." He then read 1 Timothy 3:14–15: "I am writing you these instructions so that, if I am delayed, you will know how people ought to conduct themselves in God's household, which is the church of the living God." Our ever-frank elder continued, "Since the Bible is our authority, no one person can hoard the process of setting our ministry direction as a congregation."

Based upon these principles and others, we determined together that we would engage in facilitative envisioning leadership. We would not abdicate our role of shepherding (1 Peter 5:1–5), guiding (1 Timothy 3:5; 5:17), protecting (Acts 20:13–38), and equipping the flock (Ephesians 4:11–16), but neither would we rob from our flock the privilege of studying with us God's mission, vision, passion, and commission for our church.

God's Planning and Ours

Next we probed what the Bible says about planning and purposing. One elder read Jeremiah 29:11: "'I know the plans I have for you,' declares the LORD, 'plans to prosper you and not to harm you, plans to give you hope and a future.'" Pastor Steve Viars, who I introduced you to as one of our Disciple-Making Champions, derives the following principle from this passage: "We all know that God has a plan—a strategic plan that will be carried out to perfection and on time. God is the ultimate planner. His Word gives us the instruction, motivation, cautions, and consequences—both good and bad—for planning. In many places, his Word models strategic planning and accomplishing a God-given goal."

Our elder board also examined Proverbs 29:18. "Where there is no revelation, people cast off restraint; but blessed is the one who heeds wisdom's instruction." In the context of wisdom literature, we interpreted that verse to mean we have two choices when it comes to planning: to do what is right in God's eyes as revealed in his Word, or to do what is right in our own eyes.

We applied that truth in conjunction with Proverbs 19:21: "Many are the plans in a person's heart, but it is the LORD's purpose that prevails." God wants us to plan according to his plans. And, as we saw in 1 Timothy 3:14–15, we have God's plan for his people outlined in his Word. One elder recapped our thoughts: "A church without a theology of ministry is like a ship without a rudder or a hiker without a compass. Our mission, vision, passion, and commission study will provide the spiritual glasses we need so we do what is right in God's sight."

God's Word and the Mission of the Church

Building upon our first two studies, it was easy for our elder ministry team to see that God wanted every church and every ministry team to understand its God-given mission. We quickly isolated several churchwide mission statements such as Matthew 22:34–40; Matthew 28:16–20; Acts 2:42–47; Ephesians

4:11–16; and the pastoral epistles. These became the foundation for leading our church in a joint development of our congregational mission statement.

Later, motivated by our study, we joined together to do a thorough examination of God's mission, vision, passion, and commission for our elder ministry team. We studied specific passages related to elders, pastors, and shepherds to develop the following Elder Ministry Team Mission Statement.[4]

OUR ELDER MINISTRY TEAM MISSION STATEMENT

According to God's Word, our elder ministry team exists to disciple one another as servant leaders who oversee, empower, and equip our Father's family to reproduce in themselves and others Christ-like love for Christ, Christians, and those who do not yet know Christ.

God's Word and the Vision of the Church

Exploring mission was easy. However, we started off with a little more debate regarding whether the Bible teaches that every person, church, and ministry team has a unique purpose, fingerprint, and DNA. Then, even without looking at the verses, one elder paraphrased Psalm 139:13–14; Jeremiah 1:4–10; and Ephesians 2:10. "We're each fearfully and wonderfully made. God told Jeremiah that he uniquely formed him in the womb for a specific purpose that God clearly laid out from all eternity. And we know that we are each God's workmanship—his poem—designed for a special purpose no one else can fill."

We then looked at the seven churches in Revelation 2—3. We observed how each of them had unique ministry emphases, strengths, and weaknesses.

One of our elders then mentioned how the Bible teaches that the Spirit sovereignly assembles the exact gift-mix of every congregation (1 Corinthians 12:1–31). Another chimed in with the message of 1 Peter 4:10: "Each one should use whatever gift you have received to serve others, as faithful stewards of God's grace in its various forms."

Another elder highlighted Paul's principles and practice. "Paul said that he became all things to all people so that by all means some might be saved," he

---

4. To view the complete MVP-C Statement, see Appendix 3.3 (available free online at https://rpmministries.org/ebc-resources/).

said, paraphrasing 1 Corinthians 9:19–23. Then we traced Paul's very different ministry methods throughout Acts—all based upon Paul's awareness of the uniqueness of the culture in each city he entered. Paul's practice concurred with his specific calling, which Paul described as "the sphere of service God himself has assigned to us" (2 Corinthians 10:13).

Convinced of the biblical wisdom behind the vision process, we later jointly developed our distinctive elder ministry team vision statement.

OUR ELDER MINISTRY TEAM VISION STATEMENT

It is God's plan for us to be a team of humble, caring, loving leaders united in Christ and committed to prayerfully discerning our Father's will for his family.

We will mentor faithful disciple-makers, coach committed ministers, and shepherd God's flock.

God's Word and the Passion of the Church

We were skeptical elders, so it was natural to wonder out loud, "Passion statement? Where do we see anything like that in the Scriptures?" So we started to brainstorm passages where the Bible captures the essences of individuals, churches, or ministries in succinct, captivating wording. We thought of Joshua 1:9. "Be strong and courageous." That passionate theme encapsulates Joshua's entire life.

We meditated upon Philippians 1:21. "For to me, to live is Christ and to die is gain." That thread runs throughout Paul's ministry. Paul develops his passion further in Philippians 3:13–14. He specifically communicates the "one thing" he lives for, the one purpose he is willing to die for: pressing for the prize of the high calling of God in Christ Jesus. Paul succinctly expressed to the Ephesian elders the one race—his "only aim": "testifying to the good news of God's grace" (Acts 20:24). Paul's passion was laser focused: "the apostle to the Gentiles" (Romans 11:13).

Paul could abridge the passion of the saints at Thessalonica with the phrase "your work produced by faith, your labor prompted by love, and your endurance inspired by hope" (1 Thessalonians 1:3). Jesus shared his eternal passion:

"The Son of Man did not come to be served, but to serve, and to give his life as a ransom for many" (Matthew 20:28).

These biblical insights and many more led our elder team to craft a succinct statement of our passion.

OUR ELDER MINISTRY TEAM PASSION STATEMENT

Servant Leaders Serving Our Leader

God's Word and the Commission of the Church

We explored a number of commission statements, including the Great Commission (Matthew 28:16–20). We detected not only the calling or mission, but the commission, the *how to and the follow through*: going, making disciples, baptizing, and teaching.

We noticed the same detail in what Paul described as "the commission God gave me" (Colossians 1:25). God called Paul to present to the Colossians "the word of God in its fullness" *through* making known the glorious riches of Christ, proclaiming Christ, admonishing and teaching everyone with all wisdom, presenting everyone mature in Christ, and through laboring and struggling with all Christ's energy (Colossians 1:25–29).

It was these and other scriptural statements of commission that we thought of when we summarized our ministry team commission.

OUR ELDER MINISTRY TEAM COMMISSION STATEMENT

God is calling and equipping us to fulfill our Elder Ministry Team MVP *through* ad-ministrating the ministry, organizing the organism, and overseeing the equipping of our church family by modeling maturity, mentoring disciple-makers, and mending the flock.

Our biblical study led to a systematic theology of mission, vision, passion, and commission. We weren't tied to MVP-C as an inspired outline, but we were convinced that it condensed a powerful way to summarize a consistent concept woven throughout the Bible. We were now a united team equipped and motivated to champion the MVP-C process.

DISCIPLE-MAKING CHAMPION

Dr. Deepak Reju, Pastor of Biblical Counseling, Capitol Hill Baptist Church

Dr. Deepak Reju serves as Associate Pastor of Biblical Counseling and Family Ministry at Capitol Hill Baptist Church (CHBC) in Washington, DC. A pastor-theologian, Pastor Reju's *Vision for Biblical Counseling at Capitol Hill Baptist Church* develops nine scriptural pillars "meant to be building blocks that uphold and sustain a counseling ministry over the long-haul." These pillars "paint a picture—a vision for what biblical counseling could look like" at CHBC.

These nine pillars combine to present a biblical mission and a congregation-specific vision for biblical counseling. The biblical counseling ministry at CHBC will be 1) God-glorifying, 2) Word-founded and grounded, 3) Christ-centered and honoring, 4) serious about sin, 5) serious about suffering, 6) church-based, 7) discipleship-focused, 8) change-oriented, and 9) lovingly partnering with other equipping resources.

At CHBC their passion is a *culture of discipleship*—to embed counseling into the mainstream of discipleship. Pastor Reju says biblical counseling "is a particular form of discipleship, where Christians pull off the river for a period of time to focus on the 'problems' that are slowing their movement down the river. It's a time to stop and ask, 'What slows us down from growing closer to our Savior?'"

To his nine pillars, Pastor Reju adds four strategies (his version of a commission statement). Together, they provide "a feel for what a Christ-centered vision for biblical counseling could look like in our church, and also answer some of those pesky questions" about how that counseling ministry functions.

CHBC seeks to fulfill its mission, vision, and passion for biblical counseling through 1) one-on-one counseling ministry conducted by the pastoral staff and trained counselors designed to move people back into the broader discipleship mode; 2) small groups ministry focused on aspects of the gospel that encourage members who are struggling; 3) lay members who are trained in ongoing, informal, one-another ministry; and 4) lay counselors who are trained for formal, structured biblical counseling. To each of these broad commission strategies, Pastor Reju adds several specific tactics and process steps that flesh out the how-to of their commission.

COMMENCEMENT: GOD'S PLUMB LINE

What does it mean to be a person or a church after God's own heart? David was such a man. Reflecting on David's life and death, Luke recorded, "When David had served God's purpose in his own generation, he fell asleep" (Acts 13:36a). What a fascinating, crisp portrait of mission and vision. How reminiscent of the men of Issachar in 1 Chronicles 12:32, "who understood the times and knew what Israel should do." God calls each of us to find and fulfill his explicit purpose (mission) in our distinctive time and setting (vision).

For such a time as this, in such a manner as this, God has called every congregation and every ministry team. In the fullness of time—our time— God orchestrates the mission, vision, passion, and commission of every biblical counseling ministry team. Our first role is to trust that God desires us to know his universal calling and our unique exercise of that calling. God reveals his plans to his people (Amos 3:7) as a plumb line (Amos 7:7–8). God insists that we build our ministries true to plumb by developing a biblical theology for our specific ministry—what we are calling an MVP-C Statement.

You will recall that one of my elders initially sensed that the MVP-C process might smack of being seeker-sensitive and human-centered. That same elder, after working through our biblical study and working on an elder MVP-C, a congregational MVP-C, and a LEAD biblical counseling MVP-C, had a very different take:

> This biblical process has pointed us true north. Never again will I launch any ministry without first going to the Word as my compass.

> This has been the most Bible-focused and Christ-centered time I've
> ever spent as a church leader.

The starting point for the MVP-C process involves knowing what mission, vision, passion, and commission are all about. Becoming a champion for the process requires learning the practical and biblical value of developing an MVP-C Statement.

Something imperative remains—*the how-to*. In chapter 4, we learn how to facilitate and lead a biblical counseling ministry team through the steps of collaboratively catching and casting God's mission, vision, passion, and commission.

GROWING TOGETHER: QUESTIONS FOR
REFLECTION, DISCUSSION, AND APPLICATION

1. Think about the envisioning process:

   a. Before this chapter, what was your gut reaction to mission and vision statements?

   b. Now that you've read this theological introduction to "vision work," in what ways is your mindset about the envisioning process changing and growing?

2. Think about mission:

   a. Which of the various descriptions and samples of mission embedded in this chapter most resonate with you? How? Why?

   b. In an introductory way, how would you finish the following statement? *According to the Bible, my life and ministry mission is to...*

3. Think about vision:

   a. Which of the various descriptions and samples of vision embedded in this chapter most resonate with you? Since vision is unique, what parts do not resonate with you?

b. In an introductory way, how would you finish the following statement? *In serving Christ and others, it is my life and ministry dream to...*

4. Think about passion:

   a. Which of the various descriptions and samples of passion embedded in this chapter most resonate with you? How? Why?

   b. In an introductory way, what one phrase captures your life and ministry calling?

5. Think about commission:

   a. Which of the various descriptions and samples of commission embedded in this chapter most resonate with you? How? Why?

   b. In an introductory way, how would you finish the following statement? *I will seek to fulfill my life and ministry mission, vision, and passion through...*

4

Living God's Calling

*Collaboratively Crafting Your Biblical
Counseling MVP-C Statement*

served for seventeen years as the Chair of the Christian Counseling and Discipleship department at Capital Bible Seminary. Many of my students entered seminary later in life as career-changers or as seasoned pastors seeking further theological education and ministry training. They brought to the classroom tremendous wisdom for ministry.

Their life experience and ministry involvement made my job easier. Occasionally one of my younger students with little ministry background would say, "Dr. Kellemen, why do we need to put time into the envisioning process? Can't we move right into recruiting folks, training them, and overseeing them?" I rarely had to answer that question. My established, ministry-savvy students would speak up. I love the response one mature pastor shared as he addressed a student's questions about envisioning.

> In ministry, you can take the time up front to do the hard and wise work of envisioning—of getting your MVP-C right the first time. Or, you can take twice as much time later being pulled backwards while you spend all your time cleaning up the train wreck you made with a poor launch that doesn't fit your church or match your community.

LEARNING TO LEAD THE LAUNCH

In chapter 3, we learned that a wise ministry launch requires a biblical mission, vision, passion, and commission statement. But what does it look like to facilitate this envisioning process? That's our focus in chapter 4:

- Learning *how to translate* the biblical principles of mission, vision, passion, and commission into a *practical, step-by-step process* that equips you to *lead a launch team* to collaboratively catch and cast your biblical counseling ministry MVP-C.

As I've noted, the four churches I've served were each quite different demographically. The envisioning processes in these four churches led to four distinct biblical counseling ministries. The first included a two-year training program leading to a full-blown individual and group counseling ministry where scores of people were counseled every week in formal sessions and group meetings. The second church began with time-limited equipping that led to informal but focused spiritual friendships occurring throughout the church and community—and then years later added a formal biblical counseling ministry. The third gave rise to a network of equipped believers who used their training in semiformal settings such as spiritual friends, small-group leaders, and ministers of mercy (hospital visitation, telecare). The fourth church focused on equipping equippers—nearly two dozen pastors and staff leaders—who, in turn, equipped other biblical counselors and one-another ministers.

Your church setting is different from any of the churches I've served, different from the thousands of churches where my students have ministered, and different from the hundreds of churches where I've consulted. This chapter teaches you how to launch a biblical counseling ministry *that fits your particular church*. You're about to learn *how to lead a launch team to discover together your...*

- Mission: What makes biblical counseling truly biblical?

- Vision: What's our unique biblical counseling calling in our church and community?

- Passion: Who are we as we provide biblical counseling?

- Commission: What's our MAP (Ministry Action Plan) as we launch our biblical counseling ministry?

FORMING YOUR BIBLICAL COUNSELING ENVISIONING LAUNCH TEAM

I'm amazed by God's affectionate sovereignty. As I finalized the outline for this chapter, I received an email from two people (we'll call them Brock and Michelle) in the early stages of launching a biblical counseling ministry. Their questions aligned with my planned outline. "Bob, we have four issues we're trying to sort through." Their email continued with this outline:

> 1) We already have a congregation-wide mission/vision statement, so what's the relationship between that and how we develop our ministry-specific MVP-C? 2) How do we enlist a team to a mission and vision when we want them to help us craft that mission and vision? 3) Who should be involved in the process of developing the biblical counseling MVP-C Statement? 4) How long should we allot for the envisioning process?

Brock and Michelle's four questions correspond to the four actions you need to take to form and facilitate a biblical counseling envisioning launch team:

- Building the foundation for your envisioning launch team

- Enlisting your envisioning launch team

- Organizing your envisioning launch team

- Structuring your envisioning launch team

Building the Foundation for Your Envisioning Launch Team

When Brock and Michelle told me their church already had a congregation-wide mission and vision statement that people rallied around, I told them to count themselves blessed. Ideally, a biblical counseling ministry MVP-C should build upon any churchwide statements of purpose, mission, vision, and values.

In the examples from my church in chapter 3, we saw a clear relationship in mindset and wording between the church-wide MVP-C and the two ministry-specific MVP-C Statements (LEAD biblical counseling ministry and elder ministry team). That's no accident. Throughout the process, we asked ourselves how our specific ministry could come under, support, and advance the mission, vision, passion, and commission of our church.

The envisioning process works best when leaders develop three types of MVP-C Statements:

- A Personal Ministry MVP-C Statement

- A Congregation-Wide MVP-C Statement

- Ministry-Specific MVP-C Statements

I encourage every pastor, elder, deacon, and ministry director to craft a personal ministry MVP-C Statement. I recall what motivated me to craft mine. I was in my first pastoral ministry and had just finished counseling a couple. I looked at my to-do list, pondered all the spinning plates, and asked myself, *What am I supposed to focus on in ministry?* I wasn't asking, *What activity do I do next?* Instead, I was asking, *What calling drives how I decide where to concentrate my energies as a pastor?*

Over the next several months, I stumbled through what became the MVP-C process. I crafted a statement of personal ministry mission that helped me identify what the Bible says God calls every pastor to be and do. I developed a personal ministry vision that helped me clarify how I would use my specific gifts in my unique setting to fulfill God's calling. I prayerfully created a personal ministry passion statement: *Speaking the truth in love.* Over the years it has matured into my passion to be a *coach who equips others to live the truth in love.* I created a personal ministry commission—a detailed map of how I would accomplish my mission, vision, and passion.[1] It was *after* this process that I led my team to create a biblical counseling MVP-C.

A team of church leaders each with a personal ministry MVP-C Statement is well-prepared to lead a church in developing a congregation-wide MVP-C Statement. And a church with a congregation-wide MVP-C Statement is the best context in which to build a ministry-specific MVP-C Statement.

A practical question arises: What does a biblical counseling ministry do if the church does not have a clear statement of mission and vision? First, avoid becoming too attached to the lingo in this book. MVP-C is simply one way of summarizing a common process. Don't panic if your church doesn't use my

---

1. See Appendix 4.1 (available free online at https://rpmministries.org/ebc-resources/) for my Pastoral Ministry MVP-C Statement from my ministry at Uniontown Bible Church as Congregational Discipleship Pastor (Senior Pastor).

language. Second, most churches have at least some documents related to mission. You should be able to identify some statements of purpose.

A more specific question may surface: What if our church does not consciously follow a biblically developed mission and vision? If you are *the* pastor, *a* pastor, an elder, deacon, or ministry leader, then humbly suggest that the church either revisit the existing statements or jointly develop a clear, biblical statement of purpose.

In the absence of any clearly followed biblical statements of purpose, share with the church leadership your desire to develop a ministry-specific MVP-C Statement. Invite them to participate. I've often seen this create a pocket of excellence that motivates a church to develop a congregation-wide MVP-C Statement.

Enlisting Your Envisioning Launch Team

Avoid simply recruiting people to fill an opening. Instead, recruit people to a compelling mission and vision. This relates to Brock and Michelle's second question: "How do we enlist a team to a mission and vision when we want them to help us craft that mission and vision?"

Start by clearly stating the function of this team—it is an *envisioning launch* team and not an *equipping* team. This group may not provide the training when you get to that stage. And not everyone in this group may decide to receive the biblical counseling training. Members of the envisioning team are working with you to think through what a biblical counseling ministry could look like in your church and community. To communicate the specific purpose and function of this team, you may want to call it the Envisioning Team or the Launch Team.

As you enlist team members, have just enough of a plan to give everyone some direction, but not so much that anyone is left out. This is the essence of facilitative leadership in the envisioning process. You're calling people to a big-picture idea. You're inviting people *to join you in honing a somewhat general dream* of every member a disciple-maker and of equipped members providing one-another biblical counseling for your congregation and community.

Encourage each team member to treat the team as a small group. This shifts the mindset from a work team oriented only toward getting a task done to a ministry group oriented toward experiencing one-another ministry as you plan for your church's one-another ministry.

Organizing Your Envisioning Launch Team

This leads to Brock and Michelle's third question regarding who should be involved. Should it be the pastors, elders, deacons, some members, or the whole congregation? The answer will be different for every church. To sort through the answers for your church, consider three concentric circles.

- Circle One: Church Leadership—Pastor(s), elders, deacons, ministry directors

- Circle Two: Biblical Counseling Ministry Team—People passionate about one-another ministry and disciple-making

- Circle Three: The Congregation—People who might become involved in the ministry and who might receive help from the ministry

You may find yourself in all three circles, or at the very least the second two. If you are not a part of the first circle—church leadership—then from the beginning be sure to take your biblical counseling dreams to your church leadership. A biblical counseling ministry will not thrive in a church if the church leadership, especially the Senior Pastor, is not actively engaged. I feel so strongly about this that I will not sign a consulting contract unless the Lead Pastor and other church leaders agree to be involved in the consultation.

If you are the Senior Pastor, be sure to engage your church leadership team from the ground floor. Disaster is lurking anytime a biblical counseling ministry remains the passion of only one point person. A passionate point person is needed, but that person, regardless of title, needs the support of the rest of the church leadership, and that person needs a team.

The biblical counseling ministry point person must ask several questions regarding this first circle: How can I obtain the passionate support of the church leadership? Who among the church leadership team should be invited to be part of the biblical counseling envisioning team? What role on the envisioning team should each person play?

With circle one in place, focus on building the remainder of your biblical counseling ministry team. If you do not have a team, then stop. Pray for a team of likeminded people passionate about one-another ministry. Identify people in your congregation who already provide spiritual friendship, offer encouragement, visit the sick, and take an active lead in recovery group ministries. Personally invite them to join your core envisioning team.

With the third circle—the congregation at large—you have several options. Option one is to send a congregation-wide invitation to join the envisioning team. Decide whether everyone who desires to join the team is automatically in or whether there is a size limit. Option two is to host biblical counseling envisioning meetings open to anyone in the church. I've facilitated meetings with more than one hundred people where we've worked on MVP-C Statements. Option three is for your envisioning team to interact with, engage, and interview select members of the congregation to seek their input and insight. Design these as follow-up meetings to the SWORD Heart Exam, where you now ask specific questions related to biblical counseling mission, vision, passion, and commission.

Structuring Your Envisioning Launch Team

As navigator of a crew, you now have your sailing orders. Here's your structured goal as you form your biblical counseling envisioning team:

> Facilitate the collaborative development of a biblical counseling ministry MVP-C Statement that's in sync with the churchwide MVP-C and that's crafted by some combination of church leaders, people passionate about biblical counseling, and members of the church.

Anytime you ask people to join you on a voyage, it's only fair to estimate the length of your trip. Brock and Michelle wisely asked how long they should allot for the envisioning process. When you include the congregational and community assessment, plus each step in catching and casting the MVP-C, you can anticipate six to nine months for the launch phase. When you also factor in the change management process (chapter 5) and the development of your enlisting/recruiting philosophy, policies, and procedures (chapter 6), you might add an additional three months. Overall, you can anticipate a year-long launch process. While that may seem like a long time, it's much healthier than a two-year clean-up from a ministry train wreck.

Remember this simple principle for making consistent progress: A team that does not meet is not a team. Your initial pilot envisioning team needs to schedule regular meetings. I recommend at least two meetings each month.

CATCHING YOUR BIBLICAL
COUNSELING MINISTRY MVP-C

Track with me what you've accomplished so far.

- Working within the leadership structure of your church, you have a process in place for communicating the big picture: *more than counseling, a vision for the entire church.*

- With the enthusiastic blessing and active participation of your church leadership, you've recruited a biblical counseling envisioning launch team.

- Your launch team has used your SWORD Heart Exam to interview members of your congregation and community.

- You've analyzed the SWORD results to diagnose your congregation and community's heart health, culture, readiness, and specific issues for which biblical counseling is needed.

Facilitating the Collaborative Development of Your Biblical Counseling Mission Statement

You've gathered your launch team around. They've gathered their notes from the SWORD Heart Exam analysis. They're looking at you with eager anticipation. Now what?

Envisioning is a team process where each team member contributes in different ways at different levels. Each team needs a coach, a facilitative leader, a navigator. The following material equips *you* as the leader of the biblical counseling envisioning launch team to navigate the process of *collaboratively* discovering God's MVP-C for your biblical counseling ministry.

Prepare Prayerfully and Wisely

As you convene your envisioning team, begin with a time of focused prayer for wisdom, unity, and maturity. Pray that the process itself will draw each team member closer to one another and closer to Christ. Pray for discernment to understand what God's Word says about biblical counseling in the local church.

Teach the MVP-C Concepts

If you haven't already, teach your team the meaning of mission, vision, passion, and commission. With that understanding in place, study together any documents that communicate the mission/purpose of your church.

Examine the Bible's Teaching on Biblical Counseling

Now you're ready to discover the mission of *your* biblical counseling ministry by studying what makes biblical counseling truly biblical. What is universally true about all biblical counseling ministries in the church?

This is an exciting time as your team examines what the Bible says about biblical counseling. You want to discern constant, universal, biblically central beliefs that describe God's purpose for the one-another ministry of the Word. As you study the Bible, keep the end in view. Your goal is to complete one of these sentences:

- *According to the Bible, our biblical counseling ministry exists to…*

- *According to the Bible, the mission of a biblical counseling ministry is to…*

Lead your team in brainstorming and collating passages that relate to biblical counseling. Or, as a facilitative leader, provide a collated list of passages such as the one that follows in the Disciple-Making Champions.

DISCIPLE-MAKING CHAMPIONS

Biblical Foundations for Biblical Counseling

Foundational Biblical Counseling Passages

As part of the 4E Ministry Training Strategy Questionnaire, two dozen best-practice churches answered the question, What are the Scriptures upon which you founded and base your biblical counseling ministry? Collated below are the fifty passages listed most often. These are the types of passages that your team can study to develop a biblical counseling mission statement.

Psalm 1:1–2; Proverbs 15:23; Proverbs 18:13, 21; Proverbs 25:11; Proverbs 27:6; Isaiah 9:6; Isaiah 11:1–4; Isaiah 55:11; Matthew

22:34–40; Matthew 28:16–20; Mark 12:30–31; John 1:1–18; John 6:32–33; John 8:38; John 10:10; John 14:15–31; John 17:1–26; Acts 2:40–47; Acts 20:17–38; Romans 6:1–14; Romans 8:1–39; Romans 12:1–2; Romans 12:15; Romans 15:14; 1 Corinthians 12:12–27; 2 Corinthians 1:3–11; 2 Corinthians 3:16–18; 2 Corinthians 4:16–18; Galatians 6:1–5; Ephesians 1—3; Ephesians 4:11–16; Ephesians 4:17–24; Ephesians 4:29; Philippians 1:9–11; Colossians 1:25–29; Colossians 2:1–10; Colossians 3:1–16; Colossians 4:2–6; 1 Thessalonians 2:8; 1 Thessalonians 4:13; 1 Thessalonians 5:14; 2 Timothy 2:2; 2 Timothy 2:24–26; 2 Timothy 3:16–17; Hebrews 3:7–16; Hebrews 4:12–16; Hebrews 10:19–25; James 4:1–4; 1 Peter 2:5–9; 2 Peter 1:3–4; 1 John 4:7–21.

Foundational Biblical Categories

Many participants not only included specific verses, but also categories or concepts. Collated below are biblical categories that were listed the most.

- One-another ministry passages

- Body life passages

- Comforting the suffering passages

- Counseling the sinning passages

- Sufficiency of Scripture passages

- Sanctification and growth in grace passages

- Passages on listening and communication

- Seeing God's perspective passages

- Spiritual formation/spiritual discipline passages

- Verses using *noutheteo* (Greek for "confronting out of concern for change")

- Verses using *parakaleo* (Greek for "comfort, encourage, console")

As part of this collaborative process, prepare a study guide/discussion sheet. In Appendix 4.2 (available free online at https://rpmministries.org/ebc-resources/), you'll find a sample discussion guide: Discovering Our Biblical Counseling Mission. Figure 4:1 highlights *just a few* of those questions.

FIGURE 4:1

Discovering Our Biblical Counseling Mission (Samplers)

In groups of three or four individuals, respond to these questions. Then share as a larger group.

1. According to Matthew 22:34–40 and Matthew 28:16–20, what is the end goal or mission of all life and ministry?

2. According to Ephesians 4:11–16, what is our calling from God in the body of Christ?

3. According to Hebrews 3:7–16 and Hebrews 10:19–25, what is the purpose of the personal ministry of the Word—of one-another gospel conversations?

4. Based upon your study so far:

   a. What preliminary definition of biblical counseling would you craft?

   b. What list of biblical counseling values would you develop?

5. Finish the following sentence based upon the verses you've studied: According to the Bible, the mission of a biblical counseling ministry is to...

Brainstorm a Whiteboard of Common Themes: Storyboarding

For this stage, you need all your facilitative skills. You've divided your launch team into smaller groups and assigned each group various passages and questions from your discussion guide on *Discovering Our Biblical Counseling Mission*.

The room is abuzz as group members study what the Bible says about biblical counseling.

Now, reconvene your smaller groups for a time of large-group brainstorming. Have access to a whiteboard, blackboard, flip chart, or LCD to project from your computer.

At this point, you're not focusing on your target audience, the needs of your community, or your unique gift-mix. That's vision talk, not mission work. For now, you're discerning God's timeless purpose for *every biblical counseling ministry in any local church*. Start by asking each group to share what they've discovered. Include and listen to everyone. Write summaries on the whiteboard—verses, concepts, ideas, images. Highlight and organize recurring themes. Keep the conversation moving. Have fun. Work cooperatively.

The end result of the brainstorming session should be a very messy whiteboard with lots of biblical principles about what makes biblical counseling truly biblical. Take a picture of it or somehow capture the essence. Be sure to assign someone to be the recorder or secretary. Make sure everyone has access to a copy of these brainstormed themes. Give the group time to reflect prayerfully on the themes.

Create a Straw-Man First Draft

Now, using your whiteboard summary, ask each person on your launch team to draft a straw-man biblical counseling mission statement beginning with a phrase like, According to the Bible, the mission of a biblical counseling ministry is to…

Next, ask one brave soul to volunteer to have his or her draft edited to death. Jointly shape the wording in first-draft, rough form as everyone shares input. People will be saying, "Oh, I like that!" And, "How about adding this?" Or, "Our group had an important theme we'd like to add…" And, "It seems like these five verses really stood out to all the groups…"

At some point you need to decide to close the tweaking of the first draft. Don't worry about the perfect wording. From all the scribbles on the whiteboard, facilitate the development of a rough first draft and provide each launch team member a copy. At this point, it's often wise to adjourn or at least take a break. Ask everyone to start crafting a second draft during the intervening time.

Craft a Working Second Draft

When you meet again, begin jointly crafting a second draft. Before you start, remind your team of several important points:

- The biblical counseling mission statement needs to advance the churchwide mission.

- This is still a working draft. We'll tweak it further as we develop our vision, passion, and commission.

- The overall church leadership team will weigh in on the final wording.

As you did with draft one, have your whiteboard or flip chart ready. Ask someone to share their straw-man second draft. Lead the group in commenting on and editing this draft into an agreed-upon working second draft. Aim at between fifty to one hundred words. Include supporting verses. Keep it concise, clear, and creative.

Chapter 3 shared sample mission statements from my second church. Below you'll find a sample LEAD (Life Encouragers And Disciplers) Biblical Counseling Mission Statement from my first church.[2]

OUR LEAD BIBLICAL COUNSELING MISSION STATEMENT

According to the Bible, the mission of LEAD is to equip one-another ministers, biblical counselors, and small-group leaders to speak the truth in love to people struggling with suffering and battling against sin, in order to promote Christlike maturity in the body of Christ.

LEAD exists to assist our church to

> become an equipping center (Ephesians 4:11–14), a fully functioning family (Matthew 22:34–40), a Christ-centered community (Hebrews 3:7–16; 10:19–25), a healthy body (Ephesians 4:15–16), and a teaching hospital for soul physicians healing hurting and hardened hearts (Matthew 23:23–26).

---

2. See Appendix 4.3 for the LEAD Biblical Counseling MVP-C Statement collated onto one page (available free online at https://rpmministries.org/ebc-resources/).

Facilitating the Collaborative Development of Your Biblical Counseling Vision Statement

With a working second draft of your mission in hand, your biblical counseling envisioning team is now ready to start vision catching. Your goal is to facilitate the process of discovering your team's unique biblical counseling ministry dream. What will your DNA, your fingerprint be? What sets apart your biblical counseling ministry—not as better, but as distinctive from any other church anywhere on the planet?

Prepare Prayerfully and Strategically

Pray that your team will grasp a unified sense of God's dream. Ask, "Father, what are you calling our biblical counseling ministry to be like in our congregation and community as we move forward together into the future?"

Review with your team the difference between mission and vision. Spend time studying the biblical value of mission and vision and share examples of vision in the Bible (see chapter 3). Teach your team that vision derives from a combination of prayer, the results of the congregational SWORD Heart Exam, the community diagnosis, the churchwide mission, the biblical counseling mission, and the churchwide vision. Study and discuss these documents. Summarize what they indicate about your special calling in your specific community.

Take DNA Soul Samples

Guide your envisioning team to see themselves as servants of the congregation and community. They are not simply pondering, "What is the DNA, the fingerprint, of *our* launch team?" They're seeking to represent accurately the uniqueness of your *entire congregation and community*. Rather than determine the looks of a biblical counseling ministry created in *my* image, the group will ask, "How will a biblical counseling ministry match who God has created *our church* to be in *our community*?" There's a world of difference between those two mindsets, and it takes otherworldly humility to maintain the second mindset.

Your first calling as the group leader is to model that other-centered mindset. As you respond to the whiteboard, the straw man, and the rough-draft work, your team needs to see that it's not about you. You are not manipulating them to write the statement you wanted to write all along. It's all about Christ. And it's all about your congregation serving your community in Christ's way.

Respond to vision-catching probes about your past, present, and future. Figure 4:2 provides a few samples. See Appendix 4.4 (available free online at https://rpmministries.org/ebc-resources/) for *many more* vision-catching probes/questions).

FIGURE 4:2

Vision-Catching Probes (Samplers)

Probing Our Past

1. In what unique ways has our congregation provided one-another ministry to each other?

2. What stories do we tell about special times of one-another ministry in our church's history?

3. How have we spoken the truth in love to one another in the past?

4. What words describe the ways in which we've offered biblical counseling in the past, either formally or informally?

Probing Our Present

1. What amazing work is God doing in our church through the personal ministry of the Word?

2. What are you excited about in how we currently provide one-another ministry?

3. What are some of the strengths and weaknesses in the way we currently provide biblical counseling?

4. What special "gift-mix" does our congregation have, and what biblical counseling focus would those gifts best support?

Probing Our Future

1. What are our dreams for the biblical counseling ministry in one year? Five? Ten? Twenty?

2. Read Ephesians 3:20 and dream as if we could not fail. What do you think God will do with our biblical counseling ministry in the future?

3. If time, training, and money were no objects, what would our biblical counseling ministry look like?

4. If we were to create a cover page for our biblical counseling brochure, what words might capture the essence of the ministry?

Respond representatively by answering these questions *on behalf of* your congregation and community—as you believe they would. This argues for the wise selection of group members who are representative of the diversity in your congregation and community. It also argues for the wisdom of interviewing and/or surveying your congregation and perhaps your community using probing vision-catching questions.

At the very least, you want your team to take some DNA soul samples. Either as a large group or divided into smaller groups, your team members should record their responses to vision-casting probes such as those provided in Appendix 4.4. If you use a list like this, be sure to craft the wording (biblical counseling, one-another ministry, the personal ministry of the Word) in terms that *your* people will understand.

Whiteboard and Straw Man Your Vision

Once you reconvene everyone into one larger group, follow the same facilitation principles outlined for the mission work when you brainstormed a whiteboard of common themes and created a straw-man draft. As everyone shares, highlight not only recurring themes but also imaginative, pictorial words. Fill the board with adjectives and adverbs.

After a time of sharing, ask each person to produce their own rough draft vision of twenty-five to seventy-five words beginning with this: *It is the dream of our biblical counseling ministry to...* Have one volunteer share, and then allow everyone to tinker with it. Tweak it and edit it, emphasizing richly descriptive words that make you *you*. Turn this into a first draft, and then let it simmer and percolate.

Craft a Working Second Draft

After allowing your first draft to sit either during a break or between meetings, return to craft a working second draft. After someone shares their strawman second draft, remind your team that you want this draft to advance the churchwide vision and to richly communicate in pictorial words what makes your biblical counseling ministry unique in your church and community. Lead your team in crafting a twenty-five to seventy-five-word creative second draft that points your ministry to a future possible only by the grace and power of God. Below you'll find a sample LEAD Biblical Counseling Vision Statement.

LEAD BIBLICAL COUNSELING
VISION STATEMENT

It is the DREAM of our LEAD ministry to be a maturing team of loving encouragers and dynamic disciplers equipped to make God's house a home.

We will be empowered toward personal maturity, encouraged by biblical community, and equipped for relational ministry to God's family and our community.

Through spiritual maturity, biblical wisdom, and relational skillfulness we will speak the truth in love so that we all may mature in Christ.

Facilitating the Collaborative Development of Your Biblical Counseling Passion Statement

In chapter 3, I described "passion catching" as something of an "Aha!" experience. You really can't teach that, though you can provide a relational context for it. That relationship begins with Christ as we relate in the body of Christ. Lead your team in praying that you would grasp together with all the saints God's passion for your biblical counseling ministry. Pray, "Father, help us to trust in you with all our hearts and lean not on our own understanding. Help us in all our ways to acknowledge you, so that you will direct our path."

Explore with your team biblical passion statements like the ones listed in chapter 3 and others such as Joshua 24:15; Nehemiah 2:12; Esther 4:14; Matthew 9:13; Acts 1:8; Acts 9:15; and 2 Timothy 1:6–7. These verses encapsulate the essence of someone's mission and vision—the heart of a passion statement.

Review your biblical counseling ministry mission and vision statements. Also review your church's passion statement (any brief phrase that summarizes your mission). Create a discussion guide for your team with questions such as the following:

- What phrase captures our biblical mission and unique vision?

- Which of the biblical passion statements most resonate with us?

- If we had one phrase to portray who we are to a stranger, what would it be?

- How can we communicate, in a memorable way, the essence of our calling?

- How can our biblical counseling ministry passion reflect our congregation-wide passion?

Now brainstorm possibilities, being careful not to reject anything. Often the final passion statement is a combination of several partial statements.

At my first church, we shared various phrases: speaking Christ's truth in love to love like Christ, encourage one another daily, relational ministry promoting relational maturity, equipping every member to minister maturely, changing lives, a teaching hospital training soul physicians, equipping for relational maturity leading to mutual ministry, making God's house our home, and relating God's truth to human relationships.

The process was exciting because our summary pictures confirmed that our team understood our mission and vision. Even better, the passion-catching process deepened our understanding of and our commitment to our calling.

We stopped to thank God for his calling and ask him for further clarity about our passion. Then we left...without a final passion phrase. When we met next, one of our members shared the passion statement that we all agreed captured us.

LEAD BIBLICAL COUNSELING PASSION STATEMENT

Changed People Changing Lives with Christ's Changeless Truth

DISCIPLE-MAKING CHAMPIONS

Biblical Counseling Passion Statements

As part of the 4E Ministry Training Strategy Questionnaire, two dozen best-practice churches answered the question, If you were to describe your biblical counseling training ministry in one brief phrase, how would you capture its essence? Collated below are sample passion statements.

- Promoting Heart Change That Brings Life Change

- Returning Biblical Soul Care to the Church

- Transforming Lives by the Word of God, in the Spirit of God, with the Community of God

- Bringing Christlike Comfort to the Hurting and Forgiveness to the Hardened

- Counseling in Community

- Glorifying God by Caring for Sufferers, Restoring Sinners, and Equipping the Saints

- PEACE: *P*ointing People to Christ, *E*ncouraging People to Live Like Christ, *A*ssisting the Hurting, *C*omforting with the Word, *E*quipping Disciplers

- Equipping the Church to Make Disciples Using God's Sufficient Word

- Equipping the Saints to Live Life with a Healthy Heart

- Equipping Real People to Handle Life Effectively by Handling God's Word Accurately

- Training God's People to Multiply Disciples Through Compassionate Biblical Counseling

- Bringing the Hope of Christ to the Hurting

- Connecting the Transforming Power of Christ to Everyday Life

- Personal Change through the Personal Ministry of the Word

Facilitating the Collaborative Development of Your Biblical Counseling Commission Statement

Your Commission Statement is your MAP—*M*inistry *A*ction *P*lan—that guides how you will fulfill your mission, vision, and passion. It summarizes your more detailed ministry training strategy. In your ministry training strategy, you seek to address five components represented by the acronym SMART.

- *S:* Structure: What is our overall training strategy?

- *M:* Ministers/Ministries: Who are we training for what ministry?

- *A:* Abilities/Aptitudes: What knowledge, character, skills, and relationships will our trainees need?

- *R:* Results: What ministry goals do our ministers focus on?

- *T:* Target Participants: Who do our ministers minister to?

If SMART MAP makes your head spin, set it aside. If it helps organize your thinking, wonderful. The main idea is to think through concrete, measurable action plans. The failure to outline a workable strategy is the number one reason MVP-C Statements fail. Don't waste your work. Plan your work and work your plan.

Structure: Outline Your Overall Training Strategy

With your MVP-C Statement in hand, guide your team to answer this question: Specifically, how will we accomplish our mission, vision, and passion? Use the diagnosis from your assessment process (chapter 2) to identify your current strengths, weaknesses, opportunities, and risks. That's where you are now. Your vision is where you want to go. Ask the following types of questions:

- What structures, processes, resources, and plans do we need to develop to get from here to there?

- What specific steps do we need to take to pull this off successfully for God's glory?

- How do we outline those steps in measurable ways? (I'm partial to the 4E outline of envisioning, enlisting, equipping, and empowering, but your team can draw any map it desires. Just draw something concrete and practical.)

Through my consulting ministry, I've found that in the launch-team setting it's wisest to limit your brainstorming to 1) a list of steps, and 2) Commission Statement wording. When your group has accomplished those two goals, then delegate the development of the detailed ministry training strategy. The person who assumes that task could be you as the leader; it could be a smaller group of detailed, process-oriented team members; or it could be an individual team member skilled and experienced in strategic development.

Ministers/Ministries: Identify Who You Are Training for What Ministry

In my first church, because we had an expansive view of biblical counseling, we envisioned extensive areas of ministry. We wanted every graduate to be a skilled spiritual friend regardless of their specific ministry area as an elder, a worship leader, a husband, a mother, or some other role. We also wanted some of our graduates to serve as biblical counselors, providing individual, marital, or parental counseling. Additionally, we envisioned our graduates launching new small groups, especially recovery groups, and leading existing groups. Regardless of the area of ministry, we wanted all our graduates to see themselves as soul caregivers (people who could help the suffering) and as spiritual directors (people who could help others who were struggling with sins).

Lead your team to brainstorm about current and future ministries that your graduates might launch or join. Discuss what ministry identity a graduate would have. Envisioning the successful graduate empowers you to launch with the end in view.

Abilities: Envision the Mature Graduate

In addition to knowing where your graduates might serve and in what roles, it's vital that your team members envision what the mature graduate looks like. For our LEAD ministry, we highlighted the 4Cs—biblical content (head), Christlike character (heart), counseling competence (hands), and Christian community (home)—as our four marks of a successful graduate. That guided everything we did in our selection, training, and supervising of our trainees.

Develop a succinct but concrete list of measurable objectives. These will communicate the essence of your ministry focus. Done well, they will also become the best recruiting tool you can fashion. People will clamor for your training because they want changed lives and they want to be able to change lives.

Results: Describe the Point of Your Ministry

What's the point? That's the question your launch team needs to ponder. Why are we doing this? Once our trainees graduate, once they are counseling someone or leading a group, so what? What are we equipping them to equip others to do and be?

For our LEAD ministry, the end game was *changed people changing lives with Christ's changeless truth*. People with changed lives know Christ, grow in Christ, and become Christlike disciple-makers. Changed lives occur as we apply Christ's changeless truth to help suffering people know that it's normal to hurt (sustaining) and possible to hope (healing), and as we help sinning people know that it's horrible to sin but wonderful to be forgiven (reconciling) and supernatural to mature (guiding).

Target Participants: Determine Who Your Ministers Minister To

Some biblical counseling ministries focus within the church. Others focus almost exclusively outside the church. Some focus only on certain types of issues and choose to refer other issues, and some offer only individual counseling, not marital or family counseling. Our statement focused on individuals, couples, and families in our congregation and community. Your team should determine your target participants—the people who will be ministered to by the people you train.

At one of the churches I led, our Commission Statement looked like this.

OUR LEAD BIBLICAL COUNSELING
MINISTRY COMMISSION STATEMENT

We will seek to fulfill our LEAD MVP through the 4Es of *envisioning, enlisting, equipping,* and *empowering* a congregation of one-another ministers, biblical counselors, and small-group leaders.

We will comprehensively equip soul caregivers and spiritual directors in the 4Cs of biblical *content,* Christlike *character,* counseling *competence,* and Christian *community* so they can sustain, heal, reconcile, and guide individuals, couples, and families in our congregation and community to know Christ, grow in Christ, and care like Christ.

Notice how this Commission Statement has each of the components of the SMART MAP:

- *Structure:* The 4Es of envisioning, enlisting, equipping, and empowering described how we *structured* our LEAD ministry— the big picture we used to launch and lead our ministry.

- *Ministers/Ministries:* We were training people we identified as soul caregivers and spiritual directors (*ministers*) who we envisioned ministering as spiritual friends, biblical counselors, and small-group leaders (*ministries*).

- *Abilities:* We used the 4Cs of content, character, competence, and community to identify four main *abilities* our equipping sought to impart.

- *Results:* Once trained, we released our ministers for real ministry in the real world, where they sustained, healed, reconciled, and guided people to know Christ, grow in Christ, and become Christlike disciple-makers (*results*).

- *Target:* We wanted them to reach individuals, couples, and families in our congregation and our community (*target* participants).

CASTING YOUR BIBLICAL
COUNSELING MINISTRY MVP-C

Though I'm using the standard language of "casting your vision," a better analogy is "planting your vision" (MVP-C). Vision is a seed best planted in fertile soil. When you catch the biblical counseling ministry MVP-C in community, you win over a team of committed people passionate about planting the MVP-C seed. When you involve the church leadership in catching your MVP-C, you gain influence from those who can spread the seed most broadly. When you build your ministry-specific MVP-C upon the congregation-wide MVP-C, you can plant your MVP-C seed deep in native soil.

When your vision for counseling is a vision for the entire church, your MVP-C seed spreads not to a few, but to all. When you base your MVP-C upon a biblical mission, a unique vision, a compelling passion, and a strategic commission, your seed is robust, healthy, and sure to grow. The most important principle of fruitful vision *casting* is fruitful vision *catching*.

To continue the analogy, you know that the seed of vision is bearing fruit when people own the vision by living the vision. This is imperative to remember because too many people who talk about vision casting seem more concerned about whether someone can quote the vision than whether everyone is embodying the vision. When we view vision as a seed, then we primarily focus on the internal growth of the vision—how deeply the seed is planted in each person's soul as evidenced by how much each person is growing and maturing in Christ.

When you grasp these vision principles, then vision-casting best practices flow naturally. Those best practices include real-world matters, such as when you cast the vision, who casts it, to whom you cast it, and how you cast it.

When Do You Cast the Vision?

Since biblical counseling is a vision for the entire church, ideally, people are always casting the vision for one-another ministry. Hopefully, long before you ever formulated the biblical counseling launch team, people were planting the seed of one-another ministry and discipleship. You start to cast your specific ministry vision as soon as you start forming a team, sending out surveys, interviewing church and community members, and holding churchwide envisioning meetings. Vision catching should never be done by a few behind closed doors.

Once the church leadership has officially and enthusiastically endorsed your ministry MVP-C, spread the vision seed everywhere. Announce the launch/the birth of your new biblical counseling ministry. When you start the enlisting process, spread the vision. During your equipping training, spread the vision. When you start deploying trained biblical counselors, spread the vision.

Who Casts the Vision?

Since you created the vision in community, cast the vision through community. The Senior Pastor and senior leadership should join in the task of planting the vision. Your entire envisioning team will plant the vision.

Once you begin equipping trainees, their changed lives will enflame the vision. Once your equipped ministers start counseling and discipling, the changed lives of the people they minister to will advance the vision.

To Whom Do You Cast the Vision?

Cast the vision as wide as the desired extent of the vision. If your Commission Statement identifies the target participants as your congregation and community, then you need to spread the seed far beyond the church. All vision casters always need to ask the following questions: Who do we want to minister to? How do we reach them with the word of the great work God is doing?

How Do You Cast the Vision?

So far, it's easy: Everyone always casts the vision everywhere. Though easy, a few how-tos can help.

Name your biblical counseling ministry. This is a basic idea that many ministries neglect. It helps if you have a catchy, memorable name. This is why we used an acrostic that fit our MVP-C: LEAD—Life Encouragers And Disciplers. Along with a name, create a ministry logo that captures the passion of your ministry. Spread your name, logo, and passion statement everywhere with business cards, a website, a letterhead, and training materials. Post your complete MVP-C Statement on your website, in the foyer, everywhere.

Preach it and teach it. Since your ministry is not just about biblical counseling, but about every-member ministry, pastors and teachers can embed the vision in every message. Since you have based your ministry upon foundational principles like the sufficiency of Scripture, progressive sanctification, the priesthood of all believers, and gospel conversations, your vision should naturally flow from the pulpit and the lectern, in small groups and in private conversations.

Share stories and testimonials. Start with your envisioning team sharing stories about how powerful it has been for them to study what the Bible says about biblical counseling. Your trainees can share private and public testimonies about how they are growing in the 4Cs. Once your biblical counselors start counseling, one of the most powerful ways to spread the word about your ministry is through testimonies from counselees. Many will fearlessly share, "I don't mind admitting it. I needed counseling, and God used my LEAD encourager to change my life!"

If you want your biblical counseling ministry to reach the community, the best "marketing" is word-of-mouth testimonials from the changed lives of community members. Of course, you have to "break into that market" somehow. Offer free seminars to the community on topics such as overcoming anxiety, parenting adolescents, and defeating depression. Promote these through public service radio announcements, and, most importantly, personal invitations from members. Also offer free community-based ministries (see samples from Faith Church in chapter 2). Use social media. Create a section on your church's website with information about your ministry, stories, free resources, and your MVP-C Statement. Start a blog with daily posts about biblical counseling topics. Create a Twitter account, launch a Facebook ministry group, and start a YouTube page with videos on counseling-related topics.

More than anything else, live the vision. Embody your MVP-C in how you live, relate, and do ministry.

COMMENCEMENT: LAUNCH THE
SHIP AND START THE VOYAGE

The six- to twelve-month envisioning launch is an arduous voyage. And, it's well worth it. You've been a community in order to launch a community that reaches your congregation and community. Plus, it sure beats the other option—the two-year grueling clean-up from a failed launch.

Still, the launch isn't the voyage. You've envisioned where you are, where God wants you, where God is taking you, who you are, and how you'll get there. Soon it will be time to enlist the crew members who will voyage with you in the equipping and empowering process.

You might assume that your next step is to enlist trainees. However, there's another vital phase as you start leading the revolution. You need to *foster a climate for ongoing ownership*.

One of the great failures of the "vision-casting movement" has been the lack of teaching about people's resistance to change. Chapter 5 explains why people resist change, how to prepare for change, how to manage change, and how to deal with conflict biblically. Many a ministry launch has been sidetracked by unresolved conflict. Chapter 5 teaches a proactive approach to preparing the congregation for change through strategic change management and biblical conflict resolution.

**GROWING TOGETHER: QUESTIONS FOR
REFLECTION, DISCUSSION, AND APPLICATION**

1. In forming your envisioning launch team, what specific steps do
   you need to take to...

   a. Build the foundation for your envisioning team?

   b. Enlist your envisioning team?

   c. Organize your envisioning team?

   d. Structure your envisioning team?

2. As you think about developing your Biblical Counseling Mission
   Statement:

   a. What verses and categories would you add to those listed by
      the Disciple-Making Champions?

   b. If you were creating a discussion guide, what questions would
      you use, add, subtract, or edit from Figure 4:1 and Appendix
      4.2: Discovering Our Biblical Counseling Mission?

3. As you think about developing your Biblical Counseling Vision Statement:

    a. What questions would you use, add, subtract, or edit from Figure 4:2 and Appendix 4.4: Vision-Catching Probes?

    b. Select five questions from the Vision-Catching Probes to answer now.

4. As you think about developing your Biblical Counseling Passion Statement, answer the five bulleted passion questions from this chapter.

5. As you think about developing your Biblical Counseling Commission Statement, how would your ministry answer the five SMART MAP questions?

6. Which of the vision casting (planting) principles and practices seem most important to you? Why? How could you implement them in your church?

PART 2

ENLISTING GOD'S MINISTERS FOR MINISTRY

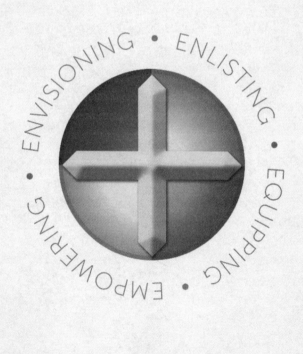

Enlisting

Decades later, they still refer to it as the miracle on ice. The 1980 US Olympic hockey team shocked the world with its epic defeat of the vastly favored Soviet team. The movie *Miracle* tells the story, beginning with head coach Herb Brooks assembling the team of amateur college players who would face the most dominant hockey team in the world.

Molding this ragtag group of *individuals* into a well-oiled, united *team* was a daunting task. *Miracle* depicts Brooks asking the players during practice, "Who do you play for?" Each player responds by naming his college team.

It took every ounce of Brooks's coaching genius and personal tenacity to unite these young men. At the end of one particularly brutal practice, they finally yell out, "I play for the United States of America!" It was a turning point, *the* turning point. They became a team that day.

You might think that the church would not need such an extreme makeover. But we all know the truth—whether it's young hockey players or seasoned members of our congregations, it's all too easy to say, like the Corinthians, "I am of Paul; I am of Apollos; I am of Cephas" (see 1 Corinthians 1:12). Because that's true, we would be naïve to attempt to move directly from envisioning to equipping. Yet many people unwisely try to do just that. The results are traumatic because the stakes are much higher than an Olympic gold medal.

Paul knew this, which is why in chapter 5 we'll learn from him and from Nehemiah how to shepherd the congregational transformation. We'll learn how to cultivate a climate where the entire congregation owns the MVP-C through...

- Transformed Lives: Changing Ministers Before Changing Ministries

- Relational Change Management: Stewarding the Change Process
- Biblical Conflict Resolution: Restoring Relationships

As amazing as that change is, like Brooks, we still realize there's more work to do. As Brooks built his dream team, he looked for players who would be more committed to the name on the front of the jersey (USA) than the name on the back. After he chose his team, some insisted that the best players were missing. *Miracle* depicts his response: "I'm not looking for the *best* players. I'm looking for the *right* players."

Paul understood that principle, which is why in chapter 6 we'll learn from him and from Jesus how to mobilize ministers. We'll learn how to nurture a family and build a team by...

- Conducting Christ's Opus: Saturating the Congregation with One-Another Ministers
- Calling People to Connection: What People Need to Know About Your Ministry
- Matching the Right People to the Right Ministry: What You Need to Know About Ministers

A coach like Herb Brooks loves measurable objectives. If he were penning this section, his ROLOs (Reader-Oriented Learning Objectives) might sound like this. Through your active reading and application of the two chapters in this part of the book, you'll be equipped to...

- Shepherd a congregational transformation that unites the entire congregation around the right Person (Christ) and the right purposes (loving God and others) (chapter 5).
- Mobilize ministers so that you are able to match the right people to the right ministry for the right reasons at the right time in the right way—relationally (chapter 6).

"Do you believe in miracles? Yes!" Play-by-play announcer Al Michaels yelled those famous words when the United States's hockey team upset the Soviets.

Do you believe in miracles? Do you believe that Christ's resurrection power is available to his church so that we can defeat the very gates of hell? *Since* you do, join me as we join Christ in building his church.

5

Shepherding the Transformation

Cultivating a Climate for Ongoing Ownership

When I teach the material in this chapter, I start with a change exercise. I ask participants to stand and face each other in pairs, observing each other's appearances. Then I instruct them to turn back-to-back and make five changes to their appearance. Typically, they roll up a sleeve, take off their glasses, loosen a tie, remove an earring, or make other basic changes.

Next, I tell them to face each other and identify the five changes their partner made. They'll laugh, point out changes, and instinctively start to change back. Before they do, I ask them to turn around again and make five additional changes to their appearance. From some people I hear murmuring; from others I observe enthusiastic creativity. Hair braids come off, pant legs are pulled up, jackets are put on backwards, pens are placed over an ear, shirttails come out or go in. Once again, the partners face each other and identify these changes.

Then I start to say, "Okay, turn around again..." Vocal resistance begins. I respond, "Just kidding. Let's sit down and talk about our CQ—our Change Quotient." We discuss the following:

- Were you comfortable or uncomfortable with the assignment?

- Were the changes easy or hard for you to make? To identify?

- Were you in a cooperative mode or in mutiny mode?

- At what point, if any, did you experience change overload?

- How quickly did you revert back to your former look?

We then discuss the implications that we can derive for change management. People mention applications such as change takes an initiator. The initiator of change must be trusted. Change requires clear instructions. People can handle only so much change—don't overload. Change takes energy and creativity. Change can be minor yet feel dramatic. Change can cause people to feel uncomfortable and even fearful about losing the old and facing the new. People focus on what they have to sacrifice. People feel isolated when they lose the familiar. People have different levels of readiness for change. Change is not one action but a journey. People often revert to their old style.

SHIFTING TECTONIC PLATES

If a little game prompts such turmoil, imagine the angst when we ask a congregation to make a major ministry mindset shift. For many congregations, it's a monumental shift to move from the pastor as the doer of ministry to the pastor as the equipper of equippers. For many church members, it's a massive shift to move from receiving counseling from the pastor to providing counseling to each other.

This is why it's unwise to move directly from envisioning to enlisting. Yet we do it all the time. We get excited after attending a seminar on gospel-centered preaching, the disciple-making pastor, or the equipping-focused church. Then we return home, gather other like-minded people, create a vision statement, tell others about it, and announce a grand new approach to church life. Instead of creating a following, we generate a family feud.

BEEN THERE, DONE THAT

I know because I just described my experience. Armed with the best of intentions but not with the greatest wisdom, I tried to shift our congregation from a pastor-centered model to an equipping-centered approach. I made enough mistakes and learned enough from those mistakes to write a book—this book.

My heart was right—I wanted to transform the way our congregation lived the gospel. My initial process was wrong—I expected people to make dramatic changes without preparing my heart and their hearts for change.

That's why I've entitled this chapter "Shepherding the Transformation." Before you seek to change church structure, seek to shepherd changed hearts. It's also why I subtitled this chapter "Cultivating a Climate for Ongoing Ownership." Before you enlist individuals to be equipped to counsel, invite a congregation to become stewards of a transformational vision.

You may say, "But haven't we done a lot of that already? We've involved the congregation in the SWORD Heart Exam and in the community assessment. We've welcomed the whole church into the envisioning process. We've cast the vision in community."

Doing all those things places you way ahead on the transitioning curve. However, so far, you've only *talked about* the future vision. What happens when Sister Gwen wants to counsel with Pastor Gordon, and instead you invite her to counsel with Sister Kirstin? What happens when Brother Dwayne expects a visit in the hospital from Pastor Varney, but instead receives a visit from Brother Thomas? Change is what has happened, and conflict is what may occur. In response, wise leaders understand that transformed lives, relational change management, and biblical conflict resolution are required.

Don't think of these as stages in a process. Though you're reading this book chapter by chapter in a linear way, life and ministry don't work like that. Though chapter 5 precedes the chapters on enlisting, equipping, and empowering, the need for transformed lives, change management, and conflict resolution doesn't stop somewhere between envisioning and enlisting. This is why the word "ongoing" is central to the title of this chapter.

Cultivating ongoing ownership is always relevant. We're going to learn that it was necessary in Nehemiah's day, it was needed in Paul's day, and it is indispensable in our day. In our changing times, we need timeless truth about change.

TRANSFORMED LIVES: CHANGING MINISTERS BEFORE CHANGING MINISTRIES

The Bible has a theology of change, which we can summarize with one word: "transformation." Transformation starts with hearts—changed leaders changing people who change churches who change communities. Before you prepare a change management plan, prepare people. Before you prepare people, prepare your own heart.

Nehemiah and Paul each led God's people through transformative change. We think of Nehemiah as a wall builder, and we sometimes use the book of

Nehemiah to distill organizational leadership principles. However, Nehemiah never prayed to be remembered as a wall builder, but rather as a people builder. In Nehemiah 5:19; 13:14, 22, and 31, he prays that God would remember him for empowering God's people to serve, for leading God's people to worship, and for motivating God's people to live transformed lives. The book of Nehemiah is not about organizational leadership. It *is* about shepherding people whose transformed lives lead to a transformed community.

Likewise, Paul's ministry in 2 Corinthians focuses not simply on conflict resolution, but on personal reconciliation—first with God and then with one another (5:17–21; 6:11–13). Paul's letter is not about transitioning ministries but about transforming ministers. In the midst of conflict, Paul fixes his eyes on the prize. "Though outwardly we are wasting away, yet inwardly we are being renewed day by day" (4:16). Paul laser-focuses his goal. "We all, who with unveiled faces contemplate the Lord's glory, are being transformed into his image with ever-increasing glory" (3:18).

Taking up the leadership mantle of Nehemiah and Paul, we must focus on transforming people before we start transitioning ministries. Transformational spiritual leaders emphasize...

- Transforming my heart

- Transforming my attitude toward God's people

- Transforming our worship of God

Transforming My Heart: Taking My Sin and Suffering to Christ

Biblical counselors don't say, "Physician, heal thyself." Instead, we say, "Soul physician, go to *the Soul Physician* for healing before counseling others." When we do, we follow the ancient path of Nehemiah. Before he implemented a single change-management principle, he prayed to the Soul Physician. "I confess the sins we Israelites, *including myself* and my father's family, have committed against you" (Nehemiah 1:6). To address his sin, Nehemiah turned to God for transformation.

Paul, perhaps the greatest human soul physician, focused first on his own heart. "We were under great pressure, far beyond our ability to endure, so that we despaired of life itself. Indeed, we felt we had received the sentence of death. But this happened that we might not rely on ourselves but on God, who raises the dead" (2 Corinthians 1:8–9). To address his suffering, Paul turned to God for transformation.

Transitioning a church is hard work. Leading a congregation through the change process of a pastor-centered church to a church where every minister is a one-another minister is demanding. It is impossible if the leader or leadership team is not addressing personal sin and suffering.

Does your team want to change lives? If so, when you meet, don't just talk about launching a biblical counseling ministry; instead, *be biblical counselors for each another.*

Transforming My Attitude Toward God's People: Seeing People as My Brothers and Sisters in Christ

Let's be honest. When people resist the changes we believe God wants us to implement, it's easy to start seeing them as the enemy. I find it fascinating that before Nehemiah dealt with change management, he *identified with* God's people. I find it instructive that before Paul dealt with conflict resolution, he *identified with* the very people who were criticizing him.

Nehemiah questioned Hanani about the Jewish remnant. Told that they were in great trouble and distress, he tells us that he "sat down and wept. For some days I mourned" (Nehemiah 1:4). Nehemiah had it made in the shade, living the life of luxury eight hundred miles away from Jerusalem. Yet he cared about his brothers and sisters. The word "questioned" (1:2) indicates much more than a passing interest. It means to inquire and express a genuine concern for the welfare of others.

When Nehemiah heard of their defeat (they were shattered and broken), when he heard of their disgrace (their reproach and shame), he mourned. He was deeply grieved and moved by the plight of God's people—of his people. His heart broke for their suffering and sin.

Paul, even with the Corinthians with whom he experienced excruciating conflict, began his second letter to them by identifying with them. Ten times in five verses he repeated a form of the Greek word for "comfort" (2 Corinthians 1:3–7). When you're in conflict with people, is your first thought (and your second and tenth thoughts) about helping them connect to Christ's comfort? We can't lead the launch of a biblical counseling ministry, which, in part, is about comforting one another in Christ, unless we can offer Christ's comfort to our brothers and sisters in Christ.

As leaders, are we making changes that are self-centered and self-focused?

Are we leading change because it's all about our leadership image? Or are we shepherding a transformative process out of a heart changed by Christ with a changed attitude toward our brothers and sisters in Christ?

Transforming Our Worship of God: Shepherding People to Christ

Nehemiah begins his ministry with worship. "LORD, the God of heaven, the great and awesome God, who keeps his covenant of love" (Nehemiah 1:5). His prayer of confession is a prayer of worship—Nehemiah links each sin to God's people's failure to respond wholeheartedly to God's holy love. Worship is embedded throughout the book, and it provides the bookends that frame the book. Nehemiah's closing prayer of remembrance is a plea that God would remember how Nehemiah purified the priests and Levites for worship.

Worship is the ultimate focus of Paul's introductory vignette concerning his despair over his suffering. Why did he share? So that "many will give thanks" (2 Corinthians 1:11). In every description Paul provides of his troubles, and there are many, his purpose is to direct people to God-dependence—to worshipping and trusting Christ alone.

The end goal of biblical counseling is worship—entrusting ourselves to God, exalting God, and enjoying God (Matthew 22:34–40). The end goal of *the process* of launching a biblical counseling ministry should be the same—to shepherd Christians to a deeper worship of Christ. Launching a biblical counseling ministry isn't a task to accomplish. It's a relationship—with God and others—to nourish and enjoy.

RELATIONAL CHANGE MANAGEMENT: STEWARDING THE CHANGE PROCESS

The most nurturing context for healthy change is a transformed congregation. It's from within that healthy environment that we plant and grow a biblical counseling ministry. Transformation is the seedbed for transition.

Still, change isn't easy. Change is like a ship that we simultaneously sail and refit. We don't get to stop the rest of life and ministry while we launch a new ministry. This is why we need wise, practical principles of relational change management.

Translate the Two Languages of Leadership: Purpose and People

Many churches spend far too little time in preparation and move far too quickly into making changes. We need to go slow if we want a biblical counseling ministry to plant deep and stay long. Other churches seem to spend forever talking about transition and never transitioning. The differences can be explained, in part, by understanding leadership styles. Some leaders tend toward a purpose-driven style and others toward a people-focused style (see Figure 5:1).

FIGURE 5:1

The Two Languages of Ministry

Purpose-Driven	People-Focused
Task	Relationship
Organization	Organism
Product	Process
Road Maker	Caretaker
Church as an Army	Church as a Body
Ministry	Maturity
Captain	Chaplain
Exhorter	Encourager
Manage (1 Timothy 3:5)	Take Care Of (1 Timothy 3:5)

Guide your leadership team to ponder the impact of their style as they interact with the congregation. Think about the following questions: Which style are we each prone to? Where did we learn and hone our style? How might a purpose-driven person lead this change in this congregation? How might a people-focused person lead in our setting? What tensions might exist on our team between the two styles? What tensions might each style create for our congregation? How will we resolve tensions biblically? What style is our congregation accustomed to? How could we wisely blend our two leadership styles?

Participate in Two-Way Conversations:
Telling Is Not Communicating

Relational change management is a continuing conversation, not a lecture. Too many churches think that they've communicated when they've posted a notice in the bulletin or on their website or made an announcement from the pulpit. Those methods are fine first steps, but they must also include an invitation to a conversation.

As you discuss the launch of your biblical counseling ministry, commit to dialogue rather than monologue. In fact, commit to trialogue—in every conversation, invite God's perspective through praying, depending upon the Holy Spirit for guidance, and seeking direction from the Word.

Where to Share

In churches where I've pastored, we used various venues to start the conversation. We offered sessions called Fireside Chats open to the entire congregation. In these informal settings, the leadership of the church and of the biblical counseling team met with the congregation to share the preliminary vision and to invite open sharing of feedback, questions, concerns, and suggestions. Other churches call these Congregational Input Nights. Still other churches choose to use business meetings as a forum for such discussions.

I've also used Leadership Community (LC) as a medium for discussion. Open to everyone in the church but especially geared to all church ministry leaders, LC meetings typically follow a vision, huddle, strategy format. The biblical counseling team shares their vision. They then huddle with participants in smaller groups to hear their responses. The larger group then reconvenes to discuss implementation strategies.

It's crucial that you work with other ministry leaders because your new ministry will impact their existing ministry. In my first church, two sisters wanted to join our LEAD biblical counseling training. The problem? They were the two primary soloists for the church choir, and choir practice met the same night as our proposed training. The worship leader and I had some planning (relational change management) to do.

Who to Share With

Your biblical counseling team needs to foster a climate of ongoing support with each group within your church. In *The Purpose Driven Church*, Rick Warren outlined five such groups: the community, crowd, congregation, committed, and the core. Your team should ask, "How are we communicating with people in each of these groups? What are we doing to nurture ownership of this ministry among the members of each group?"

You can connect with the *community* in many ways, including through the community assessment process, seminars, church outreach events, and your personal relationships with community members. The *crowd* includes those who are coming to church but are not yet members. Membership classes are a great place to discuss the vision of one-another ministry and biblical counseling. The *congregation* includes all those who are members and regular attenders. Spiritual gift classes are one means to engage them in discussions about biblical counseling.

The *committed* are the types of people you invite to LC meetings. Their ownership of and support for your biblical counseling ministry can make or break your ministry. Churches often overlook this group because they may not be official decision-makers, board members, or staff. However, they are the influencers, the doers, and the givers. And, as noted, they are often the most affected by the launch of any new ministry.

The *core* includes your church leaders, pastors, staff, elders, deacons, and board members. They must own the dual vision of every member doing informal one-another ministry and of equipped members providing formal biblical counseling. This is why you need to involve them in the envisioning process (see chapter 4).

It's especially important that you build trusting relationships with the committed and the core. Some people resist this idea because it feels like politics. However, the word "politics" comes from the term *polis*, meaning people. Communicating with the committed and core is not playing politics; it is respecting people. Committed leaders want and deserve to be informed and consulted. They want to know if their wisdom counts and whether anyone cares what they think.

Nehemiah built trusting relationships with the committed. In Nehemiah 2:16, we see his connection with the priests, nobles, and officials. He also built trusting relationships with the core. You don't get any more core than King Artaxerxes (2:1–9).

Communicate the Desperate Need for the Ministry: Holy Discontent

As you interact in various settings with different groups, discuss why the ministry is necessary. Your congregation will take ownership and invest their time and money in a biblical counseling ministry if they understand the desperate needs it will address. This occurs when people become dissatisfied with the status quo and experience holy discontent.

Nehemiah experienced this when he heard that the wall of Jerusalem was broken down and its gates burned (Nehemiah 1:3). Hearing the report, he sat down, wept, mourned, fasted, and prayed. He had a holy response to the desperate state of Jerusalem and its inhabitants.

Your congregational assessment will raise red flags of discontent. When you ask people where personal needs are not being met, they will tell you. It's easy to respond to their feedback defensively and see it as unhealthy complaining. Instead, view it as an open door, as an enormous opportunity to secure the congregation's passionate support.

Respond as Nehemiah did. After a detailed inspection of Jerusalem (Nehemiah 2:11–16), he gathered the Jews, the priests, the nobles, the officials, and others who would be doing the work and said to them, "You see the trouble we are in: Jerusalem lies in ruins, and its gates have been burned with fire. Come, let us rebuild the wall of Jerusalem, and we will no longer be in disgrace" (verse 17). The need exposed, they responded without hesitation. "Let us start rebuilding" (verse 18b). Instead of attempting to solve the problem himself, Nehemiah used the need as an opportunity to give ownership to the community.

Communicate the Amazing Benefits of the Ministry: Holy Celebration

We learn something further from Nehemiah. "I also told them about the gracious hand of my God upon me and what the king had said to me" (Nehemiah 2:18). It wasn't only holy discontent that motivated ownership; it was also Nehemiah's holy celebration.

The NIV's translation of their response is somewhat blasé: "So they began this good work" (verse 18c). We could translate the original language, "They set their hands together bravely," or "They vigorously set their hands to go about building," or "They strengthened their hands together to do God's work." That's ownership!

You might be thinking, *We haven't launched the biblical counseling ministry yet so we don't know what some of the amazing results might be.* This is why it's important to expose your key leaders to best-practice biblical counseling ministries in your area, around the country, and the world (through personal visits, reading materials, and their websites). Additionally, our Disciple-Making Champions provide the show-and-tell you need.

DISCIPLE-MAKING CHAMPIONS

Testimony Time

As part of the 4E Ministry Training Strategy Questionnaire, two dozen best-practice churches responded to the questions, What excites you and brings you the most joy about your biblical counseling ministry? How has the ministry impacted your church and community? Their answers could fill this chapter.

- "Leading this ministry has radically changed my life! It's dramatically impacting the hurting souls of men and women."

- "I love seeing the dawn of hope in the eyes of people who have been told and believe they are beyond help or hope. I love showing people that the Word of God truly has all the answers for the problems they face."

- "How exciting to know that what we share as biblical counselors carries the power of the resurrection to enable growth and change. This new growing and changing person then comes alongside another person who needs the same love of Christ lived out and helps another grow and change."

- "Seeing people understand the gospel in broader, deeper, and richer ways; seeing the Lord turn the lights on in the hearts of his people, helping them connect the dots between his grace and their daily lives, giving people a taste and zeal for gospel ministry in the body of Christ and in reaching an unbelieving world."

- "When we have eyes to see, we realize that counseling is really a ministry of spiritual transformation and discipleship. This is not about a ministry on the side. Our entire congregation has been forever changed by our biblical counseling focus."

- "It excites me to see people helping others. We're equipping members to care for one another. It has a geometric effect. When you teach a person how to grow and change to be more like Christ, you've equipped him or her to go and help someone else grow and change."

- "People share testimonies regularly about the benefits of the training—they are growing spiritually through the equipping, they feast on the depth of the relationships in our training group, and their counselees' lives are being changed forever."

- "An effective biblical counseling ministry has helped our church become known in our community as a church where people can get answers."

Communicate the Biblical Basis of the Ministry: Practical Theology

We shouldn't expect people to change because we said so, but because God says so. Through sermon series, life groups, private conversations, fireside chats, and congregational meetings, communicate the vision shared in chapter 1. Develop a common commitment that the local church *is* a biblical counseling ministry.

Assist people to grasp the direct relationship between biblical counseling and all the foundational doctrines and beliefs your church values. Discuss the sufficiency of Scripture. Do we have confidence that the Bible has answers to everyday life problems? Well, biblical counseling is the personal application of God's Word to everyday life situations and relationships.

Discuss progressive sanctification. Do we believe that God wants us to grow more like Christ every day in every way? Well, biblical counseling is a one-to-one means of helping one another to become more conformed to the image of Christ.

Discuss the priesthood of all believers. Do we believe that God calls and equips every Christian for one-another ministry? Well, biblical counseling empowers every Christian to speak the truth in love.

Address Concerns: Communicate Humble Confidence

It would be naïve to think that communication alleviates every possible concern. Your people will raise issues—some you will have thought of, and some that will be new. If you have thought through the issue previously, share your plan and seek additional feedback. If the issue is new, ask the person for their thoughts on how to address it, and commit to doing additional research.

In the Redwood National Park, there used to be a hollowed-out tree that you could drive through. There was a sign before the entrance to the tree that said, "Others Have. So Can You." That's the attitude you want to convey to your congregation. It's an attitude that says, "We're not the first people to ever launch and lead a church-based biblical counseling ministry. We don't have all the answers, but others surely know the questions. We're doing our homework, and we're willing to do more. We're confident that God, who calls us, also equips us."

Part 4 on empowering godly ministers addresses the typical concerns people raise about a biblical counseling ministry. Many of those relate to ethical and legal issues. As I note in more detail there, you should develop a written plan that clearly and honestly represents the qualifications of your counselors, the type of counseling offered, the type of issues addressed, and the ethical standards you will follow. Secure an attorney to counsel you regarding the structure and focus of your ministry and to assist you should any issues arise. I also recommend that churches purchase malpractice insurance for each person counseling in their ministry.

Prioritize the Implementation of Change: Start Small and Grow Slow

You *can* teach an old dog new tricks, but you must be very patient with the dog. Much more importantly, we are not dogs. God created us in his image. He knows us, commands us to change, and empowers us to change. Relational change management asks, "How much change can our people appropriately digest? How much change can our people realistically implement?"

If you've just launched several other ministries, it may be wise to delay the formal launch of your biblical counseling ministry. If you have a small team, it may be wise to start small and to grow slow.

I recommend equipping no more than a dozen people in the first round of training. One of my graduates started by training over two hundred women.

Because the training emphasized working on one's own struggles, she soon had scores of trainees requesting counseling. Once the training was done, she had two hundred women to supervise. She now speaks in my class and tells students, "Listen to Dr. Kellemen when he says to start with no more than a dozen trainees!"

Mourn Change: Grieve the Loss of the Old

No matter how well you prepare your people, all change involves some loss. Something new replaces or alters the old, the familiar. People will have to reckon with the fact that their pastor may not be the person who counsels them or visits them in the hospital. Someone who has been serving alongside them in ministry may leave to join the biblical counseling ministry. The church may grow and change as people are won to Christ through biblical counseling.

We would be uncaring biblical counselors if we dismissed such losses as inconsequential. We need to give people permission to grieve, and we need to shepherd the entire congregation through the grief and growth process.[1]

Call for a Vote: A Conclusive Statement of Congregational Ownership

Depending on how your church government is set up and how your church historically has launched new ministries, you may want to call for a formal vote. If so, after you've taken the steps outlined in chapters 1 through 5, your biblical counseling team and church leadership can craft the wording for a congregational vote. It will include the name of your ministry, the mission of the ministry, a summary of financial commitments, and a summary of policy and procedure matters. You can find a sample call for a vote in Appendix 5.1 (available free online at https://rpmministries.org/ebc-resources/).

Taking a vote can be valuable even if it is not constitutionally required. It communicates the central role that your biblical counseling ministry has in your vision for the entire church. It also provides a specific, tangible way for the entire congregation to express ownership of and support for the ministry.

---

1. I present a biblical model of grief and growth in *God's Healing for Life's Losses: How to Find Hope When You're Hurting* (Winona Lake, IN: BMH Books, 2010).

BIBLICAL CONFLICT RESOLUTION:
RESTORING RELATIONSHIPS

In an ideal world, the combination of transformed lives and relational change management would eliminate the need for biblical conflict resolution. Sadly, we no longer live in an ideal world. Even with a congregation that is growing in Christ and with a wise transition process, conflict can arise. When it does, biblical counselors, of all people, should be prepared for biblical conflict resolution.

Be Proactive: Respond Wisely to Potential Sources of Conflict

Nehemiah crossed all his *t*'s and dotted all his *i*'s, yet many people still resisted his ministry. Like him, when we seek to build up God's people, we may expect pockets of envy, dishonesty, apathy, fury, mockery, and hostility.

Prayerfully, you will face few or none of these. Picture the following discussion as the worst-case scenario, the perfect storm. Nehemiah models how to weather the worst storm imaginable.

Anticipate Pockets of Envy: Respond with Unity

When Sanballat and Tobiah heard that the king approved Nehemiah's plan, "they were very much disturbed that someone had come to promote the welfare of the Israelites" (Nehemiah 2:10b). They questioned Nehemiah's character not because they were concerned, but because they were afraid and envious. The intrusion of this outsider would strip away their power base and influence.

Rather than going toe to toe with these men, Nehemiah encouraged God's people to minister shoulder to shoulder (verses 11–20). He invited a trusted circle of colleagues to assess the need, and then like Shackleton, he called people to unite to conquer the problem. What he did wasn't avoidance of the enemy, but rather, a purposeful focus on God's family.

Anticipate Pockets of Dishonesty:
Respond with Humility and Integrity

When Geshem joined Sanballat and Tobiah, between the three of them, their nations nearly surrounded Jerusalem. When they saw God's people united in service, they falsely accused them. "Are you rebelling against the king?" (Nehemiah 2:19). They painted Nehemiah's good as if it were evil because Satan curses whom God blesses.

In response to their dishonesty, Nehemiah spoke the truth in love with humility and integrity. Instead of standing up for himself, he exalted God. "The God of heaven will give us success" (verse 20). Rather than exalting himself, he saw himself through God's eyes. "We his servants will start rebuilding" (verse 20).

It's not that Nehemiah stubbornly refused to search his heart. Rather, he had already been doing that, as we have seen. The same is true of Paul in 2 Corinthians 1:12. "Our conscience testifies that we have conducted ourselves in the world, and especially in our relations with you, with integrity and godly sincerity. We have done so, relying not on worldly wisdom but on God's grace." Biblical self-awareness is God's antidote for false accusation.

Anticipate Pockets of Apathy: Respond with Tenacity

Problems from without are hard enough, but problems from within are even more difficult to endure. Nehemiah launched the work with great enthusiasm only to face a potential interruption. "But their nobles would not put their shoulders to the work under their supervisors" (Nehemiah 3:5).

Interestingly, the text offers not a single word in response. The work continues unabated. While welcoming the support of all who offered it, Nehemiah had sufficient inner resources to stand alone if need be. In the tenacious discharge of his responsibilities, he was prepared to have no one but God. His energy was not dictated by others' apathy.

Anticipate Pockets of Fury: Respond with Vulnerability

In Nehemiah 3, thirty-eight diverse work crews labor harmoniously to advance God's kingdom. Then we read, "When Sanballat heard that we were rebuilding the wall, he became angry and was greatly incensed" (4:1).

When someone pushes us, our inclination is to push back. When someone gets in our face, we're tempted to get in their face. Nehemiah chose to get face to face with God. Vulnerably he prays, "Hear us, our God, for we are despised" (verse 4). "Despised" means to view someone as insignificant, useless, worthless. In the Old Testament, this frequently results in discouragement. Think of that word: dis-courage, to have your courage melt away as you curl up in a fetal position feeling overwhelmed and undermanned. Rather than give in to that, Nehemiah gave up to God.

Paul takes it a step further. He vulnerably exposes his discouragement even to his critics. He tells the Corinthians, of all people, that he despaired of life and felt the sentence of death (2 Corinthians 1:8–9). We might see that as foolish weakness, until we understand what Paul understands: "For when I am weak, then I am strong" (12:10b).

Anticipate Pockets of Mockery: Respond with God-Reality

Critics generally run in packs. Sanballat and Tobiah did. In the presence of their associates, Sanballat ridiculed the Jews. "What are those feeble Jews doing? Will they restore their wall? Will they offer sacrifices? Will they finish in a day?" (Nehemiah 4:2). Tobiah, who was at his side, said, "What they are building— even a fox climbing up on it would break down their wall of stones!" (verse 3). They pile on top of one another cruel character assaults, relentless mocking, and malicious slicing and dicing.

Drop after drop, drip after drip, it takes its toll. Verse 10 records what the people felt. Commentators believe it was actually sung as a funeral dirge. We might translate it these ways:

The strength of our burden bearing is drooping.

The rubbish heap so vast.

And we ourselves are stooping.

Unable to fulfill this impossible task.

If ever a people needed perspective—God-reality—it was them and it was then. Nehemiah looked things over, gathered his people, and said, "Don't be afraid of them. Remember the Lord, who is great and awesome" (verse 14). When life stinks, our perspective shrinks. When our perspective shrinks, we need a full dose of eternal perspective, of God perspective. We need to remember who God is, who we are in Christ, who is calling us, and what he calls us to do.

Anticipate Pockets of Hostility: Respond with Creativity

When the Israelites reached the halfway point, opposition went from bad to worse. "So we rebuilt the wall till all of it reached half its height, for the people worked with all their heart" (Nehemiah 4:6). When Sanballat and his crew heard about their progress, "they were very angry. They all plotted together to come and fight against Jerusalem and stir up trouble against it" (verses 7–8).

To make matters worse, their own people told them "ten times over, 'Wherever you turn, they will attack us'" (verse 12).

The halfway point is often the point of greatest opposition and greatest temptation to abandon our post. It's the point at which others begin to take notice of our progress, but when we begin to focus on the huge task still ahead. Great leaders respond to the potential death and destruction of a dream with life and creativity. You can define the greatness of leaders by what it takes to discourage them and by how they encourage everyone around them.

Creative thinking in a crisis requires both/and thinking, such as prayer *and* practicality. "We prayed to our God and posted a guard day and night to meet this threat" (verse 9). Nehemiah creatively suggests both working *and* protecting: "From that day on, half of my men did the work, while the other half were equipped with spears, shields, bows and armor" (verse 16). He creatively emphasizes both individuality *and* community: "Fight for your families, your sons and your daughters, your wives and your homes....We all returned to the wall, each to our own work...Wherever you hear the sound of the trumpet, join us there" (verses 14–15, 20).

Be a Peacemaker: Respond Lovingly to Resolve Conflict

A proactive approach to potential conflict prepares us so that we are not shocked if conflict occurs and so that we are able to lead effectively during conflict. However, as biblical counselors, we desire more—we desire reconciliation.

Ken Sande, in his book *The Peacemaker*, outlines a "4G" process of reconciliation. When I consult with churches ready to launch their biblical counseling ministry, I encourage them to follow Sande's biblical model:

- *Glorify God* (1 Corinthians 10:31): How can I please and honor God in this situation?

- *Get the Log Out of Your Eye* (Matthew 7:5): How can I show Jesus' work in me by taking responsibility for my contribution to this conflict?

- *Gently Restore* (Galatians 6:1): How can I lovingly serve others by helping them take responsibility for their contribution to this conflict?

- *Go and Be Reconciled* (Matthew 5:24): How can I demonstrate the forgiveness of God and encourage a reasonable solution to this conflict?

Glorify God: Pleasing God as My First Priority

Paul faced conflict with the Corinthians over several issues, especially their questioning of his integrity and authority. No small matter, Paul repeatedly clarified what motivated his ministry—God's glory. "What we preach is not ourselves, but Jesus Christ as Lord, and ourselves as your servants for Jesus' sake" (2 Corinthians 4:5). "So we make it our goal to please him" (5:9).

Paul teaches that we must always place our human conflict within the much larger context of God's eternal glory. If conflict arises in relation to your biblical counseling ministry, strive to help all parties, including yourself, by asking, "How can I please and honor God in this situation?" It's not about winning the conflict. It's not even about win/win scenarios. It's about joining together to advance God's kingdom. Sometimes that may require that we "lose" in the eyes of the world.

Get the Log Out: Examining My Heart as My First Responsibility

While Paul does not identify any particular sins, it is clear that he continually opened his heart to God's all-knowing eyes. "I call God as my witness—and I stake my life on it—that it was in order to spare you that I did not return to Corinth" (2 Corinthians 1:23). Paul lived every second aware that "we must all appear before the judgment seat of Christ" (5:10).

Paul models for us that when conflict occurs, our first responsibility is to examine our own heart based upon God's Word. If conflict arises related to your biblical counseling ministry, strive to help all parties, including yourself, by asking, "How can I show Jesus' work in me by taking responsibility for my contribution to this conflict?" When we do this, we embody the biblical counseling principles we teach.

Gently Restore: Loving Others as My First Ministry

Paul mastered the art of gentle restoration. "Even if I caused you sorrow by my letter, I do not regret it. Though I did regret it—I see that my letter hurt you, but only for a little while—yet now I am happy, not because you were made sorry, but because your sorrow led you to repentance. For you became sorrowful as God intended and so were not harmed in any way by us" (2 Corinthians 7:8–9). You can almost feel the conflict *within* Paul as he reflects on his past loving confrontation of the Corinthians. *I don't regret it. I did regret it. My letter hurt you. My letter did not harm you.*

Paul demonstrates that when conflict occurs, my first ministry, even before I launch any other ministry, is to love others with Christlike love. If conflict arises related to your biblical counseling ministry, strive to help all parties, including yourself, by asking, "How can I lovingly serve others by helping them take responsibility for their contribution to this conflict?"

Go and Be Reconciled: Restoring Relationship as My First Necessity

If Paul is the master of gentle restoration, then he's the gold standard of reconciliation. Is there a more tender yet compelling example than his words in 2 Corinthians 6:11–13? "We have spoken freely to you, Corinthians, and opened wide our hearts to you. We are not withholding our affection from you, but you are withholding yours from us. As a fair exchange—I speak as to my children—open wide your hearts also."

As if that were not enough, he pleads again, "Make room for us in your hearts. We have wronged no one, we have corrupted no one, we have exploited no one. I do not say this to condemn you; I have said before that you have such a place in our hearts that we would live or die with you" (7:2–3).

Paul not only wanted to demonstrate forgiveness, he also longed to encourage godly restoration. When the Corinthians were unrelenting in their punishment of a sinning brother, Paul taught them what to do instead. "You ought to forgive and comfort him, so that he will not be overwhelmed by excessive sorrow. I urge you, therefore, to reaffirm your love for him" (2:7–8).

Paul demonstrates that when conflict occurs, my first necessity is restoring the relationship, not pushing forward the biblical counseling ministry. If conflict arises related to your biblical counseling ministry, strive to help all parties, including yourself, by asking, "How can I demonstrate the forgiveness of God and encourage a reasonable solution to this conflict?"

COMMENCEMENT: SAIL ON

I've mentioned that change is like a ship we simultaneously sail and refit. Sometimes, in the midst of change and conflict, we just wish someone would stop the boat and let us get off!

Nehemiah and Paul surely felt the same way at times. Ultimately, their eternal goal of glorifying God kept them afloat. Their life purpose of empowering and equipping God's people kept them sailing the seas of ministry. Prayerfully, you are at the same place on your voyage.

If you are, then you're ready to expand your crew by enlisting people to your biblical counseling ministry. Chapter 6 will turn upside down the typical nonrelational recruitment process, which is often driven by the tyranny of the urgent need to find a warm body. So in chapter 6 we will replace the word "recruitment" with "connection." As a leader, you will learn how to connect to those who may join your ministry team and how to help prospective team members assess how well their gifting and calling connects to your ministry MVP-C.

GROWING TOGETHER: QUESTIONS FOR REFLECTION, DISCUSSION, AND APPLICATION

1. Share about a time in your church life when change took place and it was handled well. Or, when conflict began, and it was successfully resolved.

2. As you launch your biblical counseling ministry, what specific actions can you take and attitudes can you develop to apply the principles of...

   a. Transforming my heart: taking my sin and suffering to Christ?

   b. Transforming my attitude toward God's people: seeing people as my brothers and sisters in Christ?

   c. Transforming our worship of God: shepherding people to Christ?

3. As you launch your biblical counseling ministry, what specific actions can you take and attitudes can you develop to apply the relational change management principles of:

   a. Translating the two languages of leadership: purpose and people?

b. Participating in two-way conversations: telling is not communicating?

c. Communicating the desperate need for the ministry: holy discontent?

d. Communicating the amazing benefits of the ministry: holy celebration?

e. Communicating the biblical basis of the ministry: practical theology?

f. Addressing concerns: communicate humble confidence?

g. Prioritizing the implementation of change: start small and grow slow?

h. Mourning change: grieve the loss of the old?

    i. Calling for a vote: a conclusive statement of congregational ownership?

4. Of the six potential sources of conflict and the six positive responses, which ones might you need to apply to your situation?

5. How could you apply each of the 4Gs of biblical conflict resolution to your situation?

6

Mobilizing Ministers

Nurturing a Family and Building a Team

In my consulting ministry, I encourage church leaders to keep their eyes focused on four words that you're becoming very familiar with: "envisioning," "enlisting," "equipping," and "empowering." These words help leaders to design a straightforward process of discipling biblical counselors.

I consistently see the need for focus with the first two aspects of the process. Some churches are great at envisioning, but they get so entangled in the details that they drop the ball and never move to enlisting people. Other churches skip the envisioning process, which causes their enlisting to be more about recruiting volunteers than calling disciples.

I want to help you to simplify:

- *Connect (enlist) people to your purpose (envision).*

We birth a family and build a team not by asking, How can we recruit more volunteers? Our question is, How can we connect committed people with our disciple-making vision?

To help churches make this shift, I walk with them through the disciple-making ministries of Christ and Paul. The response to this Bible study is always the same: "It's all about connecting. Jesus called people to himself—to connect with and abide in him. It's a thoroughly relational process!" We learn together Christ's transformational, relational process: come and see me; come and follow me; come and be with me; come and remain in me; come and be like me.

This returns us to the theme we learned in chapter 1. A relationship with *the* transforming Person (Christ) produces transforming leaders (you and your team) who relationally lead a transforming process (the 4Es) that the Spirit uses in transforming your church (the body of Christ) so others (the congregation and community) are transformed also.

People display a similar response to our study of Paul's equipping ministry. They say, "Enlisting is not about mechanical recruiting; it's about connecting! Paul connected deeply with people and connected people deeply with each other. Then he made sure he connected the right people with the right calling to the right ministry."

Paul worked to ensure that everyone was equipped to do their unique work—the work that was the right fit for how God designed them—for their spiritual shape and personal calling. We see this in his ministry with Timothy, Titus, Silas, Aquila, and Priscilla. We see it in his discussion of spiritual gifts in Romans 12:3–8, 1 Corinthians 12:1–31, Ephesians 4:1–16, and 1 Peter 4:10–11. In these passages, Paul teaches that the body of Christ has many members, and though these members are one, they do not all have the same function. There are different kinds of gifts and different kinds of service. Enlisting connects people to God's unique calling.

When leaders understand this, I hear a sigh of relief. They had feared that enlisting people to their biblical counseling ministry might imply "screening people out." They think, *Who am I to tell people they can't get equipped?*

Soon they begin to understand that they want to include *everyone* in various formats that equip the whole congregation for *informal* one-another ministry. They also see that even when they enlist *some* to be equipped for *formal* biblical counseling ministry, the focus is on finding the right ministry match and fit, not on creating barricades to ministry.

As we mobilize ministers, let's keep it simple and relational. You already caught and cast your *core values* in community—*envisioning* your biblical counseling MVP-C. Now connect deeply with people and connect *committed people* to their calling—*enlisting* to your MVP-C.

NURTURING A FAMILY: CONDUCTING CHRIST'S OPUS

Christ promises that he will build his church (Matthew 16:18). Graciously, he invites us to join him as expert builders (1 Corinthians 3:10). Notice that we are not expert programmers; we are expert *builders of people* conducting a strategic relational transformation process.

To keep the process clear-cut, remember our twofold template from chapter 1:

- *The Informal Model:* Equipping *every* member for *informal* one-another disciple-making. You *nurture your church family* through saturating your congregation with passion for and equipping in every-member ministry—speaking and living God's truth in love.

- *The Formal Model:* Equipping *some* members for *formal* biblical counseling. You *build a team* by calling and connecting committed people to comprehensive equipping in in-depth, ongoing ministry as biblical counselors.

Most of this chapter and the bulk of this book focus on the formal model. However, as we saw in chapter 1, every church must be a church *of* biblical counseling—the informal model. Ephesians 4:16 points the way. From Christ, "the whole body, joined and held together by every supporting ligament, grows and builds itself up in love, as each part does its work." That pictures Christ's opus—his grand creation, his grand design for his church.

Conducting the Orchestra

You've heard it—the cacophony of noises when the orchestra begins to warm up. The disharmony is like fingers screeching on a blackboard.

Churches become like that when they are churches *with* a biblical counseling ministry but not *of* biblical counseling. The biblical counseling ministry sets up shop in the corner and competes for attention with the small-group ministry and the women's ministry and the men's ministry and the children's ministry. There's no harmony or synergy. The ministries are always tuning up, but never quite in tune with one another because no one is conducting them, so they play the same music.

The solution is not to make the biblical counseling ministry the favored ministry. The answer is to have every ministry saturated with the churchwide commitment explored in chapter 1—*every member a disciple-maker.* The women's ministry pursues that goal, the men's ministry follows that goal—everyone and every ministry aligns with that goal.

The first responsibility of pastors, teachers, and church leaders (including the leaders of the biblical counseling ministry) is to create a synchronized passion for speaking and living God's truth in love. We have seen that process in many places in chapters 1–5. We will learn how to equip and empower the biblical counseling team throughout chapters 6–12. What is missing is how to oversee that the entire church is being trained to speak the truth in love.

Training the Musicians

Even if you wanted them to, not everyone in your church would participate in your six-month, one-year, or two-year training in biblical counseling. If the whole congregation is excited about one-another ministry but only some are able to join your extensive training, now what?

Our Disciple-Making Champions (see below) offer a host of practical suggestions. I have used many of these in order to...

- Saturate the whole congregation with the mindset of one-another ministry through speaking the truth in love.

- Equip the whole congregation in basic principles of one-another ministry and biblical counseling, which they can use as spiritual friends in real-life settings.

- Whet people's appetite for more. Churches have me present a one-day "How to Care Like Christ" seminar. They use this to say, "Since you benefitted so much from one day, just imagine what could happen if you took our one-year training!"

DISCIPLE-MAKING CHAMPIONS

Saturating the Congregation

As part of the 4E Ministry Training Strategy Questionnaire, two dozen best-practice churches responded to the question, How do you assure that the entire congregation remains excited about and becomes equipped for one-another ministry? Here's a sampling of their strategies.

- Preaching on topics such as one-another ministry, the sufficiency of Scripture, body life, the priesthood of all believers, and disciple-making.

- Modeling how to apply truth to life through preaching and teaching.

- Hosting one-day seminars by nationally known leaders.

- Hosting our own seminars and in-services on one-another topics.

- Encouraging our members to attend regional/national biblical counseling conferences.

- Using Adult Bible Fellowships (Sunday school), Leadership Community, and our small-group ministry to train people in one-another ministry.

- Taking our people through DVD series on soul care, spiritual friendship, and disciple-making.

- Purchasing biblical counseling resources (books, videos, pamphlets).

- Having individuals give testimonies about how they are growing spiritually through biblical counseling.

- Counseling: People who receive counseling become our most passionate proponents of biblical counseling.

- Teaching our leaders how to implement biblical counseling principles in our deacon groups, elder groups, everywhere!

- Starting from the ground up by talking about one-another ministry in our membership class.

- Letting counseling principles inform everything we do—they are part of the typical ebb and flow of our life together.

If you're to unleash the whole congregation, then you must orchestrate a synergy between these equipping opportunities and your envisioning process. Help people make practical connections in the real world. Tell them, "The vision we've been talking about, and the training you've just received, use that in your everyday life. With your family members. With your neighbors over the backyard fence. At McDonalds and Starbucks. Be sensitive to opportunities to turn mundane conversations at work into spiritual conversations. In your small groups, enter deeply into each other's lives as you apply the Word together."

Communicate to your people that one-another ministry is just as vital as preaching from the pulpit or offering formal biblical counseling. Structure your church so that doing life together and speaking the truth in love *is* church.

BUILDING A TEAM: ASSEMBLING YOUR DREAM TEAM

Picture where you are in the process so far.

- Your whole church has a growing vision for disciple-making ministry.

- Your biblical counseling envisioning team has diagnosed the readiness of your congregation and community.

- You've jointly crafted your ministry MVP-C Statement—catching and casting it in community.

- You're working through the relational change management process and employing biblical conflict resolution principles.

- Through an ongoing strategic process, you're equipping the whole congregation to speak and live God's truth in love.

Some in your church deeply resonate with everything they're hearing. They don't know all the details yet, but the big picture draws them to want to know more. Now they hear that you're about ready to start building a biblical counseling ministry team.

Picture Myron. Part of him feels like a kid in Little League. "Pick me! Pick me!" Another part of him feels a tad reticent: "I'd better count the cost before I make any major commitment."

Part of you feels extremely excited. "I can't wait to build a team!" Another part of you thinks more strategically: "I want to be sure we match the right people to the right ministry for the right reasons at the right time." To address these dual and dueling thoughts and feelings, use the following team-building rubrics:

- Calling People to Connection: What people need to know about your ministry

- Matching the Right People to the Right Ministry: What you need to know about ministers

These two categories should work together because, whenever possible, the decision whether someone becomes a part of the biblical counseling ministry should be mutual. With Myron, ideally it would be a combination of him deciding whether he thinks he is a good match and your leadership team determining whether they think Myron is a good fit. You might even picture it as "dating" or "courtship."

Calling People to Connection: What People Need to Know About Your Ministry

I love the joy and freedom leaders experience when they see team building as calling people to connection. They no longer rely upon nonrelational, panicked recruiting of warm bodies to fill a program void. Now they focus on relationally enlisting committed people to a captivating vision.

I love the joy and freedom God's people experience when they realize that you are inviting them to consider a call to a dream team. They appreciate that you are calling them not out of desperation or as a last resort. They respect that you are asking them to consider seriously a calling to connect to a...

- People: You, your leadership team, and their fellow team members

- Purpose: Your biblical counseling ministry MVP-C Statement

- Philosophy: Your biblical approach to biblical counseling

- Profile: Your portrait of a mature trainee and a nurtured graduate

- Process: Your specific plan for training and for ministry after training

- Promise: Your covenant to fulfill your mutual commitment

If people are to make intelligent, Spirit-led decisions about whether they want to join your biblical counseling ministry, then they need clear and specific information. These six categories provide what they need to make an informed decision.

Calling to Connect to a People

Jesus always called people to himself—to be with him to become like him. While that may seem like a daunting task to us mere humans, Paul sent the same invitation. "Follow my example, as I follow the example of Christ" (1 Corinthians 11:1). Nothing is more intimidating to me as an equipper than the realization that my first responsibility is to be like Christ.

This is why the decision-making process needs to be relational. It's why I believe team leaders should be church members for at least two years and team members for at least one year. Your equipping team needs to be able to say, "You've watched our lives for some time now. We're going to be like family. You need to decide whether our lives warrant your trust and whether you want to join our ministry family."

It's also why I believe people need to be aware of who else is considering and being considered for team/family membership. Plan to have at least one in-person meeting with all prospective trainees. Tell them, "Look around the room. Here are the other folks who could potentially join our biblical counseling family. We're going to get real and raw, close and involved. Is this the group you want to call home?"

Calling to Connect to a Purpose

After you call people to yourself and your team, call them to your MVP-C. Include your biblical counseling ministry MVP-C Statement in the packet of information that every prospective trainee receives (see Appendix 6.1 for a sample Information and Application Packet available free online at https://rpm ministries.org/ebc-resources/). In your written and oral interview process, assess each person's understanding of and commitment to the MVP-C—do they own it?

Your MVP-C Statement should become the arbiter when any issues arise about the focus of your ministry. It takes personalities and power struggles out of the equation. It becomes your blueprint for how you will do ministry, and all must agree to abide by this standard.

Calling to Connect to a Philosophy

The various approaches to biblical counseling are numerous and diverse. In your packet, include a document that spells out your philosophy of counseling. Present a clear definition and a detailed description of your convictions about what makes biblical counseling truly biblical (see Appendix 6.1 for one example).

The idea is not to force everyone to walk lockstep with everything you teach. I tell potential team members, "We desire you to be Bereans (Acts 17:11), not Corinthians (1 Corinthians 1:10–17). Based upon your understanding of God's Word, test what we teach. As a Berean, we expect that you'll display a critical mind minus a critical spirit. Our team can't function biblically if any member has a Corinthian attitude of negativity, biting criticism, and againstness. If your philosophy and theology of counseling differs noticeably from what you've read about ours, then we won't be a good ministry training match."

Calling to Connect to a Profile

People deserve to know what you hope they will gain from their training. What are your anticipated goals and results? We communicate this through including in our packet and our interview process A Profile of a Nurtured LEAD Graduate (see Appendix 6.1).

This includes the heart desires that we are looking for in our trainees at entry. We are looking for answers to questions such as the following: Do you dream of being a spiritual friend who can weep deeply with those who weep? Do you desire to be a soul physician who can listen well and then wisely guide others through their problems to the Father's heart?

For some people, these descriptions resonate deeply. They are praying, "Please, Father, lead the team to invite me to be equipped." Others realize this is not exactly what they were looking for, and they self-select out of the process.

The profile also outlines the qualities that we anticipate developing in each trainee's life as a result of our equipping and empowering ministry. We briefly describe the 4Cs of biblical content/conviction, Christlike character, relational competence, and Christian community. Again, these either attract people in with enthusiasm or lead people to opt out politely.

The third aspect of the profile sketches the types of ministries that your successful graduates could become involved after their training. Your training may not be only for counselors. At my first church, of the twelve people we trained during our first two-year training, two launched and led a small group focused on sexual abuse recovery, two launched and led a small group focused on parenting adolescents, and two led a small group focused on victory over addictive behaviors. The other six graduates provided individual, marital, or parental/family counseling.

Calling to Connect to a Process

People also deserve to know what they're getting themselves into. This is part of wisely counting the cost. In our packet, we provide specific information about time and energy expectations while in training as well as our expectations after training (see Appendix 6.1).

The in-training components include how many hours each week or month the trainee would commit to lecture/lab training, meeting with an encouragement partner, meeting with a supervisor, meeting with a counselee, and outside reading. We are also very clear about the nature of the training—we say, "We're going to be real and raw, and mess with your life. Our training is not simply about academic head knowledge. We're going to speak the truth in love to one another—we're going to experience biblical counseling and discipleship. It's going to be intense and intimate."

We also expect the person to commit to ministry after they complete their training. While people can only plan "as the Lord wills," we ask that trainees commit to a year of ministry after training for every year they were in training. This includes the time they would give to counseling others or to leading small-group ministries and their preparation time for those ministries. It also includes ongoing education such as individual supervision, group supervision, and other advanced training.

Calling to Connect to a Promise

You can imagine why a good number of people self-select out of the training. They count the cost and, at least for the present training period, they opt out. You can also imagine that those who join are red-hot in their commitment to be equipped to counsel and disciple.

We think it is important to get that commitment in writing. So we create a biblical counseling ministry covenant (see Appendix 6.1).

Your Calling Cards: How You Invite People to Connection

Use all the typical means of church communication to get the word out about your training: pulpit and bulletin announcements, individual email, group e-blast, snail mail, church newsletter or e-zine, church website, church social media, and church blog. Word of mouth and personal contact remain the most productive means of communication—especially if your goal is connection.

Since our packet is pretty hefty, we don't distribute it to everyone. Our initial communications, which build upon the buzz created by the envisioning process, make people aware of how to obtain the information packet (see Appendix 6.1 for a sample cover letter). They can download it from our website, pick it up in the church office, receive it as an email attachment, or even receive it via old-fashioned snail mail. We also include information on the next steps if they resonate with our biblical counseling training process.

Matching the Right People to the Right Ministry: What You Need to Know About Ministers

In the first phase of the enlisting process, you provide people with what they need to know to make an informed decision about your ministry. After processing all your materials, some will say, "I'm interested in being considered." That leads to the second phase, where they provide you with what you need to know to make an informed decision about their fit and readiness for your biblical counseling equipping.

During the selection phase, seek to avoid ditches or extremes on either side of the enlisting process. One ditch to avoid is accepting anybody and everybody into your training. Given the commitment your equipping team is making and the expectations you have for your trainees, you need to be sure that you accept the people who best fit your ministry. Additionally, if your training emphasizes a lab/small-group component and a supervisory aspect, then realistically, you can't accept more than twelve people per trainer.

The other extreme to avoid is accepting only those people who are 100 percent ready. There's no such person—including you and me. Think about the imperfections of each of the twelve disciples Jesus called. The enlisting process is about selecting people with a maturing level of commitment to Christ, the body of Christ, and growth in Christ, and then scouting out whether their heart passion matches the passion of your ministry.

Addressing a Common Concern

You may wonder, *So what do I do if at the end of the mutual process some people want into my training, but I don't have room for everyone, or I don't think someone is a good match? How can I tell a member of my church that I won't train them?*

First, a number of people are going to opt out due to the commitment level—they simply can't commit the time and energy at this point in their life. Second, if you implement the whole-congregation training discussed earlier, then every person still has numerous opportunities for training in one-another ministry. You are not saying, "You can't be trained at all." You are saying, "At this point in time, I think it would be good if you took our thirteen-week encouragement class, then let's consider the LEAD biblical counseling training the next time we offer it."

Third, there are also many other ministries in your church where this person might be a better fit. So you are saying, "Based upon your spiritual gift analysis, the assessment you completed, and our interview, I think a better fit for you in ministry at our church could be _____."

Fourth, you could be saying, "I think you're a great fit. Unfortunately, we only have resources to train a dozen people, yet we have two dozen folks we could select. We'd like to ask you if it would be okay to put you at the head of the list for our next round of training."

Fifth, in some cases, your assessment process will raise some concerns. Some folks, *at this point in their lives*, would be better served by *receiving* biblical counseling instead of being trained to *be* a biblical counselor. Speak the truth in love to them: "Myron, we really appreciate your candor in responding to our written and verbal questions. You've mentioned a couple of specific struggles in your life that we think would best be addressed by some biblical counseling and small-group discipleship. If history is any indication, as you work through these issues, when our next round of training starts, you'll be an excellent candidate."

In more than three decades of training counselors, I've never ended the mutual process with an open conflict. Sure, a few times people were disappointed. But each time that happened, they chose one of these other options and God used them greatly. What happens more often (though not a lot) is I identify a person who I think would be an incredible biblical counselor, and for various reasons, they choose not to enter the training.

Getting from Here to There

There is no one way to discern who would be the best fit. You'll see on the next page that our Disciple-Making Champions used a great diversity of means to select trainees. They also looked for a wide assortment of qualities and qualifications. You need to build your list of qualifications based upon your ministry MVP-C, profile, and philosophy. You need to build your selection process based upon your church history, culture, and your own personality.

DISCIPLE-MAKING CHAMPIONS

Building God's Team

As part of the 4E Ministry Training Strategy Questionnaire, two dozen best-practice churches responded to the questions, What qualifications are you looking for in those you train as biblical counselors? and, What is involved in your selection, interview, and application process? No one church listed all these qualifications or included all these elements in their selection process.

The Qualifications You Are Looking For

- A Christian, growing in Christ, and a church member (some churches specified the number of years as a believer and/or as a member).

- Commitment to the church values, mission, leadership covenant, doctrinal statement, and teacher assent form.

- Enthusiastic agreement with the counseling theology/philosophy and mission/vision.

- Biblically/doctrinally sound. Able to use the Bible for real-life wisdom and discernment.

- Spiritually and emotionally mature. Godliness. Christlikeness. Growth in Christ.

- Growing demonstration of Christian character qualities

such as the fruit of the Spirit and restoring others in a spirit of gentleness (Galatians 5:22—6:2).

- Demonstrates love for people. Compassionate. Experience with the pain of life. Nonjudgmental. Relational skillfulness. Caring.

- Demonstrates ability to minister to people in informal one-another settings.

- Shows a passion for and gift for counseling/encouragement based upon service in the church.

- Demonstrates ability to handle smaller commitments. Serves faithfully in the church.

- Meets the qualifications for an elder or deacon in 1 Timothy 3.

- FITS: *F*aithfulness in training and service; *I*ntentionality in gospel growth; *T*eachable attitude; *S*kills demonstrated through small-group and one-on-one ministries.

- FAT: *F*aithful, *A*vailable, *T*eachable.

The Selection, Interview, and Application Process

- Prayer.

- Starts with self-selection: a sense of calling from Christ.

- Completion of a written biblical counseling ministry application form.

- Completion of a background check.

- Completion of a theology exam and a spiritual gifts assessment.

- Submission of one to three personal references.

- Recommendation by a pastor, elder, deacon, ministry leader, or small-group leader.

- Completion of a personal interview.

- Personal relationship—observing their life in community.

- Observation of ministry during "lower level" classes on informal one-another ministry.

- Completion of a commitment agreement/covenant.

The Qualifications/Qualities You Are Looking For

To be consistent, I find it best to align the qualifications you're looking for with the qualities you're trying to develop throughout your equipping. In my case, that means I'm looking for a *baseline level of the 4Cs* of biblical content/conviction, Christlike character, relational competence, and Christian community. If you look at the list of qualifications on the previous page, you can collate many of them into the 4Cs. As I design the written interview form, ask questions in the in-person interview, examine references, and observe people in their daily life in our church, the 4Cs are always at the forefront of my thinking.

The Selection, Interview, and Application Process

The selection, interview, and application process is how you "get at" or discern whether a candidate has the baseline level of qualifications deemed necessary to join your training. I collated thirteen common processes used by best-practice churches. Most mentioned at least half of these.

All the leaders wisely and humbly mentioned prayer. "The harvest is plentiful but the workers are few. Ask the Lord of the harvest, therefore, to send out workers into his harvest field" (Matthew 9:37–38). God not only sovereignly gifts his people; he sovereignly calls and directs his people into specific fields of service. Without a daring confidence in the Lord of the harvest, it is impossible to match the right people to the right ministry.

Depending upon the history, background, size, style, and culture of the churches I have served, I've used several of the thirteen processes. In addition to prayer and self-selection, I always use a written Biblical Counseling Ministry Application Form (see Appendix 6.1) and the completion of a personal interview. You won't be surprised when you read the application form and detect the 4Cs. If you observed a personal interview, you wouldn't be surprised to hear those 4Cs woven throughout the interview in a natural, even spontaneous way. Nor will you be surprised when you see it contains a Redeemed Personality Inventory (see chapter 9 and Appendix 6.1).

I value the input of others, so references are helpful, and recommendations from leaders in our church are beneficial. I value spiritual gifting so a spiritual gift assessment can be useful (more to indicate the style, feel, and focus of one's counseling rather than whether or not he or she would be a capable counselor). Legal and ethical issues are important to a counseling ministry, so a background check is wise.

Still, if you are skilled as a biblical counselor, if you relate with Scripture and soul (1 Thessalonians 2:8), and if your love abounds in knowledge and depth of insight (Philippians 1:9), then nothing is more suitable and valuable than the in-person interview. The other sources of information provide the context and at times do the gatekeeping. The personal interview, especially if administered by a team of leaders, provides the connection that is central to building a biblical counseling team, a family. It helps you sense the connection between your team and the candidate. It helps you discern mutually and candidly if there is a good connection between this person and your biblical counseling ministry.

COMMENCEMENT: CONNECTING FROM START TO FINISH AND EVERYWHERE BETWEEN

How you start a ministry relationship has a great influence on the ongoing shape of that relationship. It was true with Paul and the Ephesian elders. He told them at the start of his emotional farewell address, "You know how I lived the whole time I was with you, from the first day I came into the province of Asia" (Acts 20:18). Trace his ministry in Ephesus from Acts 19:1 onward, and you'll see that Paul focused on connecting, relating, and speaking the truth in love from the onset to the farewell.

Consider what characterized the last moments of Paul's ministry to the Ephesians: "They all wept as they embraced him and kissed him." What grieved them most was his statement that they would never see his face again. Then they accompanied him to the ship. "After we had torn ourselves away from them, we put out to sea" (Acts 20:37—21:1).

That's the type of relationship that should characterize every church. A church *of* biblical counseling will be so saturated with spiritual friendships and spiritual conversations that it hurts when someone leaves. The church's biblical counseling ministry should be so connected that "grief" is the only word that describes the loss when someone leaves.

For some people, when they heard "enlisting," the words "relational" and "connecting" likely were far from their minds. Words like "recruiting," "screening," "processes," "procedures," "policies," and "paperwork" were likely embedded in their minds. I pray that notion is forever changed. Enlisting is about mobilizing ministers: nurturing a family and building a team.

What a foundation that lays for equipping! You've envisioned in community, you've enlisted as a community, now you're ready to equip people for biblical content, Christlike character, and relational competence in the context of Christian community. I hope you can't wait. I can't.

GROWING TOGETHER: QUESTIONS FOR REFLECTION, DISCUSSION, AND APPLICATION

1. What difference will it make in your attitude when you think of enlisting as connecting rather than as recruiting? When you move from asking, "How can we recruit more volunteers?" to "How can we connect committed people with our disciple-making vision?"

2. Regarding saturating your congregation with one-another ministry:

   a. Of the practical suggestions from the Disciple-Making Champions, which ones are you already using? Which ones would you like to add?

   b. How could you structure your church so that doing life together and speaking the truth in love *is* church?

3. As you assemble your dream team by calling people to connection:

   a. Which of the six steps (people, purpose, philosophy, profile, process, promise) do you think would be the easiest to carry out? The hardest?

   b. What changes would you make to the sample documents in Appendix 6.1 to adapt them for your situation?

4. In matching the right people to the right ministry:

   a. What qualifications/qualities are you looking for? Why are these central?

   b. Of the Disciple-Making Champions' list of options in the selection, interview, and application process, which would you use? Why? How?

5. A shift is on the horizon—from envisioning in community and enlisting as a community to equipping within community. How could you approach equipping so that you connect as deeply to your team as Paul did to his team?

PART 3

EQUIPPING GODLY MINISTERS FOR MINISTRY

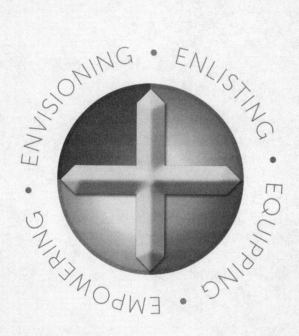

Equipping

The year was 1985—my first year out of seminary. Shirley and I had just moved to Elyria, Ohio, with our six-month-old son, Josh. We were thrilled that I'd be working at Open Door Christian School as the middle school and high school Bible teacher, guidance counselor, and high school varsity wrestling coach. We had purchased our first home—a three-bedroom, one-bath, two-car garage, brick ranch with a fenced backyard and a brand new swing set for our son.

Not only was I Coach K to three dozen young men on our wrestling team, I also launched my ministry as a coach-equipper of biblical counselors. I started PEP: *Peer Encouragement Program*. I trained a dozen high school juniors and seniors in biblical encouragement (that manual eventually became *Gospel Conversations: How to Care Like Christ*). They met with upper elementary school and middle school students to listen, care, share, and encourage.

Coaching and equipping are in my blood, in my DNA. It's who I am, who God designed me to be. Whether it's coaching wrestlers or coaching counselors, I'm always thinking about a comprehensive foundation. Whether it's the first day of wrestling practice or the first night of equipping counselors, I always start with the Vince Lombardi illustration. Lombardi, the legendary football coach of the Green Bay Packers, was frustrated after his team played a poor first half. During halftime he held a football in his hands and said to these professional athletes, "Gentlemen, this is a football." They needed a reminder about the basics—Football 101.

In part 3, I lay a comprehensive foundation for biblical counseling equipping—the 4Cs—that can constitute the focus of every biblical counseling equipping ministry.

- Biblical *C*ontent/*C*onviction: Head/Knowing—How to change lives with Christ's changeless truth

- Christlike *C*haracter: Heart/Being—How to reflect Christ

- Counseling *C*ompetence: Hands/Doing—How to care like Christ

- Christian *C*ommunity: Home/Loving—How to grow together in Christ

In chapter 7, we'll learn how the 4Cs provide our biblical counseling training *goals and objectives*. This chapter answers the questions,

- What is the purpose of biblical counseling training? What do nurtured graduates of biblical counseling training look like?

In chapters 8 and 9, we'll move from these broad goals and objectives to a focused discussion of biblical counseling training *curriculum and materials*. These two chapters address the question,

- What should biblical counselors know, be, and do, and how should they relate?

In chapter 10, we'll explore biblical counseling training *strategies and methods*. These suggest the how-to of shaping your training, and they present best-practice training methods for equipping biblical counselors. This chapter tackles the question,

- How do we structure our equipping so we effectively train biblical counselors to know, be, do, and love?

A coach like Vince Lombardi loved specific goals. If he had written this section, his ROLOs (Reader-Oriented Learning Objectives) might read like this. Through your active reading and application of the four chapters in this section, you'll be equipped to...

- Develop comprehensive four-dimensional training *goals and objectives* for equipping biblical counselors in the 4Cs of biblical content, Christlike character, counseling competence, and Christian community (chapter 7).

- Map out the focused *curriculum and materials* that will become your subject matter and lesson plans for equipping biblical counselors in content, character, competence, and community (chapters 8 and 9).

- Apply transformational training *strategies and methods* that comprehensively equip your trainees for knowing (head/content), being (heart/character), doing (hands/competence), and loving (home/community) (chapter 10).

This 4C map has served me well—from my days as the PEP equipper, to my four churches, and through my thirty years as a professor. It has served hundreds of best-practice churches well also. This comprehensive biblical guide for equipping biblical counselors can be a tool for your church too.

Competent to Counsel

The Résumé of the Biblical Counselor

Four years after I started my ministry at Open Door Christian School, I moved down the hallway one hundred yards to begin my first pastoral ministry—Counseling and Discipleship Pastor at the Church of the Open Door (COD). Though it was a megachurch of over three thousand, COD had never hired a Counseling Pastor. When they listed the position, all they knew was that they had scores of people asking for counseling and no pastors trained to counsel. The job description encompassed little more than having someone counsel people every week.

Being the guy with coaching-equipping in his veins, I prepared a packet of material proposing that they expand their vision and hire a Counseling *and* Discipleship Pastor. If hired, I would not only counsel and pastor; I would disciple and equip church members through the LEAD Ministry: *Life Encouragers And Disciplers.* I had taught, counseled, and coached the sons and daughters of half the board members, so even though I was the ripe young age of twenty-nine, they were enthusiastic about the vision and hired me.

A KID IN HIS DAD'S OVERSIZED SUIT

I'll never forget the first evening of our first LEAD class. Among my twelve trainees was my wife, but everyone else was from five to twenty-five years older than me. This was back in the day when pastors wore a suit and tie even on a

Wednesday night. I was fine the first hour of our training—the lecture/interaction hour. Then, after a short break, we switched our chairs from rows to a circle and were about to have our first counseling small-group lab.

That was when an overwhelming image struck me. I pictured myself as a ten-year-old boy dressed in my dad's way-too-large suit, the sleeves dangling over my hands, and my feet too short to touch the floor. My first inclination was to ignore the image and pretend I was fine. Then I made one of the smartest, bravest, most significant decisions of my young ministry. *I shared my image of myself with the class.*

Rather than act like I had it all together, rather than fake it, I decided to walk the talk. I had told each of them during the enlisting process that we were going to get real and talk honestly about life. That first night we did, and we were never the same because of it. We gelled, connected, bonded. We spoke the truth in love.

My honesty about my fears opened up each person to be honest about their fears. Person after person shared their story of trepidation. We laughed. We cried. We shared Scripture about our identity in Christ. We prayed. We went way overtime…and nobody noticed (except the nursery worker who was watching our newborn daughter, Marie).

A PORTRAIT OF NURTURED GRADUATES

That first night we experienced comprehensive equipping. In the context of community, we applied biblical content to our lives, encouraged one another to develop Christlike character, and began to cultivate biblical counseling competencies as we ministered to one another.

At that stage of my ministry, I wouldn't have called these goals and objectives 4C Equipping, but even then I was committed to comprehensive training. I had a picture in my mind—a portrait of a nurtured graduate of our LEAD biblical counseling ministry. I knew that I wanted to minister to the whole person—the head, the heart, and the hands in the context of God's home. Everything we did together for those two years we geared toward shaping one another into the image of that portrait.

FOUR-DIMENSIONAL EQUIPPING
VERSUS ONE-DIMENSIONAL TRAINING

In my consulting, both in churches and in seminary settings, the primary weakness we identify involves training that lacks one or more of the 4Cs. Many training programs, whether in churches or schools, tend to highlight one dimension (one of the 4 Cs) to the detriment of the other components of comprehensive biblical counseling training.

Some biblical counseling equipping tilts almost exclusively to biblical content. Trainees know the Word, which is essential, but they are mostly head and little heart (truth minus love). Lacking the competency to relate truth to life, they end up preaching *at* counselees. They are unskilled at engaging counselees in scriptural explorations that empower counselees to apply truth to their lives.

Some biblical counseling training inclines the pendulum the other direction and focuses almost exclusively on counseling competency. Training consists of the meticulous practice of skills and techniques apart from an equal emphasis on biblical wisdom, Christlikeness, and loving engagement. These trainees have big hands, if you will, but underdeveloped heads and hearts.

Still other ministries focus on the character of the counselors and their spiritual formation, which is vital. But there's a mindset that somehow by osmosis the godly person will help others to become godlier. Churches and schools end up with trainees who are all heart but lacking in biblical insight and counseling abilities.

Additionally, some training in biblical counseling tends to be a tad tone-deaf to the community or relational aspect. Perhaps because of biblical counseling's appropriate emphasis on content and the Word, an inappropriate de-emphasis results. Training becomes didactic and academic. Even the "lab" or skills component is more oriented to technique development or case-study discussions than relational depth and personal connection among group members. What's lacking is a nurturing environment that encourages group members to grow together through connecting with each other and communing with Christ. Since we counsel like we are trained, trainees end up more robotic than relational.

There are various explanations for one-dimensional equipping: the personality of the trainer, the equipping the trainer experienced, the educational philosophy of the trainer, and time limitations. Everything seeks to pull us away from comprehensive equipping.

This is why it's vital that we saturate our biblical counseling ministry with four-dimensional goals and objectives. The 4Cs should be like a neon light in our MVP-C Statement, our enlisting process, our scriptural foundation, our philosophy of education, our core learning objectives, our training itself, our evaluation of our trainees and our training—in everything. We must commit to remain on the cutting edge of biblical counseling equipping by following Christ's disciple-making model of intentionally and comprehensively training the whole person: the head (knowing/content), the heart (being/character), and the hands (doing/competence) in the context of God's home (loving/ community).

Our first task in equipping biblical counselors is to laser-focus on the four-dimensional biblical portrait. This chapter is your snapshot of the comprehensive résumé qualifications you seek to nurture in the biblical counselors you equip.

THE DIVINE COUNSELOR'S RÉSUMÉ QUALIFICATIONS: GOD'S FOUR-DIMENSIONAL MAP

Imagine that you're forwarding your résumé to the Holy Spirit—the Divine Counselor. What items would you highlight to demonstrate your eligibility to enter the ranks of biblical counselors? What do the Scriptures say? What qualifies a person for biblical counseling? What qualities make your trainees eligible to claim the mantle of soul physician and spiritual friend?

Fortunately, for those of us who train biblical counselors, Paul already completed the résumé.

> I myself am convinced, my brothers and sisters, that you yourselves
> are full of goodness, complete in knowledge, and competent to
> instruct one another (Romans 15:14).

In this verse, the surrounding context, and other biblical passages, we discover the four résumé qualifications of a nurtured biblical counselor. They supply our biblical counseling equipping *goals and objectives* (Figure 7:1).

FIGURE 7:1

*The Four Dimensions of Comprehensive
Biblical Counseling Equipping*

- Character
  "Full of Goodness"   Heart/Being

- Content/Conviction
  "Complete in Knowledge"   Head/Knowing

- Competence
  "Competent to Instruct One Another"   Hands/Doing

- Community
  "Brothers/Sisters/One Another"   Home/Loving[1]

Before we develop these characteristics, we need to consider a common reaction. The moment we start talking about training lay people as biblical counselors, we can expect pushback. People will raise numerous objections, sometimes vehemently, against our conviction that God's people can be competent counselors. We can respond to their pushback with God's Word, which settles the issue, and with research that validates the effectiveness of paraprofessional people helpers.

Confidence Based on God's Word: The Sufficiency of Christianity

Ponder who Paul is addressing in Romans 15:14 with his phrase "brothers and sisters." Are these apostles, pastors, elders, deacons, deaconesses, or former Jewish priests? Have they graduated from the exclusive training institutions of Paul's day? Are they the elite philosophers and scholars of Roman society?

No. They are average, ordinary Christians in Rome. "Brothers and sisters" was the common designation of a believer regardless of status, position, or rank. Based upon the surrounding context (Romans 16:1–16), Paul's addressees are members of small house churches spread throughout the city and dotting the countryside of Rome. These men and women, converted Jews and Greeks, slaves and free, Paul considers competent to counsel.

---

1. See Appendix 7.1 (available free online at https://rpmministries.org/ebc-resources/) for a fuller outline of biblical counseling 4C equipping goals.

Paul knew that his readers would be skeptical about their ability to counsel one another. I imagine them thinking, *Now Paul, perhaps you, a super apostle, are competent to counsel. Perhaps the other apostles also. But not us!* This is why Paul is emphatic in his language. The NIV accurately translates his emphasis, "I myself...you yourselves." Paul's addition of the personal pronoun produces emphasis by redundancy. Paul wants no mistakes. He is positive that they are powerful. "I, I myself. Inspired by the Divine Counselor, I am telling you that I am absolutely confident in you, you yourselves. Yes, you yourselves are competent to counsel one another."

Paul is not assuming here. He says that he is "convinced." He is confident in them, trusts them, and knows that he can count on them to counsel one another competently. He has faith in their spiritual ability, being inwardly certain because of external evidence. The evidence he offers provides the biblical prescription, the biblical résumé, for biblical counselors.

And the Survey Says: The Effectiveness of Paraprofessionals

While I was working on my doctorate, an article published in a major counseling journal sent shock waves through the counseling community. Its results called into question the efficacy of professional counseling training, while also distilling basic elements that qualify an individual to be an effective people helper.

The article traced the history of modern research into counselor effectiveness beginning with Durlak's work examining the results of forty-two studies that compared the effectiveness of professional helpers to paraprofessionals (laypeople helpers). The data from the study indicated that lay helpers equaled or surpassed the effectiveness of the professional therapists.[2]

Hattie, Sharpley, and Rogers attempted to refute those findings by combining the results of forty-six studies. Their data, however, supported Durlak's conclusions. Clients of lay helpers consistently achieved more positive outcomes than did clients of the professionally educated and experienced counselors.[3]

Berman and Norton reanalyzed Hattie's study. Their reanalysis indicated that lay counselors were equally effective as professional counselors in promoting

---

2. J. Durlak, "Comparative Effectiveness of Paraprofessional and Professional Helpers," *Psychological Bulletin* 86, no. 1 (1979): 80–92.

3. J. A. Hattie, H. J. Rogers, and C. F. Sharpley, "Comparative Effectiveness of Professional and Paraprofessional Helpers," *Psychological Bulletin* 95, no. 3 (1984): 534–541.

positive change. They concluded that no research currently supported the notion that professional training, knowledge, or experience improved therapist effectiveness.[4]

Herman, in his review of these studies, indicated that research suggested that professional training was not the primary means for developing competence in helping people. Rather, the personal characteristics of the helper were the greatest factors leading to competence as a counselor. In other words, the studies demonstrated that maturity, love, genuine concern, empathy, humility, and vulnerability were more important than professional training.[5]

After the appearance of these studies, Tan noted that little research had been done to assess the effectiveness of church-based Christian lay counseling programs. He rectified that through a controlled study of a church-based lay counseling program. His findings indicated that the treatment group reported significantly more improvement on all measures than the control group, and they maintained their gains at significant levels. He concluded that the study supports the effectiveness of Christian lay counseling in a local church context.[6]

Such descriptive research offers valuable support when people raise objections to the effectiveness of equipping biblical counselors for the local church. Of course, two thousand years earlier, Paul offered all the biblical validation we need when he affirmed that God's people in Rome were competent to counsel. We return now to our examination of the biblical qualifications that God's Word deems necessary to be considered a competent biblical counselor.

REFLECTING CHRISTLIKE CHARACTER:
LOVING LIKE JESUS—"FULL OF GOODNESS"

Competent biblical counselors have résumés with "full of goodness" as their first qualification. "Goodness" is the same word Paul uses in Galatians 5:22–23 as one of the nine aspects of the fruit of the Spirit. When I first read Romans 15:14, I wondered why Paul would pick the fruit of goodness. Why not love, joy, peace, or any other fruit of the Spirit?

---

4. J. S. Berman, and N. C. Norton, "Does Professional Training Make a Therapist More Effective?" *Psychology Bulletin* 98, no. 2 (1985): 401–407.

5. Keith Herman, "Reassessing Predictors of Therapist Competence," *Journal of Counseling and Development* 72 (September/October 1993): 29–32.

6. Siang-Yang Tan and Yiu-Meng Toh, "The Effectiveness of Church-Based Lay Counselors: A Controlled Outcome Study," *Journal of Psychology and Christianity* 16, no. 3 (1997): 260–267.

So I explored "goodness." The Old Testament highlights the basic confession that God *is* good because his love endures forever (1 Chronicles 16:34). It also emphasizes that our good God *does* good (Exodus 18:9). That is, he displays his goodness in active social relationships. Further, I noted Christ's statement that only God is good (Matthew 19:17). Then I noticed the linkage of goodness and godliness with godlikeness—with *Christlikeness* (Matthew 5:43–48; Ephesians 2:10; Colossians 1:10). In each of these passages, goodness displays itself in active, grace-oriented relationships, as when our good Father causes his sun to shine upon and his rain to fall on the righteous and the unrighteous.

Goodness is a virtue that reveals itself in social relationships; in our various contacts and connections with others. Biblical goodness always displays itself in relational contexts through undeserved kindness.

Equipping Christlike Counselors

Thus, in Romans 15:14, Paul is talking about *Christlike character* that relates with grace. The powerful spiritual friend reflects the ultimate Spiritual Friend, Jesus. We are powerful to the degree that we reflect the loving character of Christ. Paul is teaching us that the competent biblical counselor is the person who relates well, who connects deeply, who is compassionate, and who has the ability to develop intimate grace relationships.

In discussing goodness, Paul uses the modifier "full," which pictures a net that breaks due to the stress and tension of too much weight and a cup that is so chock-full that its contents spill over. Paul pictures mature love and godly character flowing through Christ to us, then spilling over from us into our spiritual friend's life.

To the degree that our trainees increasingly reflect Christ and relate increasingly like Christ, to that degree they will be fruitful biblical counselors. The one who is good at relating is the person whose words and actions have deep impact.

Paul's first résumé qualification teaches that knowledge and skill without character is like *one corpse practicing cosmetic surgery on another corpse.* We witnessed this truth in a counseling lab when Amber shared her deep sorrow over the loss of her mother. As a male group member, Mike, attempted to connect, it became painfully obvious that Mike was badly misconnecting because he was trying to "practice skills" instead of relating deeply out of a good heart.

So we asked, "Mike, who would you be without your skills?" Mike was dumbfounded—sincerely wanting to help but recognizing how truly unable he was to enter into Amber's world. With Amber and Mike's permission, we shifted our focus to Mike. One group member told his story of slowly learning to relate soul to soul. Another member simply hugged Mike, holding him while the dam of tears burst. A third individual painted a picture of Mike robbed of his toolbox and forced to break into his home to save his wife and children. He asked him, "Mike, what would you do if you did not have your toolbox of techniques?" One year later, Mike shared with us that our interactions with him not only changed how he offers biblical counseling but transformed how he relates to his wife and children.

Equipping Counselors Whose Inner Life Increasingly Reflects the Inner Life of Christ

Who is qualified for the task of biblical counseling? The person who increasingly reflects Christ. Through the New Covenant, God has implanted a new heart in the believer. However, as Peter reminds us in 2 Peter 1:3–8, we must cultivate growth in Christ and the development of the Christian virtues.

We need to structure our equipping in biblical counseling to encourage our trainees to discipline themselves so that in humble cooperation with the Holy Spirit the implanted Christlikeness grows. Our biblical counseling training environment should be the greenhouse where these character traits blossom as our trainees cultivate and reflect the inner life of Christ.

CHANGING LIVES WITH BIBLICAL CONTENT/CONVICTION: THINKING LIKE JESUS—"COMPLETE IN KNOWLEDGE"

Is Paul implying that the best biblical counselor is the touchy-feely person who is never dedicated to serious study of the Scripture? Not at all. Remember that God calls us to love him with our minds—with our brains (Matthew 22:37). This is why Paul lists "complete in knowledge" as the second qualification on the biblical counselor's résumé.

"Complete" does not suggest that our trainees become walking biblical encyclopedias with absolute knowledge of all theological truth. Only God has encyclopedic knowledge of all things actual and possible. Instead, by "complete" Paul means that we and our trainees become so filled with God's Word that it claims our entire being and stamps our whole life, conduct, attitude, and relationships. We are captured by God's truth.

Equipping Counselors Who Relate Truth to Life

What sort of knowledge does Paul emphasize? He could have chosen any of several words that highlight content or factual knowledge alone. However, Paul chooses a word for knowledge that highlights the combination of information and implication. Paul's word focuses upon insight and wisdom—the wisdom to relate truth to life.

Competent biblical counselors understand how to apply God's Word first to their own life. They also have the insight to see how God's Word relates to their friend's life. Additionally, they have the biblical vision to see how God is relating to their friend. They have discernment to see life from God's perspective.

In Philippians 1:9–11, Paul develops his philosophy of ministry, his conviction about what equips us for biblical counseling:

> This is my prayer: that your love may abound more and more in knowledge and depth of insight, so that you may be able to discern what is best and may be pure and blameless for the day of Christ, filled with the fruit of righteousness that comes through Jesus Christ—to the glory and praise of God.

Notice Paul's coupling of truth and love. For him, biblical counseling is never either/or—either we are loving, touchy-feely, heart people, or we are scholarly, academic, head people. Rather, ministry is both/and—we unite head and heart, love and truth in our personal ministry of the Word. When our love abounds more and more in knowledge, the result is insight—the ability to help our spiritual friends to discern not simply what is good, but what is best in their life situation.

Equipping Counselors Who Unite Scripture and Soul

We find this harmony of truth and love everywhere in Scripture. We already examined it in the core passage on local church equipping: leaders equip God's people to speak the truth in love (Ephesians 4:15). We see it again in 1 Thessalonians 2:8: "Because we loved you so much, we were delighted to share with you not only the gospel of God but our lives as well." Biblical ministry always unites Scripture and soul.

At the end of our training, we should be able to say what Paul said to Timothy at the end of his life. "You, however, know all about my teaching, my way of life" (2 Timothy 3:10a). That way, we will not be hypocritical when we encourage our trainees the way Paul encouraged Timothy. "Watch your life and doctrine closely" (1 Timothy 4:16a). Everywhere we see teaching and life, truth and love, Scripture and soul, doctrine and relationship.

We need to structure our equipping in biblical counseling so that our trainees gain deep insight into people, problems, and solutions—from a biblical perspective. And our training needs to equip prospective biblical counselors with the wisdom to relate those biblical truths to people's daily lives and relationships—changing lives with Christ's changeless truth.

CARING WITH COUNSELING COMPETENCE: SERVING LIKE JESUS—"COMPETENT TO INSTRUCT ONE ANOTHER"

Typical Christians in Rome with character and conviction are qualified to do what? Paul says they are competent to "instruct." The word "competent" means to have the power to accomplish a mission. It reminds me of Engineer Scotty on *Star Trek* yelling to Captain Kirk, "Capt'in Kirrrk. We ainta' got da poworr! Our dilithium crystal, she's breakin' up!" Competence is the dilithium crystal, the warp drive, the fuel, the power necessary to fulfill God's call on our lives.

Competence also means to have the ability, capability, resources, and strength to function and relate well. Paul is confident that believers are capable and competent in Christ.

Equipping Counselors Who Are Competent to Disciple One Another

Powerfully competent to do what? Powerful to "instruct" (Greek, *nouthetein*). Jay Adams, founder of the National Association of Nouthetic Counselors (NANC) (now the Association of Certified Biblical Counselors), described nouthetic counseling as confronting for change out of concern (see Adams, *Competent to Counseling*, *The Christian Counselor's Manual*, and *More than Redemption*). "Instruct" contains this nuance, especially when the proposed change emphasizes inner heart change leading to relational change.

The foundational meaning of *noutheteo* comes from the root *noeo*, meaning to direct one's mind, to perceive, and from *nous*—the mind, heart, seat of spiritual, rational, and moral insight and action. The mind is the place of practical reason leading to moral action. The stress is not merely on the intellect, but also on the will and disposition. *Noutheteo* means to impart understanding, to set right, to lay on the heart. Nouthetic impartation of truth can take the form of admonition, teaching, reminding, advising, urging, encouraging, and spurring on.

Paul uses *noutheteo* in Colossians 1:20–29 to describe one aspect of his pastoral ministry. God commissioned him to present Christ's gospel of grace to people (verses 20–25), infusing people with the hope of who they are in Christ (verses 26–27) with the goal of presenting them mature in Christ (verse 28) through personal, passionate, persistent involvement in their lives (verses 28–29) by Christ's resurrection power (verse 29). Believers who possess Christlike goodness (character) plus Christlike insight (conviction) are competent to disciple one another toward communion with Christ and conformity to Christ through the personal ministry of the Word—biblical counseling.

Equipping Counselors Who Are Competent to Comfort One Another

Paul never intended Romans 15:14 to be the final or only word on the nature of biblical counseling. Nor did he use *noutheteo* as the only or even the primary concept to describe the personal ministry of the Word. For instance, in 1 Thessalonians 5:14, Paul uses five distinct words for biblical counseling. "We urge [Greek, *parakaleo*] you, brothers and sisters, warn [*noutheteo*] those who are idle and disruptive, encourage [*paramutheomai*] the disheartened, help [*antechomai*] the weak, be patient with [*makrothumeo*] everyone."

Among the many New Testament words for spiritual care, *parakaleo* predominates. Whereas *noutheteo* occurs eleven times in the New Testament, *parakaleo* (comfort, encourage, console) appears 110 times. In 2 Corinthians 1:3–11, Paul informs us that we are competent to comfort (*parakaleo*) one another. Those who have humbly received God's comfort, God equips to offer comfort to others.

The word *parakaleo* emphasizes personal presence (one called alongside to help) and suffering with another person. It seeks to turn desolation into consolation through hope in God. The duty of comfort in Old and New Testament thinking fell not upon professional helpers, but upon close relatives, neighbors, friends, and colleagues. Comforters come alongside to help struggling, suffering people through personal presence coupled with scriptural insight.

When Christ ascended, he sent the Holy Spirit to be our *Parakletos*—our

Comforter and Advocate called alongside to encourage and help in times of suffering, trouble, grief, injustice, and hardship. The Spirit performs his ministry by being in us and by revealing truth to us (John 14:16–17). As the Spirit of Truth, his ministry is the exact opposite of Satan's, who is the father of lies (John 8.44). Satan's name is "the accuser" (Revelation 12:10) and his core strategy is to speak lying words of condemnation to us. The Spirit's name is "Encourager" and "Advocate," and his strategy is to speak the truth in love about our justification and acceptance in Christ.

Think about what Paul is saying to *you and your trainees*. You don't have to have a PhD in counseling to be a competent counselor. You have the *Resource* planted within you—the *Parakletos*, the Holy Spirit. You also have the *resources* planted within you—the ability to be a competent *parathetic* (combining *parakaleo* and *noutheteo*) biblical counselor who provides the following:

- Soul Care through *parakaleo*: Coming alongside hurting people in their suffering and grief, weeping with them while offering hope through your personal presence coupled with scriptural insight. Offering them tastes of Jesus' empathetic care in the *sustaining* process so they know that it's normal to hurt. Sharing with them biblical encouragement in the *healing* process so they know that it's possible to hope.

- Spiritual Direction through *noutheteo*: Entering the lives of people struggling to grow in their personal walk with Christ. Offering passionate, persistent, personal involvement in their lives as you assist them to see who they are in Christ and help them to live out their new life in Christ in communion with and conformity to Christ. Ministering to them in the *reconciling* process so they know that it's horrible to sin, but wonderful to be forgiven. Sharing Scripture and soul with them in the *guiding* process so they know that it's supernatural to mature.

We need to structure our equipping in biblical counseling so that our trainees develop the biblical counseling competencies of sustaining and healing (*parakaletic* counseling for suffering and progressive sanctification), and of reconciling and guiding (*nouthetic* counseling for sin and progressive sanctification). Our end goal is to equip our trainees to learn how to care like Christ.

GROWING IN CHRISTIAN COMMUNITY: CONNECTING IN JESUS—"BROTHERS AND SISTERS/ONE ANOTHER"

Every word Paul wrote about competent biblical counselors he penned in the plural—brothers and sisters, one another, you yourselves. The effective biblical counselor is no Lone Ranger Christian. Competent biblical counselors live and grow together in community as they commune with Christ and connect with the body of Christ.

Paul sandwiches his words in Romans 15:14 around a one-another community context. In Romans 12:3–8, he writes of each member belonging to all the others, and of using gifts in the context of the body of Christ.

In Romans 12:9–21, the context reflects one-another ministry. Be devoted to one another in love. Honor one another. Share with one another. Practice hospitality with one another. Rejoice with one another. Weep with one another. Live in harmony with one another.

In Romans 13, the context is loving one another: "Whatever other command there may be, are summed up in this one command: 'Love your neighbor as yourself.' Love does no harm to its neighbor. Therefore love is the fulfillment of the law" (verses 9–10).

Paul continues his one-another theme in Romans 14:1—15:13. Don't judge one another; instead, mutually edify each other. Bear with one another. Please one another. Build up one another. Be united with one another. Encourage one another. Accept one another. Worship with one another.

In Romans 16, Paul writes about meeting together with one another in house churches where believers connect intimately. Connecting in community is the context, before and after Romans 15:14. Effective training in biblical counseling is learned in community. Put another way, growth in character, content, and competence occurs in the context of community.

As I illustrated at the beginning of this chapter, small-group labs are a core aspect of my biblical counseling training. As part of the labs, I pair trainees as encouragement partners. These relationships blossom into some of the most meaningful aspects of our biblical counseling training. For example, the pairing of Debbie, a mid-30s Caucasian woman, and Linda, an early-50s African American woman, developed into a deep, lasting friendship. Not having known each other before September, they became so close that by December of that year, Linda asked Debbie to be her matron of honor at her May wedding. Not surprisingly, both Debbie and Linda are effective biblical counselors. They know how to connect.

One-to-one connection is vital, but so is small-group community, which is another component of the biblical counseling labs I lead. We learn to apply biblical truth, develop counseling competencies, and cultivate Christlike character as we connect in a caring community. In the context of a nurturing small-group environment, we participate in the horizontal one-another spiritual disciplines.

According to Paul, transformed lives occur as we connect together in the body of Christ (Romans 12:3—16:27) *and* as we connect with Christ (12:1–2). Conformity to Christ is the result of communion with Christ (2 Corinthians 3:16–18; 4:16–18). Effective biblical counselors add another important qualification to their résumé: connection in community. We need to structure our equipping in biblical counseling so that our trainees relate, connect, and grow together in Christ.

DISCIPLE-MAKING CHAMPION

Dr. John Henderson, Counseling Pastor

At the time of the survey, Pastor John Henderson oversaw the Equipped to Counsel ministry at Denton Bible Church in Denton, Texas. Pastor Henderson's equipping process models well the 4Cs. Pastor Henderson described the goal of his biblical counseling equipping this way:

> "Our prayer for people who complete the equipped process is for them to experience a paradigm shift in their view of God, the Scriptures, people, and counseling. We want people to be Christ-centered in their understanding of everything. We want them to see counseling as a privilege and opportunity where they live, learning to apply the gospel in every detail of life, and making 'speaking the truth in love' a priority of their lives."

When asked what *content* objectives he wanted his trainees to address, Pastor Henderson replied,

> "We want to see growth in theology/truth/biblical knowledge and practical implications of these content areas; understanding the gospel and how it speaks to daily life and struggles; understanding people and how to love, listen, and encourage them; common

errors or false teachings that assault sound biblical counseling and how to answer these from Scripture."

When asked what *character* objectives he wanted his trainees to master, Pastor Henderson shared,

"I want to see our people grow in their awe, wonder, and worship toward God. I pray our hearts would be stirred and moved by the gospel. I'd want to see our people deal honestly with the condition of their hearts and learn to minister the gospel to their own souls. I pray the Spirit would grow our love for him and one another."

Pastor Henderson summarized the *competence* objectives he seeks his trainees to gain:

"Strong listening competencies, an ability to help people tell their stories and open up; being able to address personal struggles, sinfulness, and need for change in gracious ways; learning to see where the gospel fits in someone's life; and how to make the gospel speak to others."

Related to building *community*, Pastor Henderson explained,

"We're constantly encouraging one another to apply what we're learning to our own hearts and lives and asking each other to face Christ in everything, and to listen together to him through his Word. We leave room for good group discussion; I maintain a transparent attitude as their pastor; we share testimonies and have people open up during our meetings."

A WORD TO YOUR TRAINEES: CONFIDENT COMPETENCY IN CHRIST

When someone questions the legitimacy of equipping the body of Christ for biblical counseling, direct them back to Paul and Romans 15:14. When the people you are training share their trepidation, like our group did that first night, empathize with those feelings. But don't stop there. Provide them with the same biblical affirmation that Paul offers the believers in Rome.

Say to your biblical counselors, "I'm confident that your maturing Christ-like character, increasing biblical content/conviction, and deepening Christian community connection will make you competent to counsel. Most importantly, God is confident because your competence comes from Christ. Don't take a back seat to anyone!"

And then continue, "By the way, this means that we all have work to do. God is calling us individually and jointly to *grow* in wisdom, integrity, and love. There's work to do, but we are God's workmanship created in Christ Jesus to do good works that God has prepared in advance (Ephesians 2:10). There's work to do, but it is God who works in us to will and to act according to his good purposes (Philippians 2:13). Let's start growing!"

A WORD TO YOU AS THE EQUIPPER: GROWING IN CHRIST/CLINGING TO CHRIST

Here's my hunch. At times, you're breathing a sigh of relief. A plan is coming into focus. The 4C map gives you simple yet concrete handles as you begin to shape the goals and objectives of your training.

At other times, you're feeling very much like a ten-year-old kid in his dad's oversized suit. You're beginning to realize that you won't be able to hide behind the pulpit or the lectern. You're going to have to step out, step up, and step forward—warts and all, so to speak.

I would say to you what you said to your trainees: "Don't take a back seat to anyone!" I would also say, as you said to your trainees, "There's work to do."

Imitate Christ

If we're honest, part of our trepidation arises because of a realization. If we're to equip others in the 4Cs, then we have to be growing in the 4Cs. We are to say to people what Paul said to the Corinthians: "Follow my example, as I follow the example of Christ" (1 Corinthians 11:1).

I don't have any secret steps or how-to shortcuts on that one. I will share this exhortation, however. Find a Paul and a Barnabas, or a Priscilla and a Ruth. In the classic threefold mentoring model, you already have a Timothy—a batch of them—your biblical counseling trainees.

As you build into them, who is building into you? Pray for a Paul or a Priscilla—an older, more mature saint who can disciple you. Pray for a Barnabas or a Ruth—a peer, a spiritual friend with whom you can share mutual encouragement. In conjunction with your personal walk with Christ and your relationships within the body of Christ, God will use your Paul/Priscilla and your Barnabas/Ruth relationships to mature you as a 4C biblical counselor/equipper.

Imitate Paul

I'm guessing that you realize something else. You're recognizing that you can't do this equipping stuff dispassionately, academically. As we already saw with Paul in 1 Thessalonians 2:8, equipping others requires that we give from the depths of our souls. It also requires a depth of relationship like the one we saw in the last chapter, where Paul and the Ephesian elders had to tear themselves away from each other (Acts 20:36—21:1).

There's more. Listen to Paul's description of the equipping process in Galatians 4:19: "My dear children, for whom I am again in the pains of childbirth until Christ is formed in you…" You might not have purchased this book if the title were *Equipping Counselors for Your Church: The Pains of Repetitive Childbirth*. Paul describes that labor in more detail in Colossians 1:28—2:1a:

> He is the one we proclaim, admonishing and teaching everyone with all wisdom, so that we may present everyone fully mature in Christ. To this end I strenuously contend with all the energy Christ so powerfully works in me. I want you to know how hard I am contending for you.

No, I'm not trying to scare you. Well, perhaps I am. Equipping others should scare us into dependency—Christ-dependency. Like Paul, we need to cling to Christ and his unlimited power, not depend upon our own limited strength.

Again, I have no easy formula to offer you. I will share this word of counsel, however. Practice the spiritual disciplines (1 Timothy 4:7; 1 Corinthians 9:24–27). Engage in Bible study, prayer, biblical meditation, fasting, silence, solitude, fellowship, worship, and the other historic, biblical means of growth in grace. Abide in Christ so that you connect to Christ's resurrection power (Philippians 3:10).

Like your trainees, you can do it—in Christ. Be confident in your competency in Christ.

COMMENCEMENT:
THE SOUL PHYSICIAN'S MANUAL

I think back to those early days of PEP and LEAD equipping with fond memories. Life was good because God is good—all the time. But that doesn't mean life was easy, and it doesn't mean the equipping was a breeze. At times, the training process felt like ongoing labor pains for me, just as it did for the apostle Paul.

If I was in ministry labor pains, at least there was a soul physician available—the Soul Physician. It was the Divine Counselor's 4C map that gave me hope and confidence. Sure, the birth process was messy, but at least I had access to the Soul Physician's manual, which provided me with the goals and objectives I should emphasize in my equipping ministry.

It's to that manual that we again turn our attention, in even more detail, in chapters 8 and 9. Now that we know that our biblical counseling training needs to address the 4Cs, we need to learn *what* content, character, competence, and community subject matter our trainees need to master. In the next two chapters we'll put some meat on the 4C skeleton by examining biblical counseling training curriculum and materials.

GROWING TOGETHER: QUESTIONS FOR REFLECTION, DISCUSSION, AND APPLICATION

1. As you think about equipping biblical counselors, what fears or doubts do you have? How are you handling these feelings and thoughts?

2. Of biblical content/conviction, Christlike character, counseling competence, and Christian community:

   a. Which one do you think you are most inclined to emphasize? To de-emphasize?

   b. When you were trained, which of the 4Cs was most emphasized? Least emphasized?

   c. Which of the 4Cs do you think you are best prepared to equip others to learn?

   d. Which of the 4Cs do you think you are least prepared to equip others to learn? How will you strengthen yourself this area?

3. How would equipping in biblical counseling be impacted if one of the following is overemphasized? De-emphasized? Omitted?

   a. Biblical Content/Conviction?

   b. Christlike Character?

   c. Counseling Competence?

   d. Christian Community?

4. How confident are you that...

   a. God's people can be equipped to be competent biblical counselors? On what do you base your confidence? What could increase your confidence?

   b. God has equipped *you* to be a competent equipper of biblical counselors? What can you do to further develop your confidence in your competency in Christ?

What Makes Biblical Counseling Biblical?: Part One

Theology and Methodology in Biblical Counseling

Two books are standard in any physician's office: *The Physician's Desk Reference* (*PDR*) and *The Merck Manual of Diagnosis and Therapy* (*Merck*). Both are considered bibles of medical knowledge and practice. With its three-thousand-plus pages of prescription drugs, the annually updated *PDR* is the most comprehensive, widely used drug reference available. It details the usage, warnings, and precautions for more than four thousand prescription drugs. *Merck* is the most widely used medical text in the world. It provides the latest information on the vast expanse of human diseases, disorders, and injuries, as well as their symptoms and treatments.

As the *PDR* and *Merck* are the manuals for physicians treating the body, so the Bible is God's authoritative, sufficient, relevant Word for physicians treating the soul. It is the *Soul Physician's Desk Reference* (*SPDR*) manual for dispensing grace. God's Word provides not only the latest but the eternal, enduring information on the soul's design and disease, as well as its care and cure. For equipping in biblical counseling, the Bible not only guides the curriculum, it *is* the curriculum. As we read the *SPDR*, we learn what makes biblical counseling truly biblical.

Chapter 7 introduced you to the broad portrait of what a nurtured 4C biblical counseling graduate looks like. Chapters 8 and 9 transition from big-picture *goals and objectives* to focused biblical counseling training *curriculum and materials*. These two chapters ask,

- To speak the truth in love, what do biblical counselors need to know, do, and be in the context of community (love)?

Chapters 8 and 9 provide a best-practice map for answering this question biblically. If you want your trainees to claim the label biblical counselor, then here are the 4C areas from Romans 15:14 you need to cover to equip trainees to become competent to counsel.

- Content areas you equip counselors to address: Know—chapter 8
- Competencies you equip counselors to develop: Do—chapter 8
- Character traits you equip counselors to cultivate: Be—chapter 9
- Christian community you equip counselors to participate in: Love—chapter 9

Figure 8:1 provides the outline I develop in these chapters. I am *not* suggesting exactly what to communicate in each topic area. That would be giving you a fish instead of teaching you to fish. Based on your gift-mix, specific church, and unique community, you can use these categories as your guide as *you* design the particular materials, contents, and lesson plans that are the right fit for *your* trainees.

FIGURE 8:1

*Core Proficiencies of the Competent
Biblical Counselor: Romans 15:14*

**Area #1: Content/Conviction: "Complete in Knowledge"—
Head/Knowing (How Christ Changes Lives)**

Eight Ultimate Life Questions Every Biblical Counselor Must Address

- God's Word: Where do I find wisdom for life in our broken world?

- The Trinity: What comes into my mind when I think about God?

- Creation: Who am I? Whose am I?

- Fall: What went wrong? What's the root source of my problem?

- Redemption: How does Christ change people?

- Church: Where can I find a place to belong and become?

- Consummation: How does my future destiny impact my present reality?

- Sanctification: How do I increasingly become more like Jesus?

Area #2: Competence: "Competent to Instruct One Another"—Hands/Doing (How to Care Like Christ)

Four Core Relational Competencies Every Biblical Counselor Must Develop

- *Sustaining* Biblical Counseling Competencies: Empathize/Embrace—GRACE Relational Competencies

- *Healing* Biblical Counseling Competencies: Encourage/Enlighten—RESTS Relational Competencies

- *Reconciling* Biblical Counseling Competencies: Expose/Exhort—PEACE(E) Relational Competencies

- *Guiding* Biblical Counseling Competencies: Empower/Equip—FAITH(H) Relational Competencies

Area #3: Character: "Full of Goodness"—Heart/Being (How to Reflect Christ)

Four Marks of Christlike Character Every Biblical Counselor Must Cultivate

- Relating like Christ: Loving God and others passionately

- Thinking like Christ: Renewing my mind to view life from God's eternal perspective

- Choosing like Christ: Dying to self and living sacrificially for others

- Feeling like Christ: Facing life honestly and managing my moods biblically

Area #4: Community: "Brothers/Sisters/One Another"— Home/Loving (How to Grow Together in Christ)

Two Kinds of Christian Community Every Biblical Counselor Must Participate In

- Communion with the body of Christ: Horizontal Spiritual Disciplines

- Communion with Christ: Vertical Spiritual Disciplines

BIBLICAL CONTENT: HOW CHRIST CHANGES LIVES EIGHT ULTIMATE LIFE QUESTIONS EVERY BIBLICAL COUNSELOR MUST ADDRESS

Picture it. You've led your church through the envisioning process. You've overseen the enlisting process. You have a committed biblical counseling team of a dozen people eager for your training.

Now imagine that your first equipping meeting is just three months away. You're excited, yet your mind is racing. *What do I teach them? How do I decide where to focus our content training? Where do we even begin? What material do we need to cover? What's our "curriculum" for training our biblical counselors?*

You're asking the right questions. In this section I outline an answer to the foundational question,

- What biblical content does a biblical counselor need to know?

Theology for Life

Whenever I launch my content training, I start by holding an open Bible at my eye level as I say to my trainees, "I want us to learn together how to look at life's ultimate questions through the lens of Scripture." Still holding my Bible at eye level, I continue.

> Biblical counselors are physicians of the soul. This book—God's Word—is our soul physician's manual. Together, we're going to examine God's Word meticulously, as a med-school student examines the skeletal structure of the human body. Through God's all-sufficient Scriptures, we're going to probe together the Great Physician's authoritative truth about eight ultimate life questions that every soul physician must address.

With one hand continuing to balance my Bible in front of my face, my other hand clicks the PowerPoint advance button, and my trainees and I observe the following outline (Figure 8:2):

FIGURE 8:2

*Eight Ultimate Life Questions Every
Biblical Counselor Must Address*[1]

- God's Word: Where do I find wisdom for life in our broken world?

- The Trinity: What comes into my mind when I think about God?

- Creation: Who am I? Whose am I?

- Fall: What went wrong? What's the root source of my problem?

- Redemption: How does Christ change people?

- Church: Where can I find a place to belong and become?

---

1. For a detailed development of these concepts see Bob Kellemen, *Gospel-Centered Counseling: How Christ Changes Lives* (Grand Rapids: Zondervan, 2014).

- Consummation: How does my future destiny impact my present reality?

- Sanctification: How do I increasingly become more like Jesus?

Then I wrap up my introductory thoughts with these words:

> Everybody talks about the personal ministry of the Word, but what makes biblical counseling truly biblical? How do we equip one another in a way that is truly transformational? In three decades of equipping folks like you, I've found that a crucial way to move from information to transformation is to probe the Bible's wisdom about these eight ultimate life questions. Let's learn together from the Soul Physician's manual—God's Word.

However you decide to start your first class in equipping counselors, and whatever curriculum you decide to use, my recommendation is that you seek to cover, in some form or fashion, life's eight ultimate questions. As you read the following summaries, be asking yourself,

- In my foundational course in biblical counseling theology, what content would I cover?

God's Word: Nourish the Hunger of the Soul— Preventative Medicine (Where Do I Find Wisdom for Life in Our Broken World?)

As you develop your curriculum and content related to the Bible, ask this central question:

- How do my trainees need to *view and use* God's Word in order to speak the truth in love?

The following core categories will help your trainees grow in confidence that God's Word alone has wisdom for life in our broken world.

The Sufficiency of Scripture: Anchored in Scripture

Physicians of the body determine which nutrients the body needs to remain healthy. So it is with doctoring the soul. What does the soul need? "Man shall not live on bread alone, but on every word that comes from the mouth of God" (Matthew 4:4). We must communicate to our trainees that God's Word is absolutely necessary and totally sufficient (2 Timothy 3:16–17) for addressing all matters of the soul.

Our trainees need to feast on God's Word. They need to develop the conviction that the deepest questions in the human soul are God-questions, and that we find our deepest answers in God's Word. The Reformers used the term *sola scriptura* (by Scripture alone) to communicate their confidence in the robust wisdom for living found only in the Bible. Our equipping should help our trainees share Paul's certainty that in Christ are hidden *all* the treasures of wisdom and knowledge (Colossians 2:3–10).

The Nature of Scripture: The Narrative of Relationship

If our trainees are to use the Bible to nourish hungry souls, they must hear the Bible's story the way God tells it. And God tells it in story form, as a *narrative of relationship*. More than 75 percent of the Bible is narrative, and the rest of the Bible involves passionate psalms, wisdom applied to life, and personal letters to real people in real-life situations and real relationships. The Bible is 100 percent relational (Matthew 22:34–40).

We need to trace the Bible's story with our trainees. The Bible begins by telling the story of relationship initiated and rejected (Genesis 1–3). After those first three chapters, the rest of the Bible tells the story of God wooing us back to himself, all the while fighting the evil one who wants to seduce us away from our first love. Ever since Genesis 3, *life has been a battle for our love*—the ageless question of who captures our heart: Christ or Satan.

Our trainees need to understand that their biblical counseling will be sterile and dead if they see the Bible as a textbook. But if they read and use the Bible as the story of the battle to win our hearts, then their biblical counseling will come alive.

The Relevancy of Scripture: Truth and Love Must Kiss

We want to communicate that the Word of God is profound—it deeply addresses the real-life issues of real people in a really messy world. As we minister God's Word to people's suffering and sin, our trainees need to make truth and love kiss. Throughout your training, make Philippians 1:9–10 your prayer: "This is my prayer: that your love may abound more and more in knowledge and depth of insight, so that you may be able to discern what is best."

Create in your trainees the longing to share Christ's changeless truth to change people's lives. Help them think through what that means. Does dispensing God's Word mean that they tell their counselees, "Take two Scriptures and call me in the morning"? Does it mean that life is so simple that it consists of a one-problem-one-verse-one-solution formula? We need to train biblical counselors to use the Bible in *relationally relevant* ways.

The Trinity: Know the Creator of the Soul—the Great Physician (What Comes into My Mind When I Think About God?)

As you develop your curriculum and content in this area, ask,

- How can I help my trainees to know the Soul Physician personally in order to be a soul physician?

This question, like the others, is not simply about teaching content but about cultivating conviction through applying truth to life.

The Trinity as Our Model for Ministry: Before God Created, He Related

The Bible is our relational manual written by the most relational being in the universe. By answering the question, Who is God? we also answer the question, What is love? Through exploring the eternal community within the Trinity, our trainees begin to see that they must relate soul to soul because God is Trinitarian (John 1; John 17).

The Character of God: Holy Love

A person's image of God is central to their growth in grace. Our trainees need to ponder how the character, attributes, and works of God the Father, Son, and Spirit impact their lives and the lives of their counselees.

The Person and Work of Satan: Spiritual Warfare

For a story to be great, there must be a plot filled with conflict and a fiendish enemy. By beginning before the beginning, our trainees not only understand the

Bible's Protagonist—Christ; they learn about his antagonist—Satan. Through probing the fall of Satan, we expose the hidden spiritual warfare at work behind every temptation to sin. We learn not only the onset of the evil disease that infects image bearers, but also how Satan attempts to spread the virus of sin.

Creation: Examine the Spiritual Anatomy of the Soul— People (Who Am I? Whose Am I?)

I still remember the day I was introduced to the Creation/Fall/Redemption outline of Scripture. It was the first day of my first Bible college class. More than one hundred intimidated freshmen awaited the arrival of Dr. Lawler. The bespectacled, diminutive Old Testament scholar's reputation preceded him. When he entered, all chatter ceased. Staring us down, he said, "Repeat after me: Creation. Fall. Redemption."

"Creation. Fall. Redemption," we mimicked in unison.

"Never forget those words," he instructed us. "They summarize the entire story of the Bible."

These three categories also form the core of biblical counseling: *people, problems, and solutions.* Everyone involved in the personal ministry of the Word must ponder:

- Creation: How to understand *people* biblically—
  The nature of human nature

- Fall: How to diagnose *problems* theologically—
  The root causes of sin and suffering

- Redemption: How to prescribe *solutions* scripturally—
  The pathway to growth in grace

Equipping in biblical counseling helps trainees acquire a biblical understanding of who we are—learning from the Creator who the creature is. It helps trainees develop a biblical diagnosis of what went wrong—why people do the things they do. It also helps trainees offer a biblical prescription of the source of true, lasting heart and life transformation—care and cure in Christ.

We start with Creation. As you develop your curriculum and content in this area, ask,

- How do my trainees need to view people in order to know, love, and minister to them God's way?

Pursue God's Target: The Image of God

Sometimes in biblical counseling we start with the fall into sin and what went wrong. Instead, we would be wise first to explore with our trainees the creation narrative. It teaches how we were meant to live life with God and each other. It teaches God's original design for the soul—the nature of human nature as bearers of God's image. It enables us to answer the questions, What is health? And, What does a healthy image bearer look like?

Knowing who God designed us to be provides us with our target, our purpose in life. The goal of biblical counseling is *our inner life increasingly reflecting the inner life of Christ*. Our goal is not simply symptom relief, but Christlikeness. Equip your trainees to be *soul-u-tion-focused*, not solution-focused.

Comprehensive Biblical Counseling: Understanding People

For our trainees to move others toward this target, they must grasp God's comprehensive original design for the human personality. We need to explore with our students the Bible's teaching about who we are as

- Relational Beings: Created to love passionately

  » Spiritual Beings: Created to love God

  » Social Beings: Created to love one another

  » Self-Aware Beings: Created to know who we are in Christ

- Rational Beings: Created to think wisely

- Volitional Beings: Created to choose courageously

- Emotional Beings: Created to experience deeply

- Physical Beings: Created to live fully

Fall: Diagnose the Fallen Condition of the Soul—Problems (What Went Wrong? What's the Root Source of My Problem?)

As you develop your curriculum and content in this area, ask,

- How do my trainees need to view suffering and sin in order to counsel people with compassion and discernment?

Biblical Sufferology: Not the Way It's Supposed to Be

As important as it is to return to creation, we would be naïve to end our journey there. God didn't. The true story of life must include the sad story of our descent into the abyss of sin.

Skip the fall, and we skip relevant answers to real life questions. Our trainees need to understand that though sad and tragic, without this story, they could never make sense of life. The fall is the only reasonable explanation for suffering and sin. By dissecting the fallen planet, trainees are able to diagnose the reasons for suffering and develop a biblical approach to grieving with hope.[2]

Diagnosing Sin Biblically: Why We Do What We Do

By dissecting the fallen *soul*, our trainees are able to diagnose the impact of sin on the human personality and predicament. Their biblical insight begins as you help them to see the depth of heart sin and the comprehensive nature of sin.

- Relational Sin: Idols of the heart/false lovers of the soul

- Rational Sin: Foolish beliefs

- Volitional Sin: Self-centered choices

- Emotional Sin: Ungoverned emotions

Redemption: Prescribe God's Cure for the Soul—Solutions (How Does Christ Change People?)

As you develop your curriculum and content in this area, ask,

- What comprehensive understanding of salvation do my trainees need to grasp in order to counsel people toward progressive sanctification?

Our Complete Salvation: Justification, Regeneration, Reconciliation, Redemption

If the Bible ended with the fall, life would be hopeless and we would despair. Thankfully, God's story moves to Redemption. It addresses the questions we all want answered: Can I change? How does Christ change people?

---

2. For a detailed development of a "biblical sufferology," see Bob Kellemen, *God's Healing for Life's Losses* (Winona Lake, IN: BMH Books, 2010).

Our trainees need to understand that biblical counseling applies our salvation, comprehensively understood, to our progressive sanctification. At times, new biblical counselors mistakenly counsel Christians as if they were non-Christians. They view their spiritual friends only through the lens of depravity. That would be like a heart surgeon transplanting a perfectly healthy new heart into her patient, but then treating her patient as if he still has his old heart.

To avoid this, your trainees need to understand what took place at salvation. They need to grasp the fourfold nature of biblical salvation (justification, regeneration, reconciliation, and redemption) and the implications of each for daily growth in Christ. How do people change? By applying justification, reconciliation, regeneration, and redemption to their daily lives.

Church: Embed Counseling in the Body of Christ—Community (Where Can I Find a Place to Belong and Become?)

As you develop your curriculum and content in this area, ask,

- How can my trainees begin to understand that growth in grace is a community journey?

Trainees need to know that sanctification is neither a self-improvement project nor an individual process. We grow in community. Our trainees need the big picture of the relationship of biblical counseling to the rest of the life of the church. Our trainees need to know the role of the church in the life of the Christian.

Consummation: Envision the Final Healing of the Soul— Glorification (How Does Our Future Destiny Impact Our Present Reality?)

As you develop your curriculum and content in this area, ask,

- How could knowing the end of the story impact how my trainees live and counsel?

Trainees need to see the big picture. Creation, fall, and redemption summarize life on planet Earth. However, we are everlasting beings. When our trainees remember to read the end of God's story, then God opens the eyes of their hearts to see the day-by-day story in a new light. Our eternal future addresses the question, Where am I headed? The biblical answer to that question ought to impact drastically how our trainees live and counsel today. Heaven is not only the end of suffering and sinning; heaven is the motivation for endurance of suffering *today* and for fighting against sin *today*.

Sanctification: Dispensing Grace—Growth in Grace (How Do I Increasingly Become More Like Jesus?)

As you develop your curriculum and content in this area, ask,

- What do my trainees need to understand about gospel-centered growth in grace so they can empower others to put off the old way and put on the new person in Christ?

Our trainees need to think biblically about progressive sanctification. It involves the Christian's inner life increasingly reflecting the inner life of Christ relationally (spiritually, socially, self-aware), rationally, volitionally, and emotionally.

Trainees need to understand the process of growth in grace, including issues such as mind renewal, putting on/putting off, and the spiritual disciplines. What biblical truth do our trainees need to understand in order to help others to move from conviction of sin, to repentance, to receiving the Father's forgiveness, to putting off sin, and to progressively putting on holiness?

DISCIPLE-MAKING CHAMPIONS

Equipping for Biblical Counseling Content

As part of the 4E Ministry Training Strategy Questionnaire, two dozen best-practice churches responded to the question, What content (theology, truth, doctrine, biblical knowledge) do you want to equip your graduates to address? The following list collates the most common themes.

- Sufficiency of Scripture: Distinctiveness of biblical counseling

- Relevancy of Scripture: How to relate truth to life

- Nature/Purpose of the Bible: Bible as story, relationship focus

- Hermeneutics: Principles of biblical interpretation and application

- God/Trinity: Implications of the Trinity on biblical relationships, God's character

- Christology: Christ's sinless life, sacrificial death, resurrection, return

- Holy Spirit: Comforting and sanctifying work, power, filling, fruit

- Creation: God's design of the soul, understanding people, the image of God

- Fall: Sin, depravity, idols of the heart, diagnosing problems

- Redemption: Salvation in Christ, the new person in Christ, prescribing solutions

- Gospel: Work of Christ, forgiveness, grace, faith, our complete salvation

- Sanctification: Progressive growth in grace, putting off/on, heart change, repentance, forgiveness, mind renewal, loving God/others, spiritual disciplines

- Church: Body life, the role of the church in discipleship/ counseling

- Spiritual Warfare: Role of Satan, victory over the world/ flesh/devil

- Various Specific Counseling Issues

- Suffering: Biblical teaching on grief, hope, and healing

- End Times: Heaven, hell, consummation, glorification, eternal perspective

What About *You*?

You've read my outline of eight theology-for-life categories for biblical counseling content equipping. You've seen more than a dozen content areas from best-practice disciple-making champions. What truth-for-life wisdom content will *you* teach your biblical counseling trainees?

COUNSELING COMPETENCE:
HOW TO CARE LIKE CHRIST
FOUR CORE RELATIONAL COMPETENCIES EVERY
BIBLICAL COUNSELOR MUST DEVELOP

We want our trainees to become soul physicians who understand people, diagnose problems, and prescribe solutions—biblically. A soul physician is like a doctor at a teaching hospital or a brilliant surgeon who can diagnose and treat the most obscure illness.

We all know of brilliant surgeons with horrific bedside manners, just as we all know of scholarly people who can't relate well. The *comprehensive biblical insights* of the soul physician must morph together with the *compassionate, competent Christian engagement* of the spiritual friend. This is exactly what Paul models in 1 Thessalonians 2:8. He loved people so much that he was delighted to share with them not only the gospel of God (Scripture), but his own life (soul) as well because they had become so dear to Paul.

Biblical counseling is not either/or: either a brilliant but uncaring soul physician, or a loving but unwise spiritual friend. God calls our trainees to be wise *and* loving soul physicians *and* spiritual friends. So now we consider what counseling competencies every trainee needs to develop in order to *care like Christ* by becoming spiritual friends who empathize (sustain), encourage (heal), exhort (reconcile), and empower (guide) their counselees.

One Map of Counseling Interventions and Interactions

In chapter 7, I outlined a biblical, historical (church history), and practical map: counseling for suffering through sustaining and healing (*parakaletic*), and counseling for sin through reconciling and guiding (*nouthetic*).[3] I develop this further in Figure 8:3. This is not *the model*, but *a map*. The suggested competencies listed with sustaining, healing, reconciling, and guiding are one way to conceptualize the types of counseling competencies your training could seek to cultivate. The idea is *not* that a biblical counselor *only* uses those skills within sustaining, or healing, or reconciling, or guiding. Life and counseling are much more complex and relational than that. Each competency is valuable throughout the entire biblical counseling relational process.

As you read the following counseling competency summaries, be asking yourself,

- In my foundational course in biblical counseling methodology, what counseling competencies would I equip my trainees to develop?

FIGURE 8:3

Twenty-Two Biblical Counseling Relational Competencies

Sustaining Biblical Counseling Competencies
Empathize and Embrace—GRACE Relational Competencies

- *G:* Grace Connecting—Galatians 6:1–3

- *R:* Rich Soul Empathizing—Romans 12:15

- *A:* Accurate Spiritual Listening—John 2:23—4:43

- *C:* Caring Spiritual Conversations—Ephesians 4:29

- *E:* Empathetic Scriptural Explorations—Isaiah 61:1–3

---

3. For a detailed training manual in sustaining, healing, reconciling, and guiding see Bob Kellemen, *Gospel Conversations* (Grand Rapids: Zondervan, 2015).

Healing Biblical Counseling Competencies
Encourage and Enlighten—RESTS Relational Competencies

- *R:* Relational Treatment Planning—John 2:23–25

- *E:* Encouraging Communication—Ephesians 4:29

- *S:* Story Reinterpreting—Philippians 3:7–15

- *T:* Thirst Spiritual Conversations—Hebrews 10:24–25

- *S:* Stretching Scriptural Explorations—Ephesians 3:15–21

Reconciling Biblical Counseling Competencies
Expose and Exhort—PEACE(E) Relational Competencies

- *P:* Probing Theologically—Ephesians 4:17–19

- *E:* Exposing Through Confronting Wisely—2 Timothy
  2:22–26

- *A:* Active Softening of Stubbornness—Hebrews 3—4

- *C:* Connecting Intimately—2 Corinthians 6:11–13

- *E:* Enlightening Spiritual Conversations—Hebrews 3:12–19

- *E:* Empowering Scriptural Explorations—Hebrews 4:12–16

Guiding Relational Counseling Competencies
Empower and Equip—FAITH(H) Relational Competencies

- *F:* Faith-Based Interventions—2 Corinthians 5:17

- *A:* Activating Envisioned Maturity—2 Timothy 1:5–7

- *I:* Insight-Oriented Treatment Planning—Colossians 3

- *T:* Taking Action—Ephesians 4:17–32

- *H:* Holiness Spiritual Conversations—Romans 5—8

- *H:* Heroic Scriptural Explorations—Hebrews 10—11

Comprehensive and Compassionate Biblical Counseling

Frank Lake summarized the personal ministry of the Word well when he wrote, "Pastoral care is defective unless it can deal thoroughly both with the evils we have suffered and with the sins we have committed."[4] Historically, biblical counseling has always dealt with *both* suffering *and* sin.

Our trainees need to learn the art of comforting suffering people. This includes the competencies of *sustaining*, where they listen to the earthly story of suffering, communicate that it's normal to hurt, and empathize with the agony of living in a fallen world. It also includes *healing* competencies, where they stretch their spiritual friend to the heavenly, eternal story, communicate that it's possible to hope, and encourage people to find God in the midst of their suffering by looking at life with spiritual eyes.

Trainees also need to learn how to practice the art of counseling people battling besetting sins. This includes the competencies of *reconciling*, where they expose the twofold truth that it's horrible to sin, but wonderful to be forgiven. It also includes *guiding* competencies, where they empower people to live out the truth that it's supernatural to mature—through Christ's resurrection power counselees can be victorious over the world, the flesh, and the devil.

Equipping in biblical counseling is much more than teaching a trainee how to implement a technique or skill. I prefer using the phrase *relational competencies*. Rather than a mechanical technique we pull out of our toolbox of skills, relational competencies are wise and compassionate ways of speaking the truth in love.

Sustaining Biblical Counseling Competencies: Empathize and Embrace—GRACE Relational Competencies

What does it look like to engage and embrace a suffering person with wisdom and compassion that sustains their faith? When trying to capture the essence of sustaining, I find it helpful to encourage my trainees to picture grace that helps others in their time of need—Hebrews 4:14–16. Jesus is the perfect picture of sustaining relational competency, of grace relating. Our sympathetic High Priest is not aloof, distant, or removed.

In his incarnation, Christ went through the heavens to earth sharing in our humanity, becoming like us, so that he might help us (Hebrews 2:14–18). Jesus is touched with the feelings of our infirmities. He is able to suffer with and be affected similarly to us. He offers grace to help in our time of need—well-timed

---

4. Frank Lake, *Clinical Theology* (London: Darton, Longman & Todd, 1966), 21.

help, help in the nick of time, words aptly spoken in season and seasoned with grace. Our trainees can become Jesus with skin on.

In equipping for sustaining competencies, I train biblical counselors to address the question, *How can my counselees and I experience GRACE relationships that sustain their faith through the trials of life?* GRACE summarizes five sustaining relational competencies.

- *G:* Grace Connecting—Galatians 6:1–3

- *R:* Rich Soul Empathizing—Romans 12:15

- *A:* Accurate Spiritual Listening—John 2:23—4:43

- *C:* Caring Spiritual Conversations—Ephesians 4:29

- *E:* Empathetic Scriptural Explorations—Isaiah 61:1–3

Grace Connecting: Committed Involvement—Galatians 6:1–3

Grace connecting is personal involvement with a deep commitment to the maturity of another person. It includes connection through communication. Your trainees have love in their hearts for their spiritual friends, but how do you equip them to convey it? Grace connection allows their passionate love to touch their spiritual friends through incarnational, face-to-face relating. Through grace connecting, trainees develop the relational competency of intimate interaction where they display the courage to talk seriously and to offer to go deeper.

Galatians 6:1–3 captures the attitude. Trainees restore others gently and humbly, carrying their burdens patiently and persistently. They communicate, "I love you in Christ for the long haul, like a marathon runner."

Rich Soul Empathizing: Climbing in the Casket—Romans 12:15

Empathy is the ability to sense a person's inner response to external suffering and to communicate, "It's normal to hurt." It's the capacity to mourn with those who mourn.

I help trainees picture the depth of this concept by portraying it as "climbing in the casket." Paul needed such comfort when he wrote, "We were under great pressure, far beyond our ability to endure, so that we despaired of life itself. Indeed, we felt we had received the sentence of death" (2 Corinthians 1:8–9). How will you equip your trainees to develop the capacity to share in the sorrows of others—communicating that they feel and experience their spiritual friend's pain?

Accurate Spiritual Listening: Faith-Drenched Alertness— John 2:23–4:43

Biblical counseling trainees need to develop the competency of accurate spiritual listening: listening to God's Word as they listen to people's words. Your training needs to demonstrate that listening is vital because words are meaningful (Proverbs 18:4; 20:5) because words convey issues of the heart (Matthew 12:34) and, therefore, our words are worthy of soulful attentiveness (Proverbs 18:13; James 1:19) because they reflect either God's interpretation of life or Satan's (Job 42:7).

Caring Spiritual Conversations: Sustaining Theological Trialogues—Ephesians 4:29

In a monologue, I speak to you. In a dialogue, we speak to each other. In a trialogue, together we listen to God through his Word. In caring spiritual conversations, your trainees learn to use biblical wisdom principles to engage their spiritual friends in interactions that help them think through their external suffering and internal grief from God's perspective.

Your trainees need to learn to use sustaining spiritual conversations to help their friends face their suffering face to face with God. Spiritual conversations in sustaining encourage others to invite God into their casket.

Empathetic Scriptural Explorations: Sustaining Biblical Trialogues—Isaiah 61:1–3

Spiritual conversations use *broad biblical principles* to prompt people to ponder their walk with God. Scriptural explorations use *specific applicable passages* to help people relate God's truth to their life.

How will you equip your trainees to learn to use sustaining scriptural explorations to help their spiritual friends lament to God candidly, crying out to him for his comfort? They need to learn not to use the Bible to preach at people in their suffering; instead, they learn to explore God's Word together with counselees to encourage them to relate God to their suffering.

Healing Biblical Counseling Competencies: Encourage and Enlighten—RESTS Relational Competencies

Through sustaining relational competencies, your trainees learn how to help counselees face the truth that life is bad and that in a fallen world it's normal to hurt. Having learned how to climb in the casket, your trainees now need to learn how to celebrate the empty tomb. They need to develop healing relational competencies that help their counselees see that even when life is bad, God is good—all the time—and that even in a fallen world it is possible to hope—because of Christ.

In equipping for healing competencies, we train biblical counselors to address the question, *How can my counselees and I engage in RESTS relationships that heal their faith by offering hope in Christ?* RESTS summarizes five healing relational competencies.

- *R:* Relational Treatment Planning—John 2:23–25

- *E:* Encouraging Communication—Ephesians 4:29

- *S:* Story Reinterpreting—Philippians 3:7–15

- *T:* Thirsts Spiritual Conversations—Hebrews 10:24–25

- *S:* Stretching Scriptural Explorations—Ephesians 3:15–21

Relational Treatment Planning: Mutuality in Hope Building— John 2:23–25

Relational treatment planning is much more than altering symptoms or offering short-term solutions to circumstances and problems. In relational treatment planning, the counselor and counselee cooperate with God in the process of sanctification, defined as moving toward communion with and conformity to Christ.

How will you equip your trainees to develop the competency of helping people move from the smaller earthly story to the larger eternal story? They need to be able to assist counselees to expand their goals beyond changed circumstances and fixed feelings to transformed hearts and renewed relationships. They then need to learn how to journey with counselees toward progressive sanctification as they deal with suffering and sin biblically and practically.

Encouraging Communication: Hope-Based Interactions— Ephesians 4:29

Since people typically come to counselors with problem-saturated stories, our trainees must learn how to infuse hope. Though we encourage trainees to empathize with hurting people, we don't want them to join people in their shrunken perspective.

Encouraging communications infuse hope by cropping Christ back into the picture. Satan attempts to deceive people into believing that since life is bad, God must not be good. How will you equip your trainees to develop the competency of undeceiving people by helping them look at life with spiritual eyes, with faith eyes, with 20/20 spiritual vision.

Story Reinterpreting: Coauthoring Resurrection Narratives— Philippians 3:7–15

When Paul despaired of life, he came to understand that God allowed his struggles so he would not rely upon himself, but upon God who raises the dead (2 Corinthians 1:9). Biblical counselors need training in coauthoring resurrection narratives. From within the casket of despair, they encourage people to see life from God's eternal perspective. How will you equip your trainees to develop the competency of story reinterpreting—using the benefit of faith to see the benefit of trials?

Thirsts Spiritual Conversations: Healing Theological Trialogues— Hebrews 10:24–25

Created for paradise and now experiencing desert living, suffering people thirst. Satan desires to direct people in their thirsts to drink from broken cisterns that hold no water (Jeremiah 2:13). Thirsts spiritual conversations encourage hurting people to recognize their deepest spiritual longing for God and enlighten them to see Christ as the only One who could ever satisfy their soul. How will you equip your trainees to direct people to God, the Spring of Living Water?

Stretching Scriptural Explorations: Healing Biblical Trialogues— Ephesians 3:15–21

In stretching scriptural explorations, trainees learn how to explore together with counselees relevant biblical passages that enlighten counselees to see their suffering from a hope-filled and grace-focused perspective. How will you equip your trainees to use healing biblical trialogues that encourage people to see what God is doing behind the scenes and what God might want to do in their heart?

Reconciling Biblical Counseling Competencies: Expose and Exhort—PEACE(E) Relational Competencies

Training in biblical counseling should equip people to become soul caregivers who compassionately identify with people in pain and redirect them to

Christ and the body of Christ to sustain and heal their faith (*parakaletic* counseling for suffering). Biblical counseling training should also equip people to become spiritual directors who understand spiritual dynamics and discern root causes of spiritual conflicts, providing loving wisdom that reconciles and guides people (*nouthetic* counseling for sinning).

Biblical counseling for sin involves the twin processes of reconciling and guiding. In reconciling, trainees learn how to expose their spiritual friend's sin and Christ's grace. In guiding, trainees learn how to empower people to live out their new life through Christ's resurrection power.

In equipping for reconciling competencies, we train biblical counselors to address the question, *How can my spiritual friends and I engage in relationships that produce PEACE (shalom) as they experience reconciliation with God and others?* PEACE(E) summarizes six reconciling relational competencies:

- *P:* Probing Theologically—Ephesians 4:17–19

- *E:* Exposing Through Confronting Wisely—2 Timothy 2:22–26

- *A:* Active Softening of Stubbornness—Hebrews 3—4

- *C:* Connecting Intimately—2 Corinthians 6:11–13

- *E:* Enlightening Spiritual Conversations—Hebrews 3:12–19

- *E:* Empowering Scriptural Explorations—Hebrews 4:12–16

Probing Theologically: Theory-Guided Awareness— Ephesians 4:17–19

Before trainees can expose sin, they have to understand biblical diagnostic categories of sin. Through the relational competency of probing theologically, trainees learn the art of relating the theology of the fall to a person's life by diagnosing sin comprehensively and specifically. How will you equip your trainees to help their counselees see that their sin is not a surface issue, but a heart issue that relates comprehensively to how they relate, think, choose, and feel?

Exposing Through Confronting Wisely: Disclosing Discrepancies—2 Timothy 2:22–26

Trainees need equipping in loving, wise biblical care-fronting. They need to learn that confronting wisely helps people see where they are intoxicated by the lies of the world, the flesh, and the devil so they can come to their senses and escape the devil's trap.

Active Softening of Stubbornness: Loosening Resistance to Repentance—Hebrews 3—4

Confrontation attempts to help people see what they are unaware of. Softening stubbornness attempts to help people face things they are aware of but refuse to change. Our trainees need equipping to help people when they are resisting the Spirit's work of conviction, change, and growth.

Connecting Intimately: Relating in the Moment— 2 Corinthians 6:11–13

Perhaps one of the most difficult competencies to learn is also one of the most important ones to develop—connecting intimately. It is more caught than taught by how we relate to our trainees and by the environment we cultivate in our training groups and labs.

In connecting intimately, trainees learn how to handle what is occurring in their relationship right now with their counselee. They learn to discuss the here and now with a view toward the implications for the counselee's other relationships.

Enlightening Spiritual Conversations: Reconciling Theological Trialogues—Hebrews 3:12–19

Through enlightening spiritual conversations, trainees learn how to help their counselees see their sin and their Father's amazing grace. This includes training in how to explore and apply biblical principles of confession of sin, repentance, and receiving God's grace and forgiveness.

Empowering Scriptural Explorations: Reconciling Biblical Trialogues—Hebrews 4:12–16

Empowering scriptural explorations continue the process, but instead of applying general biblical principles of sanctification, trainees learn how to explore and apply specific biblical passages relevant to confession, repentance, grace, and forgiveness. How will you equip your trainees to help their counselees apply God's Word to their struggles with sin?

Guiding Relational Counseling Competencies: Empower and Equip—FAITH(H) Relational Competencies

In biblical guiding, trainees learn how to collaborate with counselees in applying principles and passages from God's Word to their lives and relationships. In equipping for guiding competencies, we train biblical counselors to address the question, *How can my spiritual friend and I engage in relationships that nourish FAITH active in love?* FAITH(H) encapsulates six guiding relational competencies.

- *F:* Faith-Based Interventions—2 Corinthians 5:17

- *A:* Activating Envisioned Maturity—2 Timothy 1:5–7

- *I:* Insight-Oriented Treatment Planning—Colossians 3

- *T:* Taking Action—Ephesians 4:17–32

- *H:* Holiness Spiritual Conversations—Romans 5—8

- *H:* Heroic Scriptural Explorations—Hebrews 10—11

Faith-Based Interventions: New Covenant Living— 2 Corinthians 5:17

Having confessed the horrors of sin and having received God's grace, counselees need biblical wisdom in applying progressive sanctification principles to their specific heart and relationship issues. Trainees need equipping in faith-based interventions that help counselees live out their new nature and their new relationship with Christ by putting off the old patterns of relating and putting on the new person in Christ.

Activating Envisioned Maturity: Stirring Up God's Gifts—2 Timothy 1:5–7

We need to equip our trainees to envision their spiritual friends walking in maturity and then to stimulate that maturity by stirring up the gift of God. How will you equip your trainees to help people see their universal identity in Christ and recognize their unique calling from Christ?

Insight-Oriented Treatment Planning: Collaborative Spiritual Direction—Colossians 3

In insight-oriented treatment planning, biblical counselors work with their counselees to map out a personal spiritual growth process. How will you equip your trainees to help their spiritual friends establish realistic and specific plans for ongoing growth in grace?

Taking Action: Homework That Works—Ephesians 4:17–32

Trainees need to master the art of helping their counselees apply New Covenant truth to the specifics of their daily lives. How will you equip your trainees to shape homework that works in the real world?

Holiness Spiritual Conversations: Guiding Theological Trialogues—Romans 5—8

In holiness spiritual conversations, trainees learn how to explore with their counselees general biblical principles of growth in grace. How will you equip your trainees to help counselees relate God's Word to the specifics of suffering and sin?

Heroic Scriptural Explorations: Guiding Biblical Trialogues— Hebrews 10—11

Faith active in love involves trusting God while engaging in deep relationships with others. In heroic scriptural explorations, trainees learn how to empower their spiritual friends to be God's heroes. How will you equip your trainees to explore with counselees specific, relevant biblical passages that help their counselees courageously apply God's truth to their relationships?

DISCIPLE-MAKING CHAMPIONS

Equipping for Counseling Competence

As part of the 4E Ministry Training Strategy Questionnaire, two dozen best-practice churches responded to the question, What counseling competencies (relational competencies, methods, skills, counseling abilities) do you seek to equip your graduates to develop? The following list collates the most common themes.

- Four Stages: Love, know, speak, do

- Four Es: Empathize, encourage, exhort, equip

- Six Ls: Love, listen, learn, label lies, lecture, launch

- Building Involvement: Developing a trusting relationship, caring interaction

- Empathy: Feeling with others; connecting with hurting people

- Encouraging Hope: Instilling, building, infusing, and offering hope

- Drawing People Out: Helping people tell their stories

- Listening Skills: Understanding people and the complexities of their individual situations

- Gathering Data: Asking effective probing open-ended questions, using data well

- Interpreting Data: Compassionate discernment, interpreting personal information

- Isolating the Problem: Discovering where change is needed, determining direction

- Providing Biblical Encouragement: Helping people see life from God's perspective

- Targeting the Heart: Discerning root issues, applying truth to the heart

- Biblical Discernment: Understanding how to relate biblical principles to people's lives

- Spiritual Conversations: Connecting biblical principles to life

- Scriptural Explorations: Exploring pertinent passages, discussing relevant verses

- Speaking Truth in Love: Sensitive and gentle speech that blends grace and truth

- Providing Instruction: Empowering the counselee to discover and apply biblical truth

- Reconciling: Helping people confess sinful patterns, repent, and receive forgiveness

- Confronting in Love: Care-fronting, graciously addressing personal sinfulness

- Guiding: Equipping to put off/put on, helping people apply growth-in-grace principles

- Assigning and Assessing Homework: Extending the application process into daily life

What About *You*?

You've read my outline of four truth-to-life categories for biblical counseling competency equipping. You've seen nearly two dozen competency areas from best-practice Disciple-Making Champions. What truth-to-life relational competencies will *you* equip your biblical counseling trainees to develop?

COMMENCEMENT: A ROBUSTLY HEALTHY TRAINEE

When I teach on the 4Cs, I also like to use the imagery of the 4Hs—head, hands, heart, and home. The 4Hs help people picture what happens when an area is emphasized or de-emphasized disproportionately. If I'm using a whiteboard or PowerPoint, I'll draw a stick figure or show a picture of a body with a huge head and a tiny heart, for example. That pictures training that is tilted too much toward academic content and not enough toward character development. Take a moment to imagine the other stick figures and body images that would depict a distorted training emphasis of any of the 4Hs.

Comprehensive training is not easy. It takes quality and quantity time. However, it's worth the effort because it results in a robustly healthy trainee—one whose head, hands, heart, and home are proportional. There's no distortion. That doesn't mean perfection, but it does imply holistic training. The whole person is equipped to minister the whole gospel to bring wholeness to hurting and hardened people.

Chapter 9 continues our comprehensive training. Our trainees need to cultivate good heart health—Christlike character. They also need to participate in a healthy home—Christian community. Chapter 9 suggests the types of character traits and Christian community that complete our comprehensive training curriculum.

GROWING TOGETHER: QUESTIONS FOR REFLECTION, DISCUSSION, AND APPLICATION

1. Of the eight ultimate life questions and their content areas:

    a. Which ones surprise you? Why?

    b. Which ones have you taught on? How has your focus been different from the way that area was developed in this chapter? What would you teach in that content area?

    c. Which ones haven't you taught on? Why?

    d. What content area, if any, would you not include in your training curriculum? Why?

    e. What content area would you add for your training ministry? How would you develop it?

2. Of the collated list of biblical counseling content from the Disciple-Making Champions:

    a. Which ones surprise you? Why?

b. Which ones haven't you taught on? Why?

c. Which content area, if any, would you not include in your training curriculum? Why?

3. Of the four counseling areas and the twenty-two relational competencies that every biblical counselor must develop:

a. Which ones surprise you? Why?

b. Which ones have you equipped people for? How has your focus been different from the way that competency was developed in this chapter?

c. Which ones haven't you equipped people for? Why?

d. Which competency, if any, would you not include in your training? Why?

e. What competencies would you add in your training? How would you develop it?

4. Of the collated list of counseling competencies from the Disciple-Making Champions:

   a. Which ones surprise you? Why?

   b. Which ones haven't you equipped people for? Why?

   c. Which competency, if any, would you not include in your training? Why?

What Makes Biblical Counseling Biblical?: Part Two

Spiritual Formation and Spiritual Fellowship in Biblical Counseling

Equipping Christians for biblical counseling requires the vision of Gutzon Borglum, the creative genius behind the presidential carvings on Mount Rushmore. Someone once asked him, "How did you ever create those faces out of that rock?" Borglum replied, "I didn't. Those faces were already in there. Hidden. I only uncovered them."[1]

As equippers of Christians, we should never forget the freeing truth that the face of Jesus is already in every new creation in Christ (2 Corinthians 3:17–18; 5:17). We don't have to implant the 4Cs into our trainees. Instead, God calls us to stir up and fan into flame the gifts he has already implanted in every believer (2 Timothy 1:5–7).

This is especially true regarding the areas of Christlike character and Christian community. Figure 9:1 outlines the equipping objectives we pursue in these two areas.

---

1. From a film showed at the Mount Rushmore museum in 1996.

FIGURE 9:1

*Equipping in Christlike Character
and Christian Community*

**Reflecting Christ's Character:
"Full of Goodness"—Heart/Being**

How to Reflect Christ: Spiritual Formation

*Four Marks of Christlike Character Every Biblical Counselor Must
Cultivate*

- Relating Like Christ: Loving God and others passionately

- Thinking Like Christ: Renewing the mind to view life from
  God's eternal perspective

- Choosing Like Christ: Dying to self and living sacrificially
  for others

- Feeling Like Christ: Facing life honestly and managing
  moods biblically

**Growing Together in Community:
"Brothers/Sisters/One Another"—Home/Loving**

How to Grow Together in Christ: Spiritual Fellowship

*Two Kinds of Christian Community Every Biblical Counselor Must
Participate In*

- Communion with the Body of Christ: Horizontal spiritual
  disciplines

- Communion with Christ: Vertical spiritual disciplines

CHRISTLIKE CHARACTER:
FOUR MARKS OF CHRISTLIKE CHARACTER EVERY
BIBLICAL COUNSELOR MUST CULTIVATE

The premise of this section is simple. *As biblical counselors, before we can help others to become more like Christ, we need to be growing in Christlikeness.*

It's not, "Physician, heal thyself." It is, "Soul physician, become like the ultimate Soul Physician."

This is why the biblical counseling movement has a long history of "self-counsel"—equipping counselors to apply God's Word to their own growth in grace. As we equip biblical counselors, we must emphasize their growth in Christlike character. Spiritual formation, transformation into the image of Christ, is the ultimate goal of biblical counseling—first for the counselor, and then for the counselee.

As you read the following counselor character summaries, be asking yourself,

- In my foundational course in biblical counseling, what Christlike character qualities would I seek to cultivate in my trainees?

Picturing the Spiritually Mature Biblical Counselor[2]

To move toward this goal, we have to ask and answer several related questions:

- What is our definition of a spiritually mature Christian?

- How do we measure spiritual maturity?

- What is our target, our goal in progressive sanctification?

- What does Christlikeness look like?

These are foundational questions, aren't they? Yet our answers to these questions are often abstract, nebulous, vague, and ill-defined. This is why all too often we end up working toward surface *solutions*—changing circumstances, fixing feelings, or modifying external behaviors. We should be working toward *soul-u-tions*—comprehensive inner-life transformation.

---

2. For a fuller development of a biblical theology of the spiritually mature Christian, see Bob Kellemen, *Gospel-Centered Counseling* (Grand Rapids: Zondervan, 2014).

That's why in chapter 8 we offered a succinct and focused definition of Christlikeness: *our inner life increasingly reflecting the inner life of Christ.* And it's why now in chapter 9 we're painting four snapshots, four tangible portraits of Christlikeness:

- Relating Like Christ: Loving God and others passionately

- Thinking Like Christ: Renewing my mind to view life from God's eternal perspective

- Choosing Like Christ: Dying to self and living sacrificially for others

- Feeling Like Christ: Facing life honestly and managing my moods biblically

Speaking of pictures, picture yourself on your first day of equipping a new group of biblical counseling trainees. Now picture their "graduation" day. Would you have been successful if your graduates knew a lot of biblical content and could practice a lot of counseling methods, but their lives didn't reflect Christ? Of course not. So in addition to spending time determining what content to teach trainees and what skills to help trainees develop, let's spend time—like we are now—focusing on discipling trainees to relate, think, choose, and feel like Christ.

Relating Like Christ: Loving God and Others Passionately

Relating like Christ is the first mark of Christlike character that every biblical counseling trainee must cultivate. In Matthew 22:34–40, Christ summarized the entire Old Testament with the two commands to love God wholeheartedly and to love our neighbor as ourself. God created us as three-dimensional relational beings. We relate to him (spiritual beings), to one another (social beings), and to ourselves (self-aware beings).

We want to design our curriculum and training in such a way that our trainees grow spiritually in their love for God. We want them to be cultivating a godly heart response to questions like these:

- Like Christ, do I increasingly exalt, enjoy, love, and find satisfaction in God more than in anything or anyone else?

- Do I increasingly cling to God the Father, running home to him as my Father, like a faithful son or daughter?

- Do I increasingly enjoy Christ more than any other joy?

- Do I increasingly depend upon the Holy Spirit to make me holy, beautify me, empower me, and equip me?

As social beings, we want to help our trainees love one another sacrificially as Christ models for us. How will you design your curriculum so your trainees can cultivate a godly heart response to the following question?

- Like Christ, am I increasingly loving others deeply and sacrificially from the heart?

As self-aware beings, God calls us to think of ourselves accurately according to who we are in and to Christ (Romans 12:3). How will you craft your training so your trainees can cultivate a godly heart response to the following question?

- Am I increasingly resting confidently in who I am in and to Christ?

Thinking Like Christ: Renewing the Mind to View Life from God's Eternal Perspective

Thinking like Christ is the second mark of Christlike character that every biblical counseling trainee must cultivate. God calls us to renew our minds so that in our relationships with God and one another we have the same mindset as Christ Jesus (Philippians 2:5).

Rationally, mentally, we want our trainees to value what God values. The Reformers and Puritans called this "thinking God's thoughts after him." How will you assist your trainees to be cultivating a godly heart response to the following question?

- Like Christ, do I increasingly view life from the Father's eternal, gracious, and good perspective?

We want our trainees to see life with spiritual eyes, with faith eyes, with 20/20 spiritual vision. We want God's Word to enlighten them to the reality that God's larger story interprets their smaller story (Romans 8:17–18). We want the end of the story to impact how they live today (Revelation 7:9–17; 21:1–7). So how will you organize your training so your trainees can be cultivating a heart response to the following questions?

- Like Christ, do I increasingly grasp the holy love of God together with all the saints?

- Like Christ, do I increasingly allow God's eternal story to invade my earthly story?

- Like Christ, do I increasingly renew my mind according to God's Word?

- Like Christ, do I increasingly live by every word that comes from the mouth of God?

Choosing Like Christ: Dying to Self and Living Sacrificially for Others

Choosing like Christ is the third mark of Christlike character that every biblical counseling trainee must cultivate. Christ's life mission must become our life mission. "Whoever wants to become great among you must be your servant, and whoever wants to be first must be slave of all. For even the Son of Man did not come to be served, but to serve, and to give his life as a ransom for many" (Mark 10:43–45). "Greater love has no one than this: to lay down one's life for one's friends" (John 15:13).

Volitionality relates to our will, choices, motivations, purposes—why we do what we do. Volitionally, we want our trainees to choose the courageous path of sacrificial living. How will you mentor your trainees to cultivate a godly heart response to the following questions?

- Like Christ, do I increasingly die to self and live for God and others?

- Am I increasingly trusting Christ courageously and taking risks to minister to others?

- Am I increasingly finding my life by dying to myself, taking up my cross, and following Christ?

- Am I increasingly living to shepherd and minister to others?

- Am I increasingly serving Christ and others out of a pure heart, a good conscience, and a sincere faith?

Feeling Like Christ: Facing Life Honestly and Managing Moods Biblically

Responding to our feelings like Christ is the fourth mark of Christlike character that every biblical counseling trainee must cultivate. As I typed that sentence, I imagined pushback from some readers. We've become accustomed to assuming that all feelings, all emotions, are bad. Nothing could be further from God's truth. God designed us as emotional beings.

The issue is not whether we have emotions, but how we handle our emotions. This is true even for one of the most intense of emotions—anger. "In your anger do not sin" (Ephesians 4:26). Jesus practiced what Paul preached. "He looked around at them in anger and, deeply distressed at their stubborn hearts, said to the man, 'Stretch out your hand.' He stretched it out, and his hand was completely restored" (Mark 3:5). Jesus experienced and expressed his emotions motivated by his commitment to minister to others.

Emotionally, we want our trainees to face life honestly and to manage their moods biblically. So how will you design your time together to equip your trainees to cultivate a godly heart response to the following questions?

- Like Christ, do I increasingly respond to and express my emotions with a ministry focus?

- Am I increasingly soothing my soul in my Savior?

- Am I increasingly developing emotional empathy for others?

- Am I increasingly developing emotional savvy—handling my relationships well?

- Am I increasingly developing emotional self-awareness, understanding my moods?

DISCIPLE-MAKING CHAMPIONS

Equipping for Christlike Character

As part of the 4E Ministry Training Strategy Questionnaire, two dozen best-practice churches responded to the question, What Christlike character do you seek to equip your graduates to cultivate and manifest? The following list collates the most common themes.

- Christlikeness: To be more like Jesus, growing mature in Christ, loving like Christ

- Spiritual, Relational, Emotional Maturity/Intelligence

- Fruit of the Spirit/Filled with the Spirit

- Christian Virtues/Beatitudes

- First Timothy 3 and 2 Peter 1 Character Qualities

- Love: Love God, his Word, and people

- Worshippers: Growing in their awe, wonder, and worship toward God

- Intimacy/Relationship with Christ

- Gospel-Centered Lives: Ministering the gospel to their own souls

- Self-Counseling: Applying what they're learning to their own heart/lives

- Living Faith: Living out faith in their families, churches, and communities

- Personal Holiness: Striving to live for God's glory, growing in grace

What About *You*?

You may be wondering, *But Bob, how do we go about this type of heart training?* Great question—one we'll answer in chapter 10.

For now, I have some questions for you: Is character training on your radar? Is character training an essential aspect of how you plan your equipping times together?

It must be. In Romans 15:14, Paul's first qualification to become a biblical counselor focuses on character—"full of goodness"—Christlikeness.

When we sit down to craft our counseling curriculum, we tend to spend the bulk of our time on content and competency. I'm suggesting we expend at least as much time and energy on character—thinking through how we shape our curriculum and our time together so that we encourage and empower each other to become soul physicians who increasingly reflect the inner life of the great Soul Physician.

CHRISTIAN COMMUNITY:
TWO KINDS OF CHRISTIAN COMMUNITY EVERY
BIBLICAL COUNSELOR MUST PARTICIPATE IN

Just as we must maintain consistency between our theology and methodology, we also need to maintain consistency between our definition of biblical counseling and our equipping of biblical counselors. Revisiting our definition of biblical counseling, especially the last sentence, makes this clear.

> Christ-centered, church-based, comprehensive, and compassionate biblical counseling depends upon the Holy Spirit to relate God's Word to suffering and sin by speaking and living God's truth in love to equip people to love God and one another (Matthew 22:35–40). *It cultivates conformity to Christ and communion with Christ and the body of Christ leading to a community of one-another disciple-makers* (Matthew 28:18–20).

When I counsel, I always have the end in view. I want to help counselees cultivate conformity to Christ—their inner life increasingly reflecting the inner life of Christ (spiritual formation). I also want to help them cultivate communion with Christ and the body of Christ (spiritual fellowship). I don't want to point people to myself or to never-ending meetings with me. I want to point them to the ultimate Spiritual Friend (Christ) and to ongoing spiritual friendships (within the body of Christ).

If this is what we want our trainees to do with their counselees, then it makes sense that we would equip our trainees in the same way with the same goals. If the end goal of biblical counseling in the church is the creation of a community of one-another disciple-makers, then our *biblical counseling equipping group must become a one-another community*. We cannot effectively equip competent biblical counselors apart from the context of intimate biblical one-another community.

A word to professors: We must train people in the Christian college and seminary setting in the same way that we want students to train people in their churches. When we train pastors-to-be only in a didactic, lecture-oriented, brain-dump, content-exclusive model, then that's exactly what pastors will do *to* their people.

The model you're learning throughout this book is the model that I've implemented in four churches *and* that I implemented when I launched and led the MA in Christian Counseling and Discipleship program at Capital Bible Seminary. The 4Cs, including the C of Christian community, have been the core components in each setting.

A word to everyone—remember the imagery that one of my students used:

Community is the container for the other 3Cs.

Christian community is the growth-enhancing context, the fertile soil, the healthy environment for equipping people in biblical content, counseling competence, and Christlike character. Every biblical counseling trainee must participate in two kinds of Christian community: communion with the body of Christ and communion with Christ.

Communion with the Body of Christ: The Horizontal Spiritual Disciplines

Don't take my word for it. Take God's Word and its teaching about one-another community. Consider the classic passage where Paul talks about God bringing glory in the church and in Christ Jesus and doing so immeasurably beyond anything that we could ask or imagine. Notice the *container* in which that occurs.

I pray that you, being rooted and established in love, may have power, *together with all the Lord's holy people*, to grasp how wide and

long and high and deep is the love of Christ, and to know this love
that surpasses knowledge—that you may be filled to the measure of
all the fullness of God (Ephesians 3:17–19).

How do we understand who God is? How do we grasp His love? How do
we become more like Christ? We do so *together with all the saints*. Sitting in
rows and being lectured at for the entire equipping process does not count as
together with all the saints.

Consider the classic passage about living out our new nature in Christ and
being renewed in the image of Christ (Colossians 3:1–17). How does that work
itself out in the real world? By being united with one another across ethnic bar-
riers, by bearing with one another, by forgiving one another, and by loving one
another (verses 11–14). It doesn't occur only through the pulpit ministry of the
Word. In this passage, Paul emphasizes the personal ministry of the Word. "Let
the message of Christ dwell among you richly as you teach and admonish *one
another* with all wisdom through psalms, hymns, and songs from the Spirit,
singing to God with gratitude in your hearts" (verse 16). Progressive sanctification, whether for our counselees, our trainees, or ourselves, occurs in the context of one-another community.

Consider the classic passage that teaches how Christians experience victory
over sin. "See to it, brothers and sisters, that none of you has a sinful, unbelieving heart that turns away from the living God. But encourage one another daily,
as long as it is called 'Today,' so that none of you may be hardened by sin's deceit-
fulness" (Hebrews 3:12–13). What softens the heart? What counteracts sin's lies?
Daily one-another encouragement in Christian community.

Consider the classic passage that teaches how Christians experience healing
hope in the midst of devastating suffering. "Let us consider how we may spur
one another on toward love and good deeds, not giving up meeting together, as
some are in the habit of doing, but encouraging one another—and all the more
as you see the Day approaching" (Hebrews 10:24–25). In suffering and in sin,
we need ongoing one-another community.

In the next chapter, we'll learn best-practice biblical counseling training
methods and strategies for cultivating community. There, we'll learn that we
nurture community by being a community; we cultivate community in community. In my training of students at Faith Bible Seminary, I say it like this:

> *"To become effective biblical counselors, we must give and receive bibli-
> cal counseling in community."*

What does that look like? As a training small group, we experience one-another empathy (sustaining), encouragement (healing), exhortation (reconciling), and empowerment (guiding). We lead our group in such a way that together we experience group biblical counseling—group sustaining, healing, reconciling, and guiding.

We create a safe equipping environment where we weep with one another—communicating that it's normal to hurt (sustaining). We cultivate an equipping environment where together we explore life from God's perspective—communicating that it's possible to hope (healing). We nurture a grace environment where the faithful wounds of friends communicate that it's horrible to sin but wonderful to be forgiven (reconciling). We promote an environment where we stir up one another, communicating that it's supernatural to mature (guiding). We are real and raw as we speak the truth in love to one another with authenticity and intimacy.

This soul-to-soul connecting doesn't imply any lack of curriculum, content, or materials about one-another ministry. In the training groups I facilitate, we explore and apply passages such as the ones we just examined: Ephesians 3:17–19; Colossians 3:1–17; Hebrews 3:12–13; Hebrews 10:24–25; and many more.[3]

Additionally, via outside reading, I include teaching about the theology and practice of the spiritual disciplines.[4] Through individual supervision and through a writing project, I also have each trainee develop their own Personal Spiritual Workout Routine/Plan. They craft a spiritual development plan that includes individual spiritual disciplines and corporate spiritual disciplines.

Communion with Christ: The Vertical Spiritual Disciplines

Our definition of biblical counseling highlights not only communion with the body of Christ, but also communion with Christ. These vertical spiritual disciplines are essential to conformity to the image of Christ. Sometimes people assume that the vertical spiritual disciplines are always and only practiced individually. That need not and often should not be the case.

All four of the passages we examined in the previous section have elements of communion with Christ experienced together with the body of Christ. Hebrews 10:22, in the plural, exhorts, "Let us draw near to God with a sincere heart with the full assurance that faith brings." As a training group, group

---

3. See Bob Kellemen, *Gospel Conversations* (Grand Rapids: Zondervan, 2015).

4. See Donald S. Whitney, *Spiritual Disciplines for the Christian Life* (Colorado Springs: NavPress, 2014).

communion with Christ in prayer should become an essential component—both planned and spontaneous. Many times our groups have been engaged in counseling vignettes when it becomes obvious that one of the members needs prayer. The vignette stops and prayer begins.

Colossians 3:15–17 merges seamlessly from one-another teaching and admonition to mutual worship through psalms, hymns, and spiritual songs with gratitude in our hearts to God. Many times I have been lecturing, a question is asked, a discussion begins, and spontaneous praise erupts. Other times I build in planned times of singing, praising, and group worship (more on this in the next chapter).

Again, this shouldn't imply that there's no curriculum, content, or materials about communion with Christ. In fact, creative Bible teaching should always relate truth to life. If we are talking about the Trinity and implications for biblical counseling, it is almost unimaginable that we wouldn't also discuss individual and group life application (again, more on this in the next chapter).

As described in chapter 8, biblical counseling values the role of homework. Just as one hour of counseling per week is not enough for ongoing growth in grace, so two hours of training is not enough. So in conjunction with the training in spiritual disciplines mentioned above, trainees have homework assignments in the practice of the private and corporate spiritual disciplines that enhance their communion with Christ and help them tap into Christ's resurrection power.

DISCIPLE-MAKING CHAMPIONS

Equipping for Christian Community

As part of the 4E Ministry Training Strategy Questionnaire, two dozen best-practice churches responded to the question, What community-building objectives and activities (group connecting, team-building, creating a homelike atmosphere, practicing private and corporate spiritual disciplines) do you seek to equip your training group to experience and your graduates to participate in? The following list collates the most common themes.

- We work to create the proper atmosphere so mutual ministry occurs in our training.

- Everyone is encouraged to experience and flourish in gospel community—a mutual care and bearing of burdens with one another both within and outside our training.

- Our training groups build on a churchwide culture of mutual discipleship.

- We strive to experience and practice one-another ministry so every trainee feels wanted, valued, respected, appreciated, and ministered to.

- Character is shaped in community over time, so we strive to cultivate a synergistic, group environment where there's trust, risk, and whole-group involvement.

- We employ a body life approach and emphasize loving connection within our training.

- We teach encouragement and community as a high value.

- We share testimonies of God's work in our lives through the training.

- We encourage people to share openly during our meetings.

- As leaders, we share our lives and struggles to encourage a community of authenticity.

- We create groups among our counselors-in-training and give them exercises to complete together to demonstrate the effectiveness and benefits of small-group interaction.

- Within the group time we practice spiritual disciplines like corporate worship and prayer, mutual fellowship, and biblical encouragement.

- We consider the biblical one-another commands to be part of corporate spiritual disciplines—what we teach our trainees to do we experience together each time we meet.

- We require our trainees to read books on the spiritual disciplines.

- We encourage our people to practice spiritual disciplines such as silence, solitude, service, worship, confession, repentance, fellowship, and biblical meditation.

What About *You*?

By talking about the two kinds of Christian community that every biblical counselor must participate in, I've outlined an *atmosphere or attitude*. Like the other 3Cs, these two kinds of community are simply one map to address Christian community in biblical counseling training. Two dozen best-practice churches added their perspective. What about you? Your task is to weigh the combined advice in this chapter as you develop the community-building aspect that best matches your ministry context.

OUTSIDE RESOURCES
AND REQUIRED READING

Chapters 8 and 9 have focused on *curriculum and materials* with an emphasis on mapping out and outlining the 4C categories you need to consider covering. So far, I've purposefully not focused on outside training materials. It's unhelpful to decide on outside sources until you've decided what 4C categories your training ministry needs to cover.

To their credit, every one of the twenty-four best-practice churches developed their own in-house curriculum materials: outlines, handouts, notes, manuals, or videos. Their typical best-practice method was to use outside resources to supplement and fill in their in-house materials.

In Figure 9:2, I've collated introductory biblical counseling equipping resources. These come from a combination of my survey of the Disciple-Making Champions and from my *Annual Guide to Biblical Counseling Resources.*

FIGURE 9:2

Introductory 4C Biblical Counseling Equipping Resources

Content: Theology of Biblical Counseling

- Adams, Jay E. *A Theology of Christian Counseling*

- Kellemen, Bob. *Gospel-Centered Counseling*

- Kellemen, Bob, and Jeff Forrey, editors. *Scripture and Counseling*

- Kellemen, Bob, and Kevin Carson, editors. *Biblical Counseling and the Church*

- Kellemen, Bob, and Steve Viars, editors. *Christ-Centered Biblical Counseling*

- Lambert, Heath. *A Theology of Biblical Counseling*

- Lelek, Jeremy. *Biblical Counseling Basics*

- Powlison, David. *Seeing with New Eyes*

Competence: Methodology of Biblical Counseling

- Adams, Jay E. *The Christian Counselor's Manual*

- Adams, Jay E. *Competent to Counsel*

- Emlet, Michael R. *CrossTalk*

- Emlet, Michael R. *Saints, Sufferers, and Sinners*

- Eyrich, Howard, and William Hines. *Curing the Heart*

- Henderson, John. *Equipped to Counsel*

- Kellemen, Bob. *Consider Your Counsel*

- Kellemen, Bob. *Gospel-Centered Family Counseling*

- Kellemen, Bob. *Gospel-Centered Marriage Counseling*

- Kellemen, Bob. *Gospel Conversations*

- Pierre, Jeremy, and Deepak Reju. *The Pastor and Counseling*

- Powlison, David. *Speaking Truth in Love*

- Scott, Stuart, and Heath Lambert, editors. *Counseling the Hard Cases*

- Tripp, Paul David. *Instruments in the Redeemer's Hands*

Character: Growth in Christlikeness

- Cheong, Robert K. *Restore*

- Lane, Timothy S., and Paul David Tripp. *How People Change*

- Pierre, Jeremy. *The Dynamic Heart in Daily Life*

- Powlison, David. *How Does Sanctification Work?*

Community: Communion with Christ and the Body of Christ

- Packer, J.I. *Knowing God*

- Tautges, Paul. *Counsel One Another*

- Whitney, Donald S. *Spiritual Disciplines for the Christian Life*

- Welch, Edward T. *Caring for One Another*

- Welch, Edward T. *Side by Side*

COMMENCEMENT: HOW DO WE
GET FROM HERE TO THERE?

I thank God that the face of Jesus is already in every Christian we train to become a biblical counselor. I enjoy stirring up what God has placed within. Old Faithful at Yellowstone National Park also communicates the idea of releasing something that is already within. Like clockwork, the geyser explodes upward because of the contents stored deep within.

When I taught that image in our church, one of our elders got excited. "Men," he said to the rest of our elder ministry team, "do you understand this idea from 2 Timothy 1:5–7 that Pastor Bob is picturing with Mount Rushmore and with Old Faithful? *It's in there!* Our job as elders, coaches, and counselors isn't to put maturity into people. That would be impossible. Our role is to fan into flame and stir up the Christlikeness that's already in there!"

In chapters 7 through 9, we've seen "what's in there." In chapter 7, we learned how the 4Cs provide our biblical counseling training *goals and objectives.* In chapters 8 and 9, we focused on the 4Cs of biblical counseling training *curriculum and materials.*

Because I've taught this so many times, I know what some of you are thinking: *All of that is great. It clarifies a lot for me. But…how do I move from goals, objectives, curriculum, and materials to the actual process of training folks in these core 4C areas?*

Glad you asked. Chapter 10 explores biblical counseling training *strategies and methods.* We'll address the question, How do we effectively train biblical counselors to know, be, do, and love? We'll apply best-practice transformational training concepts that comprehensively equip your trainees for biblical content, counseling competence, Christlike character, and Christian community.

GROWING TOGETHER: QUESTIONS FOR REFLECTION, DISCUSSION, AND APPLICATION

1. Before reading this chapter, how would you have answered the following questions? What is your definition/description of a spiritually mature Christian? How do you measure spiritual maturity? What is your model, target, goal of spiritual maturity?

2. Now that you've read this chapter, in what ways, if any, would you answer those questions differently?

3. As briefly as possible, what would you say the ultimate goal of biblical counseling is?

4. Below, take a Redeemed Personality Inventory evaluating your current progress toward Christlikeness. Use a 10 for "Most Like Jesus" and a 1 for "Least Like Jesus."

   _____ Like Christ, do I increasingly exalt, enjoy, love, and find satisfaction in God more than in anything or anyone else?

   _____ Like Christ, am I increasingly loving others deeply and sacrificially from the heart?

   _____ Am I increasingly resting confidently in who I am in and to Christ?

   _____ Like Christ, do I increasingly view life from the Father's eternal, gracious, and good perspective?

_____ Like Christ, do I increasingly die to self and live for God and others?

_____ Like Christ, do I increasingly respond to and express my emotions with a ministry focus?

5. Of the two kinds of Christian community and their development in this chapter:

   a. Which ones surprise you? Why?

   b. Which ones have you focused on? How has your focus been different from the way that area was developed in this chapter? What would you teach in that content area?

10

Equipping Competent Biblical Counselors

*Transformational Training
Strategies and Methods*

I was profoundly impacted by the research and writing for the book *Beyond the Suffering: Embracing the Legacy of African American Soul Care and Spiritual Direction*. The book depicts the amazing mutual ministry of the Black Church during the horrors of enslavement. In a chapter entitled "The Old Ship of Zion," my coauthor and I describe the *Invisible Institution*—the hidden worship and fellowship meetings that occurred in the cabins and woods of the slave plantations.

Pastor Peter Randolph pictured the situation. "Not being allowed to hold meetings on the plantation, the slaves assemble in the swamps, out of reach of the patrols. They have an understanding among themselves as to the time and place of getting together."[1] Once gathered, Randolph explained their *spontaneous yet structured* gatherings.

> Arrangements are then made for conducting the exercises. They first ask each other how they feel, the state of their minds, etc. The male members then select a certain space, in separate groups, for their division of the meeting. Preaching in order by the brethren; then

---

1. Bob Kellemen and Karole Edwards, *Beyond the Suffering* (Grand Rapids: Baker, 2007), 130.

> praying and singing all around.... The preacher usually commences by calling himself unworthy.[2]

Their practice reminds us of the early church in Acts 2.

> They devoted themselves to the apostles' teaching and to fellowship, to the breaking of bread and to prayer....Every day they continued to meet together in the temple courts. They broke bread in their homes and ate together with glad and sincere hearts, praising God and enjoying the favor of all the people (Acts 2:42, 46–47).

If any two churches could have been all spontaneity and no structure, we might think it would have been the early church in Acts and the Black Church under American slavery. Yet we discover in both cases the art of *organizing the organism*. They made arrangements for conducting the exercises. They devoted themselves to the apostles' teaching. Though valuing spontaneity and the leading of the Spirit, they also treasured purposeful planning and ongoing training.

We so easily swing the ministry pendulum between structure *or* spontaneity, yet God's Word cherishes the *structured spontaneity of the organized organism* (Acts 6:1–7; 1 Corinthians 14:26–40; 1 Timothy 3:5, 14–15; 2 Timothy 2:2; 4:2; Titus 2:1–8). God calls leaders to prepare his people for works of service so the body of Christ might be edified and equipped with the result that Christians speak the truth in love as the whole body joined and held together grows and builds itself up in love—the organized organism (Ephesians 4:11–16).

In my consulting ministry, I tend to see churches swinging the pendulum toward the extreme of spontaneity without structure, organism without organization, and experiences without equipping. Relative to biblical counseling, that would result in being a church *of* one-another ministry (which is vital) but never becoming a church *with* an envisioned, enlisted, equipped, and empowered biblical counseling ministry. We should cultivate an environment where *informal one-another ministry* spontaneously saturates the entire congregation. We *also* can oversee a ministry where *equipping in formal biblical counseling* provides the entire congregation with access to believers who are competent to counsel. It is never either/or.

In chapter 7, we learned how the 4Cs provide our biblical counseling training *goals and objectives*. In chapters 8 and 9, we moved from these broad goals

---

2. Ibid., 130–32.

and objectives to a focused discussion of biblical counseling training *curriculum and materials*. Now in chapter 10, we explore biblical counseling transformational training *strategies and methods*. This chapter presents best-practice answers to the question,

- How do we *structure* our training so we comprehensively equip biblical counselors to know, be, do, and love?

To answer that question, we'll think through transformational strategies, methods, and structure using three broad categories.

- Organizing for 4C Equipping: Levels of training, length of training, and schedule, scope, and sequence of training

- Meeting for 4C Equipping: Transformational teaching-oriented training and transformational small-group lab-oriented training

- Outside Training for 4C Equipping: Supervision, spiritual friendship, protégée meetings, and assignments

ORGANIZING FOR 4C EQUIPPING

Before you read what I have to say about how to do it, remember this: *Don't do it like I do it.* There's no cookie-cutter approach, no one-size-fits-all training model. I've already testified about how I blundered when I tried to plop a successful large church model on a much smaller church. You'll be reading principles and best practices that you need to interpret and implement to fit *your* biblical counseling ministry in *your* church.

Levels and Styles of Training: The Informal Model and the Formal Model

Throughout this book, I've compared and contrasted training in informal one-another ministry and training in formal biblical counseling. Every member of every church should be equipped to speak the truth in love in small groups, in the foyer, over the backyard fence, at the dinner table, and at the diner—*the informal model*. Additionally, some members with gifting, passion, calling, and commitment can focus their ministry on intentional and intensive ongoing biblical counseling—*the formal model.* While this chapter focuses on equipping in the formal model, it's important that we not forget the need to equip the entire congregation to speak the truth in love to each other.

Length of Training in the Formal Model

Informal training is typically of a shorter duration, more periodic, offered on an elective basis, and used in everyday-life situations. Formal training, to which we now turn our attention, meets regularly over an extended period of time. How much training is enough; how much is too little; how much is too much? Initially, when you read the average length of training in best-practice churches, you might be taken aback. Don't read ahead until you've considered some important points.

First, don't dumb down. Keep your expectations high. Formal biblical counseling is serious. People's lives matter. Comprehensive equipping is essential.

Second, factor in what a committed member would be doing if not in your training. Most committed members would likely be dedicating a couple of hours per week either to a ministry they were involved in or to a small group they participated in. Most would do so on an ongoing, open-ended basis—year after year.

Third, don't apologize. Don't be sheepish about insisting on commitment—both quality and quantity.

Fourth, communicate the amazing benefits of the training. Your meetings, done right and run well, will become the most powerful small-group time that your trainees have ever experienced. Your trainees will say years later, "To this day, I miss our training small group and see it as the most amazing time of personal growth and group connection that I have ever experienced!"

Now you're mentally prepared. For the twenty-four best-practice churches, the average time spent meeting was one hundred hours.[3] That includes lecture, lab, and counseling observation. It does *not* include time spent outside the actual meetings in reading assignments, meeting with supervisors, and meeting with lab partners/spiritual friends. The lowest reported time in training was forty hours, the highest was one hundred and fifty hours, and the mean was seventy-five hours.

The average length of training was one-and-a-half years. The most frequent

---

3. By comparison, in Tan's survey (*Lay Counseling*), the average in-meeting time was seventy-two hours. The minimum was forty to fifty hours. His training of lay counselors lasted 108 hours.

length was one year. The shortest length was three months—but that was intensive training in which the trainees met twelve hours each day, one day a week. The longest length was three years. Additionally, almost every best-practice church also required ongoing supervision and/or continuing education as long as the biblical counselor still provided formal biblical counseling.

While I've structured my equipping ministry differently in each of my four churches, whenever I've offered formal training it typically ran two years, meeting once per week over nine months each year. That's one hundred and forty-four hours of in-meeting time.

What do you do for that long? You comprehensively equip one another in the 4Cs of biblical content, Christlike character, counseling competence, and Christian community.

Is that too much for people? The attrition (dropout) rate is an excellent measure to answer that question. In my four churches, less than 4 percent have ever dropped out. Over 96 percent of the people who started the training continued for two years to graduation and beyond. Compare that to the percentage of people who stay in a small group for two years, or frankly, who do anything consistently for two years. The key to retention is careful selection, plus comprehensive equipping in the context of loving community that impacts the trainee's life so the trainee can impact the lives of others.

Schedule, Scope, and Sequence of Training in the Formal Model

Every time I've trained biblical counselors in the local church, my meeting schedule and training scope and sequence have been different. I offer the following schedule simply as one representative sample—from my first church LEAD biblical counseling equipping group. It was what fit best for that church with that MVP-C Statement with those trainees in our community.

We met every Wednesday night from September through May (other than holidays) for two hours for two years. We divided each year into semesters. I required attendance at 90 percent of all meetings. Our average attendance over the two years was 98 percent—our meetings became "can't miss."

LEAD Year One, Semester One

During our first hour we met for interactive applicational lectures covering a theology of four of life's eight ultimate questions. During the second hour we met for intensive small-group lab interactions focused on character and competence development. There, we covered the counseling competencies associated with sustaining and healing.

Since that first training group, I've altered how I schedule each evening. Now I normally have the interactive lectures for two hours one evening (with a break in the middle), and the next week I facilitate two-hour intensive small group labs. I've found that a two-hour slot for the labs is more conducive to relationship building, connecting, intense interaction, and live counseling of one another.

Another best-practice alternative is to cover all the lecture/content material first—either the first year or the first semester—and then focus on the lab/competency area next. This method has the advantage of covering all the content first so that trainees are solidly grounded in biblical counseling theology/theory. However, in my thinking, that's outweighed by the disadvantage of an extended amount of time with a predominantly cognitive focus without the intimate relationship/community building time and without the focus on character and competence.

During this first semester, outside the meetings, trainees averaged one hour per week in assigned reading. They also were required to meet every other week with an assigned encouragement partner/spiritual friend (of the same gender) from the class. Trainees also met with me (or another mentor/supervisor) for one hour every other week.

LEAD Year One, Semester Two

During the second semester, our meeting schedule remained the same. The content focused on the final four of life's eight ultimate questions. Our training labs highlighted continued community building, character growth, and the development of the counseling competencies of reconciling and guiding. Trainees continued to spend one hour each week in outside reading and continued to meet every other week with their encouragement partners and every other week for supervision. They also completed a project where they developed their personal spiritual disciplines/spiritual workout routine.

At the end of the first year, every trainee was assessed in each of the 4Cs (see Appendix 10.1, available free online at https://rpmministries.org/ebc-resources/). They evaluated themselves, the group shared evaluations, their encouragement partner evaluated them, their supervisor/mentor evaluated them, and they completed a written exam. Each trainee then received a Level One LEAD Graduate Certificate in a formal ceremony during a church service.

LEAD Year Two, Semester One

The second year's meeting schedule remained the same. The content now focused on marriage and family life, while the small-group lab focused on marriage and family counseling.[4] We based the decision to focus on marriage and family issues on our congregational and community assessments.

Trainees continued to spend one hour each week in outside reading. They now began approximately two hours each week in supervised ministry. Some provided individual counseling, some offered marital or parental/family counseling, and some facilitated recovery/care/support groups. They learned how to lead groups by being a part of our intensive group labs. Trainees also met every other week for supervision. Most trainees voluntarily chose to continue meeting every other week (or even more often) with their encouragement partner, although they were now required to meet just once each month.

LEAD Year Two, Semester Two

The second semester's meeting schedule remained the same. The content and competence training now focused on depression and anxiety. The small-group labs also continued to be a place where community was built and character was molded. We based the decision to focus on mood disorders on our congregational and community assessments. As I noted in a previous chapter, I believe trainees gain more from extensive training in one issue than they do from brief coverage of many issues. They learn how to study and use the Scriptures to develop a helping approach to other issues.

In addition to one hour each week in outside reading, trainees wrote a paper where they developed their model of biblical counseling theory and practice related to a counseling issue of their choice. They continued providing two hours each week of supervised ministry, either in individual, marital, or parental counseling, or in small-group ministry. They also continued meeting for supervision and meeting with their encouragement partner for mutual spiritual friendship.

At the end of the second year, every trainee was again assessed in each of the 4Cs through self-assessment, group assessment, encouragement partner assessment, assessment from their supervisor, and a written exam (see Appendix 10.1). At the end of the training, each graduate received a Level Two LEAD Graduate Certificate.

---

4. For the material covered in these labs see Bob Kellemen, *Gospel-Centered Marriage Counseling* (Grand Rapids: Baker, 2020) and *Gospel-Centered Family Counseling* (Grand Rapids: Baker, 2020).

MEETING FOR 4C EQUIPPING

We can divide our thinking about in-person group meetings into teaching-oriented training and small-group lab-oriented training. However, they often morph into one another. In a lesson where truth is applied to life in the context of community, the class sometimes shifts spontaneously to a lab-like counseling time. At other times, the class shifts purposefully to a small-group discussion time or partner counseling time. Also, in a ministry where God's Word is viewed as relevant and sufficient, small-group labs have content components and material to cover, meaning that, at times, teaching modes are included in the lab training.

Transformational Teaching-Oriented Training

A confession: I don't like the word "lecture." It connotes being talked at—listening to a monologue. Too often that's our image of training in biblical counseling. That needs to change.

One section of one chapter can't address everything that a transformational teacher might want to implement. What it can do, and what I will do, is share five foundational transformational teaching principles that can shape how you equip your biblical counseling trainees. (See Appendix 10.2 for a sample lesson plan and lesson outline, available free online at https://rpmministries.org/ebc-resources/.)

Transformational Bible Teaching Is Comprehensive

We need to start with a definition of transformational teaching:

- Creative, interactive, engaging joint-exploration and two-way communication of truth (content) related to life (character) and ministry (competence) in the context of relationship (community).

Notice in this description that teaching is not simply about covering content. Instead, it comprehensively addresses all 4Cs. To train biblical counselors, we must think like and teach like biblical counselors—always relating truth to life in the context of relationships.

Transformational Teaching Is Student-Oriented

Notice from the definition that transformational teaching is not teacher-oriented, but student-oriented. Just like each section of this book begins with a list of ROLOs (Reader-Oriented Learning Objectives), so every lesson we teach should start with a list of SOLOs (Student-Oriented Learning Objectives) (see Appendix 10.2).

Those SOLOs should complete the following sentence for the 3Cs in the context of the fourth C. In the context of community, and based upon active engagement and participation in this lesson:

- The student will be able to know (content)…

- The student will be able to do (competence)…

- The student will be able to be (character)…

By thinking like this, we shift our focus from information to transformation. We no longer ask, "What information do I need to dump and download into my student's brain?" Instead, we pray, "Father, how can our time together (home) transform our heads, hearts, and hands?"

Transformational Bible Teaching Is Big-Picture Focused

What's the big idea? That's not a question asked by an agitated friend. Instead, it's the question asked by Haddon Robinson in his classic text on biblical preaching.[5] Effective communication demands a single theme. While your lesson will engage students in thinking about many ideas and applications, and while it will address all 4Cs, each lesson needs cohesiveness. What is the dominant idea or theme that unites the various points of the lesson?

For example, when I teach on the Trinity, I start with a simple big idea. *The Trinity is our model for biblical counseling ministry.* We discuss that single idea from a host of different perspectives, looking at a number of different passages. But everything zeroes in on how the relationship within the Trinity models the soul-to-soul connecting required of the caring, competent biblical counselor.

Transformational Bible Teaching Is Life-Changing

Thirty years ago, I learned four rhyming words that sound like a line from a Dr. Seuss book: hook, book, look, took. This little memory device from Larry Richards has shaped my teaching for three decades.[6]

---

5. Haddon Robinson, *Biblical Preaching* (Grand Rapids: Baker Academic, 2014).

6. Lawrence Richards and Gary Bredfeldt, *Creative Bible Teaching* (Chicago: Moody, 2020).

"Hook" engages students in considering the *why* questions: Why is this lesson important to me? Why should I even listen? In a sermon, it's the riveting illustration that introduces the vital importance of the message. In a lesson, it's the opening discussion/interaction question that helps students to ponder the real-life significance of the upcoming lesson material.

When teaching about the Trinity as our model for biblical counseling ministry, I tell my students about sixteen-year-old Aminah McKinnie of Madison, Mississippi, who confesses in *Newsweek* that she is beset by feelings of isolation mixed with longings to be connected.[7] I then propose that the solution to her disconnected soul is nothing less than Trinitarian theology. Next, I have students divide into pairs or small groups to discuss the following questions:

- Who do you know that is like Aminah—experiencing fleeting, fragmented relationships?

- To what degree does it shock you that Trinitarian theology is the solution to disconnected, unanchored souls?

Prepared to ponder the relevancy of the topic, we next turn to "the Book" (the Bible) and address what Richards calls "book." This answers the *what* question: What does the Bible say about our topic? What does the Bible teach about the Trinity?

Likely this is the part of a lesson that most of us think about when we think about teaching. It is the main thing, but it is *not* the only thing. It is central, but it is *not* exclusive.

Even with the content/book aspect of the lesson, creativity and engagement are essential. It still is not simply a lecture (see below for an introduction to creative Bible teaching methods).

Theologically speaking, this part of the lesson is *academic* theology—the vital foundation for teaching in biblical counseling. It includes *systematic* theology, where you outline the entire New Testament's teaching on the Trinity. It includes *biblical* theology, where you explore one author's teaching on the Trinity (I typically highlight John). It includes *exegetical* theology, where you explore in depth the teaching about the Trinity from one or two central passages (I typically highlight John 1, where you examine the mutual intimacy within the Trinity and John 17, where you explore the mutual glory shared by the Trinity). It also includes

---

7. Sharon Begley, "A World of Their Own," *Newsweek*, May 7, 2020, 52–56.

lexical theology, where you examine specific words used to describe the relationship within the Trinity ("glory" used numerous times in John 17, being one example).

As vital as "book" is, we don't stop there. Instead, interspersed throughout the lesson is the "look" element. "Look" addresses the *so what* question: So what difference should this make to my life? What personal application could I make to my life? I use PDQs—Prompting Discussion Questions—built into every lesson outline to help students ponder either individually or together how to apply the truth to their lives.

In theology, this is known as *spiritual* theology. It's a missing ingredient in much theological education. It links the head and the heart. It moves from information about God and the Bible to transformational application of the Bible to my life and relationships. I might ask a PDQ like, "Think of someone you could begin to enjoy more fully. How could that relationship more fully reflect the mutual enjoyment of the Trinity as described in John 1 and John 17?"

The "took" aspect of the lesson asks the *what now* question: What could I do with this truth now in my ministry? What are the ministry implications of this truth?

Theologically, this is *practical or pastoral* theology. It relates truth not just to our lives, but to how we do ministry. When we explore John 17, we note that the Trinity is an eternal mutual admiration society. Father and Son in John 17 are passionate about spreading each other's fame. We summarize that by noting that *it's all about him.* Life is not ultimately about us. So in a "took" ministry implication, we ponder a question such as, How would our counseling look different if we realized that counseling is not about us or about our counseling, but ultimately about helping our counselee to glorify God in the midst of their struggle with suffering and sin?

Transformational Bible Teaching Is Creative

The methods for creative Bible teaching are almost limitless. It's less important that we master all of them than it is that we're aware that lecturing is only one method among many. Consider a few methods for creative Bible teaching in biblical counseling:

- *Lecture:* Done well—with handouts, PowerPoint, illustrations, CDs/music, video/DVDs, teaching to the right brain and left brain, personal sharing, and passion—the lecture method is one of the most efficient ways to communicate blocks of truth.

- *Student Interaction:* I've already noted many examples such as opening "hook" discussions, interspersed "look" PDQs, and lesson ending took ministry application questions. You can group students in pairs, in small groups, or have the entire class interact. You can have prepared questions and/or allot time for spontaneous questions and answers.

- *Student Teaching:* We learn best what we teach, so assigning students parts of lessons to study, prepare, and present is very effective.

- *Student and Teacher Sharing:* Personal examples, stories, and illustrations enhance acquisition of knowledge, skill, and character.

- *Case Studies, Role-Playing, Counseling Observation, and Live Counseling:* While sometimes reserved for lab learning, I often incorporate these into the teaching-oriented training.

- *Fellowship and Worship:* I include prayer/praise, cheers/tears, worship CDs and DVDs, and testimony times in the teaching component.

- *Outside Assignments:* Required reading, research projects, personal application projects, ministry implication projects, and written papers are all effective methods to enhance learning.

- *Assessments:* Quizzes and exams keep students accountable and stretch their learning, especially when questions go beyond mere rote learning to concept understanding and application.

Transformational Small-Group Lab-Oriented Training

Two questions will help us organize our thinking about transformational small-group lab training. What is the climate or environment we hope to develop, and how do we cultivate it? What training methods can we use, and how do we implement them?

The Transformational Small-Group Lab Climate and How to Cultivate It

I've used the words "lab," "small group," and "small-group lab" interchangeably. Used alone, "lab" can have a clinical feel to it. Instead of real life lived together and *experiential* learning, it might picture artificial, forced connection and *experimental* learning. Saying "small-group-oriented training" might cause some to think that we are training people only or primarily to be small-group leaders. I use the phrase "small-group lab" to convey themes you've previously heard:

- Community is the container for equipping in content, character, and competency.

- We become effective biblical counselors by giving and receiving biblical counseling in community.

The authentic, intimate small-group environment provides the fertile soil in which we nurture competent biblical counselors.

In teaching, if we become overly dependent upon the lecture mode and content communication, then we suck the life out of our biblical counseling training. In small-group labs, if we become overly dependent on skill development, then we suck the air out of the one-another community environment. The lab as a place only to discuss case studies, or only to observe experts counsel, or only to practice skills through role-playing, becomes a sterile environment. Those are essential components of lab work, but they must exist within a genuine, secure small-group community.

So, in lab training, my first goal is to cultivate a climate where we experience biblical counseling together. We grow more like Christ as we receive *parakaletic* soul care for our suffering and as we receive *nouthetic* spiritual direction for our struggle against sin. We become more competent biblical counselors as we sustain, heal, reconcile, and guide one another.

How do we do this? It begins with a mindset, with a vision communicated consistently. The vision is that we are not a pack of lab rats. We are image bearers. We are here not simply to learn skills, but to minister to one another.

As leaders, we must model that vision. I did that when I shared with my first training group my image of myself as a ten-year-old boy in my father's oversized suit. In my first seminary small-group lab, two of my students had so caught the vision that on the first day they invited me to open up. One was a pastor's wife and the other was a pastor, and when the lab began, they asked me what the transition was like from pastor to professor and who was currently building into my life.

Rather than dismiss their care and concern so I could focus on the lesson plan, I shared openly. The group focused on me. I was on what became affectionately known as "the hot seat." The hot seat refers to *anytime the group shifts its focus from discussing the material to offering sustaining, healing, reconciling, and guiding to an individual.*

By responding to their invitation, I modeled the priority of "presence"—staying in the moment, dealing with what is happening in the room, focusing on the people in the group and the relationships among group members. Whether in the seminary setting or the local church setting, I've found that you rarely need to role-play because when you prioritize presence, you experience and engage in live biblical counseling with one another.

Authentic community is caught and learned by experience more than taught or read. When I consult, churches often bring me onsite to lead a small-group lab. In a lab, we'll talk about a question from *Gospel Conversations* or dabble in a role-play assignment. I'll say something like, "Bill, that question seems like it really hits home for you. Would you like to talk about it a bit more at a personal level?" After an hour of counseling Bill on the hot seat, he'll say, "Wow! In a second, we went from talking about counseling to my *being* counseled. That was amazing and so helpful personally."

Then someone else will chime in, "Bill, thank you for your courage to be so vulnerable and open. Not only did it help you personally, but I learned more in one hour of watching you being counseled than I would ever learn in hours of reading about counseling."

This also illustrates the need to invite intimacy, not to force it. While some labs stay clinical forever, I've observed others that are so bent on experiencing deep relationships that people feel guilty if they are not ready to go deep, or feel coerced into going deeper faster than they're ready. Knowing the difference is not always easy, but it begins with creating a safe environment—safe to go deep or safe not to until a person is ready.

The Transformational Small-Group Lab Methods and How to Implement Them

Don't think that the hot seat is *the* method you use. That turns a spontaneous, divinely appointed connection into a method. A grace-oriented community in which group members feel safe to speak the truth in love is the context for using a variety of lab-based methods.

Some methods are best used in conjunction with a training manual or book. I will use my biblical counseling training books *Gospel Conversations*, *Gospel-Centered Marriage Counseling*, and *Gospel-Centered Family Counseling* to illustrate some of these methods and how you could use them.

- Trainees come to class having read assigned content sections of *Gospel Conversations*. I facilitate discussions and respond to questions about principles and methods of biblical counseling. Often these quickly morph into real-life counseling situations.

- Before class, trainees complete a series of character development questions. We use this section of *Gospel-Centered Marriage Counseling* in several ways. Sometimes students pair up with their encouragement partners to share. Other times we start with a particular question, and the discussion soon morphs into live counseling. Other times I simply invite people to share: "Is there a particular question that raised something in your heart and life that you want us to help you with?" Again, these often shift spontaneously into real-life counseling interactions.

- Before class, trainees answer questions related to competency development. Some of these require the students to share how they might respond to a person with a particular issue. Others ask students to evaluate or discuss a case study. Still others suggest role-plays that they can practice with their encouragement partner or with the group.

- With any book or training manual, remember that it's a guide to prompt discussion, not a list of questions you must cover in an allotted amount of time. Allow the material to prime the pump and get the discussion going, and then use your biblical counseling skills to invite people to go deeper.

- Hold one another accountable for having read and engaged the material thoroughly *before* class. Then you don't have to cover all the content *in* class. You can accomplish this through the honor system, through quizzes covering the material, or through trainees showing you, their encouragement partner, or the group that they've completed the chapter questions.

We can categorize additional lab-training methods by thinking through increasing levels of on-the-job training.

- *Discuss Case Studies:* Facilitate a discussion of a case study with background information and presenting problem and have the group explore relevant biblical principles (theory) and how they would intervene and interact (methods).

- *Practice Meta-Skills:* Give students specific, brief assignments to practice specific skills such as listening or spiritual conversations. Often it's helpful to do this in triads: one person is the counselor, one person is the counselee, and the third person provides feedback. Then have the students rotate so that each person has occupied each role.

- *Use Triad Role-Play Counseling:* This combines and goes beyond case studies and meta-skills. Share a prepared case study, then have one student play the counselee, another student play the counselor, and a third student provide feedback.

- *Use Group Observation Role-Play Counseling:* Here, instead of just one person observing, the entire class observes one student role-play counseling another, and then they all provide feedback.

- *Use Observation of Live Counseling by the Trainer:* Either a class member, a church member, or a member of the community is counseled live by the trainer while the class observes. After the session ends, the trainer/counselor, the counselee, and the class interact about what they observed and learned and ask questions for clarification and instruction.

- *Use Live Counseling by the Trainee with the Trainer Sitting In:* The class observes while a trainee counsels either another class member, a church member, or a member of the community. The trainer/supervisor is in the room and periodically offers feedback, shares probing questions, and occasionally and briefly counsels and then hands things back to the trainee. Everyone interacts about the counseling afterward.

- *Use Live Counseling by the Trainee Without the Trainer Sitting In:* The trainer and the class observe the student counseling someone live and all interact at the end of the session.[8]

---

8. See Appendix 10.1 for a sample Biblical Counseling Competency Evaluation Form.

Again, in the counseling labs I lead, the vast majority of counseling is live counseling of one another. Some of the live counseling is preplanned. At other times, the live counseling occurs spontaneously through the hot-seat method described previously.

Frequently during the discussion of the live counseling, the trainee/counselor ends up on the hot seat. A group member might note, "Barb, you seemed a tad disengaged in the session. Did you sense that at all?" Perhaps Barb acknowledges her disengagement and the group invites Barb to ponder with them what may be happening in her heart that she wants to work on.

Or, going even deeper, perhaps Barb does not acknowledge that she was relationally distant. Other group members express a similar experience of Barb keeping them at arm's length. As the discussion unfolds, Barb disengages from the group. As the leader, you may discern that the timing is not right and you need to address this later. Or you may invite Barb either to discuss it now with you in front of the group or later in supervision. "Barb, it seems that you may be disengaging a bit with us *even while we give you feedback about disengaging*. Would you like to talk with me about that now, would you like for us to interact about that later during supervision, or would you like to think about it, ponder it, pray about it, and maybe share with us next week?"

Now your small-group lab has gone full circle. You created a safe place to speak the truth in love. Barb spoke the truth in love to her counselee, but this raised issues that appear to be present in Barb's life. Now you've invited Barb to allow you and the group to enter her life. This is the essence of transformational small-group lab-oriented training in biblical counseling.

OUTSIDE TRAINING FOR 4C EQUIPPING

Small-group labs in which members sustain, heal, reconcile, and guide one another are foundational for equipping in biblical counseling. To that foundation you can add training that occurs outside the context of your meetings. Two categories summarize this area: meetings with a Paul, a Barnabas, and a Timothy, and completing outside training assignments.

Transformational Meetings with a Paul, a Barnabas, and a Timothy

I've always used the time-honored, biblical, threefold equipping model.

- Meeting with a Supervisor/Mentor: A Paul or a Priscilla

- Meeting with an Encouragement Partner: A Barnabas or a Ruth

- Meeting with a Protégée: A Timothy or a Euodia—Philippians 4:2

Depending on the size of your group and whether you've trained any co-trainers, you may be the only supervisor. If you are, then keeping your training group to a maximum of twelve is essential. In my model, you'd meet every other week with each person, in addition to your other ministry commitments. Twelve is also an ideal maximum size for the joint small-group meetings.

If you do have co-trainers, then you can train more than twelve people at one time because you can divide the supervisory roles and the small groups. Where possible, it's helpful if each trainee at some point in the course of their training has access to each supervisor. It's also helpful if each supervisor/trainer facilitates each small group at some point.

Transformational Supervision Meetings

In my model of supervision, the supervisory role is multifaceted, and it evolves over the two-year period. I'm *always* seeking to help each trainee mature in each of the 4Cs. We meet every other week and spend time discussing questions about the content we've covered and its application to life. During these meetings, I also provide sustaining, healing, reconciling, and guiding—biblical counseling. These meetings assist in the development of Christlike character. They also develop counseling competencies because one of the best ways to learn to be a biblical counselor is to be counseled by an experienced biblical counselor.

During consultation, I'm sometimes asked, "Are your trainees really open to being counseled? Do mature people like this really have enough issues to work on?" Once you start teaching about truth applied to life, once you start opening up illustratively about your own life, and once you create a safe small-group atmosphere, trainees open up. And when we realize that biblical counseling is simply intensive and intentional focused discipleship, then we know that we all have enough issues to work on until we reach heaven.

By the second semester of training, I have encouragement partners record their counseling of each other. Much of my supervision now involves listening to portions of recordings and helping trainees to assess and develop their counseling. As with the labs, many times the way trainees relate as a counselor opens windows to their own heart issues. So listening to a recorded counseling session can quickly shift to counseling the trainee. By the second year, trainees are being recorded offering live counseling to church and/or community members.

Transformational Encouragement Partner Meetings

During the first year, I have trainees meet with their encouragement partners every other week. In the first semester, trainees provide mutual sustaining, healing, reconciling, and guiding for each other.

By the second semester, they are more focused on developing counseling competencies. At times, they work through role-play assignments from *Gospel Conversations*. Most of the time, they take turns counseling one another over real-life issues.

As I noted earlier, the second year they're required to meet only once per month. They decide what they want to focus on. Typically they've built such strong spiritual friendships that they meet almost weekly and continue to discuss and apply content, encourage one another in Christlike character development, and develop their counseling competencies—often by continuing to counsel one another.

Transformational Protégée Meetings

Normally I do not have trainees meet with protégées until the end of the first year. (I discuss in the next two chapters the appropriate paperwork and safeguards once these meetings begin.) These meetings involve live-recorded counseling. I screen and assign all counselees based upon their issues and the expertise of the trainee.

The trainees listen to their recordings and evaluate themselves. I listen to portions of the recordings with the trainees, and we assess and evaluate their counseling competencies. Often this discussion shifts to issues in the trainee's life, and we shift back to their character development.

In consultation I'm often asked, "But will people really agree to counsel with a layperson?" Most do, especially when they understand the level of training, know it's supervised, and understand that the supervisor can become involved. I'm also asked, "Don't people feel squeamish about being recorded while being counseled?" Some may at first, but they report that they barely think about the recording once the session begins. They know how we safeguard the recordings and how the recordings assist their biblical counselor to help them more effectively.

Transformational Training Assignments

I've used a wide variety of outside training assignments. Required reading is standard. Completing assignments from *Gospel-Centered Counseling* and *Gospel Conversations* is standard. Periodic quizzes are typical and year-end exams are standard.

Homework assignments vary from semester to semester and group to group. The first year, students develop their own spiritual disciplines/spiritual workout routine. The final semester of the final year, students research and write a twelve- to fifteen-page project on a counseling issue they choose. By choice, many students attend local, regional, or national counseling conferences or our weekend conferences.

While it is not an assignment per se, at least once each semester we plan a fun event. It might be attending a sporting event, dining out together, enjoying a cookout at someone's home, or throwing a seasonal party. Counseling is serious ministry. Counselors need to have fun. And counseling training groups need to understand that they don't have to go deep every second.

DISCIPLE-MAKING CHAMPIONS

Transformational Training Methods

As part of the 4E Ministry Training Strategy Questionnaire, two dozen best-practice churches responded to the question, What equipping methods/means/style do you use to accomplish your content, competence, character, and community objectives? The following list collates the most common themes.

- *Transformational Teaching:* Creative PowerPoint lectures, discussion groups, video presentations, question-and-answer sessions, case studies, brainstorming, personal application, ministry implications, Bible studies, quizzes, exams, student teaching.

- *Transformational Small Groups/Labs:* Observing experienced counselors, case studies, role-playing, completing practice exercises, sharing authentically, being counseled, doing personal-growth exercises, triads, and sharing personal stories, prayer, and praise.

- *Transformational Outside Equipping:* Meeting with supervisors/mentors; completing homework assignments, required reading, research papers; completing personal improvement projects and personal sanctification projects; having accountability partners; creating self-counsel projects; counseling under supervision; fellowshipping and scheduling fun times; attending outside conferences; journaling.

COMMENCEMENT: ORGANIZING THE ORGANISM

Pastor Peter Randolph described how in the *Invisible Institution* arrangements were made for conducting the exercises. Following in their footsteps, this chapter helps us organize the organism and structure for spontaneity. In fact, the whole book has offered that focus.

Tracking where we've been so far:

- We've learned how to help an entire congregation catch and cast a vision for informal one-another ministry and formal biblical counseling—Envisioning.

- We've learned how to cultivate a climate where the entire congregation owns the MVP-C vision and how to nurture a family and build a team—Enlisting.

- We've learned how to oversee comprehensive, transformational 4C training—Equipping.

From my research and consulting, I can guarantee you that if you've taken your church this far, you're far ahead of the vast majority of churches. I can also tell you that many of the churches that get this far experience a bit of panic once their first group graduates and they start training their second group. They say, "Too many spinning plates! How do we shepherd our graduates while we also train our second equipping group? Help!"

Help is on the way. We now shift to our fourth E—Empowering godly ministers for biblical counseling ministry.

In our final two chapters, we'll learn how to oversee the ongoing organizing of the organism by leading ministries that are built to last, that grow from good to great, and that leave a legacy of loving leaders.

Don't feel overwhelmed. By God's grace, in his strength, and for his glory others have succeeded—and so will you. Not somehow, but triumphantly.

GROWING TOGETHER: QUESTIONS FOR REFLECTION, DISCUSSION, AND APPLICATION

1. On the continuum of spontaneity and structure, where would you place yourself? How might that impact how you process and apply this chapter?

2. Regarding the average length of training in biblical counseling:

   a. How surprised are you at the typical duration (one hundred hours over one to two years)? How do you think your congregation would respond to that? How could you prepare them?

   b. As you reflect on your biblical counseling training in your church, what duration do you think is most appropriate? Why?

3. Of the elements of transformational teaching-oriented training:

   a. Which do you think are most important?

   b. Which is already naturally your strength? Which might you need to work on, and how?

4. Regarding the transformational small-group lab training:

   a. How surprised are you by the relational focus of the lab

training? How similar or dissimilar is it to what you have experienced? To what you would have anticipated?

    b. What elements of the lab training would you most want to incorporate? Why? How will you do that?

5. Concerning the threefold equipping model:

    a. How have Paul/Priscilla, Barnabas/Ruth, and Timothy/Euodia relationships impacted your life and ministry?

    b. How could you use each of these transformational relationships in your biblical counseling training?

PART 4

EMPOWERING GODLY MINISTERS FOR MINISTRY

Empowering

When I arrive at the fourth E in my seminar "The 4E Ministry Training Strategy," I show two PowerPoint slides that picture two forces fighting against the successful oversight of equipped biblical counselors. One slide pictures spinning plates, the other slide shows an elephant in a living room.

SPINNING PLATES AND
ORGANIZING THE ORGANISM

When I talk about spinning plates, I share that I have good news, bad news, and more good news. The good news: If you've progressed through envisioning, enlisting, and equipping, then you are far ahead of the curve. Your church will be one of the few that comprehensively addresses envisioning, enlisting, and equipping.

The bad news: Some that do get this far sometimes crash and burn shortly after takeoff. Why? No one has thought through what it means to organize the organism.

Not one to end on bad news, I share more good news: There are answers to practical questions about overseeing biblical counseling ministries—questions like these:

- Now that we've launched the ministry, how do we keep it running—especially while we have a myriad of other plates spinning?

- How do we balance structure and spontaneity?

- How do we nourish the relational focus while addressing procedural and policy issues?

Chapter 11 portrays the relational processes that help churches to deploy and employ empowered ministers for ministry to the congregation and community. It explores the proactive mindset that's necessary to move from training to implementation, from implementation to ongoing growth, and from growth to passing the baton of ministry. It demonstrates how to oversee the biblical counseling ministry by organizing the organism through launching ministries built to last, leading ministries from good to great, and leaving a lasting legacy of loving leaders.

ELEPHANTS IN THE ROOM
AND PROTECTING MINISTRIES

No one likes to talk about ethical and legal concerns. They're often the unspoken elephants in the room that motivate church leaders to squelch biblical counseling ministries. While we cannot allow the unwise and unnecessary fear of people to stop us from serving God, we must take ethical and legal concerns seriously. Even more importantly, we must take seriously God's law of love that demands that our ministry remain above reproach.

Chapter 12 explains that by following sound principles of ethical behavior, legal norms, wise practices, and biblical standards, churches can confidently launch and lead biblical counseling ministries. Chapter 12 teaches us how to care carefully.

EMPOWERED BY GOD FOR GOD'S GLORY

I intend the word "empowering" to indicate that our work is not done after we've envisioned, enlisted, and equipped our biblical counseling team. We need to deploy them into ministry. We need to develop the type of ongoing ministry structures that enable our biblical counselors to employ their gifts for God's glory through God's power.

With this understanding in mind, one final time we consider our ROLOs: Reader-Oriented Learning Objectives. Through your active reading and application of the two chapters in this section, you'll be equipped to...

- Oversee the ongoing organizing of the organism through God's empowering for God's glory by administrating ministries, mentoring/supervising ministers, and passing the baton of ministry (chapter 11).

- Care carefully by following sound principles of ethical behavior, legal norms, wise practices, and biblical standards (chapter 12).

How do you oversee people in a caring way that builds community as you impact your community? How do you care carefully? Section 4 teaches us how.

11

Overseeing Ministries
for God's Glory

Organizing the Organism

I was the ripe young age of thirty-one when our initial two-year LEAD biblical counseling group graduated. All twelve members who started went on to finish. All twelve spent at least the next two years ministering to members of our church and community.

One graduate led our New Hope Fellowship group, ministering every week to twenty people who were seeking to overcome various addictions. Two female graduates launched and led a Beauty for Ashes group, working each week with ten women who had been sexually abused. Another graduate led a weekly Parenting Adolescents group, ministering to twelve parents each week. One graduate became my co-trainer for the next round of teaching. He ministered to twelve trainees and counseled two counselees per week. The other seven graduates provided an average of two biblical counseling sessions per week for a total of fourteen people counseled weekly. That's more than seventy people ministered to each week by our biblical counseling team.

I share this story to illustrate the following:

- By God's empowering, it can be done—and you can do it too.

- Even with God's empowering, there's still work to be done.

- To oversee the work that needs to be done, we need to organize the organism—for God's glory.

HOW DO YOU PULL IT OFF?

You may say, "Well, Bob, your process was made much easier by the fact that you were in a large church." Perhaps. Yet, a host of circumstances made it a wild ride as we simultaneously sailed and refitted our ship. Our church had never had a Counseling Pastor, much less tried to launch a counseling ministry. At the time, there were few books or churches we could turn to for wisdom. We weren't quite making it up as we went along, but it was close.

Though my title was Counseling and Discipleship Pastor, only 25 percent of my time was allotted to the LEAD ministry. The other 75 percent included my schedule of counseling twenty people per week, leading an Adult Bible Fellowship of more than four hundred people (a church within a church), performing all the traditional pastoral-shepherding functions, and that dreaded *m* word: "meetings." In addition to ongoing supervision of the twelve LEAD graduates, one graduate and I were co-leading a second group of twenty-four LEAD trainees.

While I enjoyed the blessing of an excellent administrative assistant, her role was part-time and she also served two other pastors. She was able to devote just three hours weekly to the LEAD ministry.

We had no budget. Paperwork costs came out of a general staff fund, and the only biblical counseling resources we had were books I bought and donated to the church library.

Now you may say, "Okay, Bob, I guess the process wasn't all that easy. In fact, now you're scaring me. How in the world can people pull off the oversight of a biblical counseling ministry?"

You Are Not Alone

If you're concerned about how to oversee your biblical counseling ministry, you are not alone. Our Disciple-Making Champions share your struggle.

DISCIPLE-MAKING CHAMPIONS

Overseeing the Ministry

At the end of the 4E Ministry Training Strategy Questionnaire, I asked the two dozen best-practice churches to share the strengths and weaknesses of their equipping ministries. By far the greatest weakness related to overseeing people once they moved from train-ees to graduates. Leaders shared struggles such as the following:

- We start well with those interested in biblical counseling, but the ministry seems to fizzle after the initial equipping push.

- Overseeing the ministry is an area of particular weakness for us right now.

- Our greatest weaknesses relate to administrative structures and systems.

- We've grown quickly, which has allowed many things to slip through the cracks, and we don't feel we're where we need to be in terms of ongoing oversight.

- We don't really have the organizational skills or administrative personnel to oversee our growing ministry as well as we'd like.

- We don't have the policies and procedures in place yet that allow us to provide the type of oversight that we know we need.

Clearly there's a need for organizing the organism. It does no good and wastes valuable time to envision, enlist, and equip, only to stop short of the ongoing administrating of the ministry.

God-Sized Dreams Bring Glory to God, Not to Us

The challenge is so large that we have no hope of achieving it *apart from* God's empowering. That's why *before* God calls us to equip his people in Ephesians 4:11–16, he reminds us in Ephesians 3:20 that he "is able to do immeasurably more than all we ask or imagine, according to his power that is at work within us." He also reminds us that it's not about us. It's all about him. "To him be glory in the church and in Christ Jesus throughout all generations, for ever and ever! Amen" (verse 21).

Yes, we'll explore our role in overseeing the biblical counseling ministry. However, we must see our role as God-glorifying, Christ-centered, and Spirit-dependent. We don't empower, employ, and deploy people in our power. We empower people with and through God's empowering for God's glory.

Let's orient ourselves again. You have these equipped biblical counselors, and now you need to learn how to oversee the shepherding of these ministers. As you do, you can shape your thinking about organizing the organism around three relational practices.

- Launching Ministries Built to Last: Administrating ministries

- Leading Ministries from Good to Great: Mentoring and supervising ministers

- Leaving a Lasting Legacy of Loving Leaders: Passing the baton of ministry

LAUNCHING MINISTRIES BUILT TO LAST: AD-MINISTRATING MINISTRIES

As explained earlier, I sometimes hyphenate the words "ad-ministrating" and "ad-ministering." I do this to indicate that there is nothing inherently non-ministerial or nonrelational about administration. Paul penned the pastoral epistles to mentor Timothy and Titus to be relational overseers: "I am writing you these instructions so that, if I am delayed, you will know how people ought to conduct themselves in God's household, which is the church of the living God" (1 Timothy 3:14–15). "The reason I left you in Crete was that you might put in order what was left unfinished and appoint elders in every town, as I directed you" (Titus 1:5).

Ad-ministrating a biblical counseling ministry requires that we proactively and relationally address unfinished matters left after our envisioning, enlisting, and equipping. As you deploy biblical counselors, I recommend that you…

- Evaluate: Testing ministers

- Graduate and Congratulate: Commissioning and affirming ministers

- Designate: Connecting ministers to assigned ministries

- Create: Implementing new ministries

- Automate: Organizing ministry policies and procedures

- Formulate: Developing a ministry budget

- Communicate: Telling your ministry story

Evaluate: Testing Ministers

In organizing the organism, it helps to think chronologically and sequentially. Imagine that you've just concluded your last meeting of your nine-month or two-year equipping ministry. Now what? What needs to happen before you can deploy your equipped counselors?

First, you need to evaluate them to be sure that they are indeed equipped counselors. There are many reasons to assess trainees before they become graduates, and there are many potential areas of assessment to consider. Nothing tells us why to assess and what to assess better than Romans 15:14. Remember that in this verse Paul says he is convinced that the believers at Rome are competent. "Convinced" means to be inwardly certain because of *external evidence*. While Paul does not tell us how he assessed their competency, he does tell us what evidence he looked for—the 4Cs of biblical content, Christlike character, counseling competence, and Christian community.

There are also legal/ethical reasons to evaluate trainees (see chapter 12). You want to be able to demonstrate, objectively, their level of qualification for biblical counseling. There are practical reasons for assessing trainees. When you see weaknesses, you can focus on helping them to grow and mature in those areas. When you see a pattern of weakness, it helps you to assess the effectiveness of *your* training. It demonstrates areas where you need to grow as a trainer, in ongoing supervision and in the next round of training.

Yet there's no better reason to evaluate trainees than the biblical reason. Before you say to someone, "I am convinced that you are competent to counsel," you need to be able to back up those words with external evidence. And there is no better assessment model than the biblical 4Cs.

If in your training you use something other than the 4Cs, be sure to communicate your training goals throughout the enlisting and equipping process. From your profile of a nurtured graduate (see Appendix 6.1) onward, everyone should know what a successful graduate looks like. That portrait of a nurtured trainee becomes your gatekeeper, your standard that you use to evaluate trainees.

Evaluating Biblical Content

As chapter 10 illustrated, at the end of each year of training, I assess every trainee in each of the 4Cs (see Appendix 10.1 for sample assessments). Quality assessment focuses on the specific student-oriented learning objectives and specific content taught during the training. In the case of my training, that means assessing mastery of the material related to life's eight ultimate questions.

Written assessment can include objective sections such as true/false, multiple choice, fill-in, and matching. They also can include subjective sections with short answer and essay questions that seek to discern how well the student relates truth to life and ministry (as Appendix 10.1 demonstrates, this is the focus of my exams). In addition to written assessment, you can measure content acquisition and application through your observation of the trainees during lab and through listening to your trainees' recorded sessions.

Evaluating Counseling Competence

Your evaluation will target the areas of competency that you focused on in your training. In my setting, that means assessing how well trainees demonstrate the sustaining GRACE relational competencies, the healing RESTS relational competencies, the reconciling PEACE(E) relational competencies, and the guiding FAITH(H) relational competencies (see Appendix 10.1).

There are several effective ways to measure relational competencies. During your group time, if you have role-playing and live counseling, then you and the entire group can offer immediate, specific feedback of strengths and weaknesses. Additionally, at the last meeting of each year, your group can spend the entire time sharing candid feedback about the competency growth you've seen and the areas of growth you believe each person needs to develop further.

If you pair your trainees with partners for role-playing and live counseling, and if these are recorded, then you, the partner, and the trainee can all share verbal and written feedback. If during your training the trainees provide any live recorded counseling, then you, the trainee, and the counselee can all provide feedback. (See Appendices 10.1 and 11.1 for sample evaluation forms, available free online at https://rpmministries.org/ebc-resources/.)

Evaluating Christlike Character

There are various assessments that seek to measure levels of spiritual maturity. In my training, I do a pre-training, mid-training, and post-training comparison using the Redeemed Personality Inventory (RPI) that builds upon my training focus (see Appendix 6.1). Trainees complete a self-assessment at the three points noted. Their encouragement partner and I also complete an RPI assessment of the trainees at the end of the first and second year of training.

Given the relational component discussed in chapters 8 and 9, I also use feedback from the trainer(s), the encouragement partner, and from the group. Throughout the training, as different trainees are counseled in class, they receive loving feedback about perceived areas of spiritual maturity—both strengths and areas for further growth. As with competency issues, at the last meeting of each year we spend our entire time sharing candid feedback about Christlike character growth and development.

Evaluating Christian Community

While somewhat subjective, there are ways to get at a trainee's level of growth in Christian community. Measures include attendance, attitude, and engagement in the lab small groups, in the supervision meetings, and in the encouragement partner meetings. Assessment in this area addresses more than whether trainees are *practicing* the skills of sustaining, healing, reconciling, and guiding. It evaluates how well, in a *one-another context*, the trainees are *embodying* sustaining, healing, reconciling, and guiding.

My definition of Christian community emphasizes the horizontal spiritual disciplines of communion with the body of Christ and the vertical spiritual disciplines of communion with Christ. Therefore, I ask each graduate to assess how well they are implementing their Personal Spiritual Workout Routine/Plan (see chapter 9 and see Appendix 10.1).

What If a Trainee Is Not Approved?

This chapter focuses on the formal model of equipping trainees for ongoing, intensive biblical counseling. In the informal model of saturating the congregation with one-another ministers, I don't suggest a pass/fail assessment. If there is any assessment, it should focus on the quality of the training so it can be continually improved.

In the formal model, if the trainee is approved, then we joyfully move to the next step of graduate and congratulate. But what happens if your various means of evaluation blend together to suggest that the trainee is not ready to become a graduate?

First, pre-warn. Even in the initial interview process you should make it clear that graduation is based upon assessment in the 4Cs. Then, throughout your training, discuss any patterns of weaknesses and co-create a plan of growth. It should never come as a surprise to trainees that their graduation is in jeopardy.

Second, be gentle. Affirm their growth and worth in Christ. Lovingly explain the objective and subjective measures that indicate any lack of readiness. Help them to assess their own self-assessment. Do they think they are ready? Are there areas they think they need to work on?

Third, plan together the possible next steps. If it is a personal or character issue, then receiving biblical counseling may be in order. If it is a competency issue, then perhaps retaking the training would be suggested. Or, it is possible that the person should be matched with another ministry. They could still use their training in one-another ministry, but they would not offer ongoing biblical counseling under your ministry.

However, in my four church ministries, I've never had a trainee not graduate. I've had situations where, at the end of the first year, both the trainee and I saw red flags that needed to be addressed. By God's grace they were addressed, and the trainee graduated and was used by God.

What If a Trainee Drops Out?

On a few rare occasions, I've had trainees stop the training. If that occurs, the first response should be a candid conversation discussing the trainee's reasons for wanting to stop along with a reminder of the initial commitment that the trainee made. In some cases, the person may recommit at this point. If not, then an exit interview is important. Seek to be sure that no bridges are burned, and seek to learn what your ministry might be able to do better in the future.

Graduate and Congratulate: Commissioning and Affirming Ministers

The more likely and likable occurrence involves your trainees becoming graduates. That requires celebration! At the very least, provide them with a certificate. If at all possible, offer a public commissioning with prayer and testimonies.

As I noted in the introduction, some churches provide a full-blown graduation ceremony. While I've never done that, I have always hosted a party for graduates and their families.

Designate: Connecting Ministers to Assigned Ministries

When someone graduates from high school, college, or graduate school, the obvious questions are, What's next? What am I qualified to do? Where and how do I use my training? The same is true with your biblical counseling graduates.

To answer those questions, return to a form like the Profile of a LEAD Nurtured Graduate (Appendix 6.1). What were the initial options—individual counseling, marital counseling, family/parental counseling, small-group leadership, or something else?

Within those parameters, you want to garner a mutual decision between the graduate and yourself about the best fit for them in the biblical counseling ministry. Based upon your church and community assessments, where are the needs? What is the graduate passionate about and best gifted and equipped to offer?

Create: Implementing New Ministries

In some cases, the placement answer may be simple. Individual counseling may be the extent of your biblical counseling ministry—and that is wonderful. In other cases, as has often been the case with my graduates, we determined that they should start a new ministry—often a group-focused ministry.

I previously mentioned two female graduates who used their LEAD training to launch and lead a Beauty for Ashes group for women who had been sexually abused. Since our church never had such a ministry, we were creating an entirely new ministry. We used a modified 4E process in launching it. In three months, we worked through the envisioning and enlisting process.

For further equipping, they immersed themselves in an intensive one-week Christian training course on sexual abuse recovery. They had each done their second-year research project on this issue, and they continued to read and develop their awareness. They also spent time that summer observing me counseling people who had been sexually abused.

For the fourth E of empowering, we developed expectations, reporting responsibilities, paperwork, policies, and procedures. We obtained approval from the church for the launch of this new ministry. We decided how they would lead the group and what materials they would use. We obtained a place to meet that would maintain privacy and confidentiality. We developed a plan for how they would communicate about the group's launch, purpose, and function. And we created a safe, confidential system for women who were interested to contact them. We also organized our plans for my ongoing supervision of these two graduates. Three months after graduation, they launched Beauty for Ashes and ministered to ten women every week.

Automate: Organizing Ministry Policies and Procedures

"Automate" may seem like an odd label. However, I use it to stress that organizing ministry policies and procedures streamlines your process *so that you have more time for people.* This is where many people get confused and many training ministries make a major mistake. The false mindset says, "I don't want to focus all my time on paperwork. I just want to do people ministry." I would counter, "Get your systems in place and they will run themselves so you can focus your time and energy on people—organize the organism."

Appendix 11.1 provides a thorough, detailed Policy and Procedure Manual. Since every church situation is unique, no policy and procedure manual fits everyone, so simply view Appendix 11.1 as one sample. The Policy and Procedure Manual highlights three areas: intake procedures, welcome form/consent form, and record keeping. Because these are detailed in the appendix, the following material simply highlights how they are used and why they are important.

Intake Procedures: Triage

I think of intake procedures as triage—who is counseled, by whom, when, and why? Through the Intake Procedure Form, the Initial Intake Form, and the Ministry Guidelines Form (see Appendix 11.1), you develop a step-by-step policy that determines how you handle requests for counseling. Your intake policies and procedures should include the following:

- *Who is counseled?* Only church members/attendees? People from the community?

- *How are counseling requests prioritized?* By severity of the issue? By the ability, giftedness, and training of the team members? By whether the person is a member/attender or from the community? By the availability of the counseling team?

- *Who provides the counseling, and why?* Is referral made to one of the staff pastors? The counseling pastor? One of the trained LEAD counselors? An outside counseling agency? A medical doctor?

- *Who makes the decisions?* The counseling pastor/LEAD director? A trained administrative assistant?

- *What steps are taken when a counselee is assigned to a LEAD counselor?* What are the step-by-step procedures that the counselee must take? That the trainer, director, or administrative assistant must take? That the LEAD counselor must take?

- *What forms must be completed?* Who completes which forms? Where are they kept? Who sees which forms, and why?

- *What is the reporting structure?* How is information about counseling cases conveyed, and to whom?

- *Where do counselors and counselees meet?* What are the policies regarding proper meeting etiquette, safeguards, privacy, meeting with a person of the opposite gender, and confidentiality?

- *What is the supervision policy?* Who sees whom, and how often?

Welcome Form/Consent Form

Chapter 12 expands upon the legal and ethical issues related to informed consent—counselees have a right to know the scope and nature of the biblical counseling you offer. Appendix 11.1 contains a Welcome Form, a Consent Form, and a Consent to Minister to a Minor Child Form. The forms must be read, explained and discussed, completed, signed, dated, and kept in the counselee's file.

The Welcome Form describes in two pages or less your philosophy and practice of biblical counseling. Through the Welcome Form and Consent Form, prospective counselees gain an introduction to what types of counseling you offer, your definition of biblical counseling, what you call your counseling, what your goals are, your confidentiality policy, your appointment structure, the training level of your counselors, what commitments you make to your counselee, and what commitments you expect of your counselee.

Record Keeping

Proper record keeping not only maintains ethical and legal standards, it enhances communication and streamlines your processes. I include the following record keeping forms in my Policy and Procedure Manual (see Appendix 11.1):

- LEAD Biblical Counseling Ministry Goals Form

- LEAD Biblical Counseling Ministry Personal Information Form

- LEAD Permission to Record and Review Meetings Form

- Authorization for Release of Information (to Your Counseling Ministry)

- Authorization to Release Information (from Your Counseling Ministry)

- LEAD Biblical Counseling Record Sheet

- LEAD Biblical Counseling Tape Self-Evaluation

- LEAD Individual Biblical Counseling Evaluation

- LEAD Marital Biblical Counseling Evaluation

- LEAD Family Biblical Counseling Evaluation

- LEAD Biblical Counseling Commencement Summary

Formulate: Developing a Ministry Budget

As I noted, in my first ministry, we barely had a budget. I'm not saying this is the best-practice model, but I am saying you can run an excellent biblical counseling ministry on a limited budget if need be.

Other churches have a more extensive budget designated for their biblical counseling ministry. Faith Church in Lafayette, Indiana, organizes their budget around initial expenses, the annual counseling budget, and next steps.

Initial Counseling Ministry Expenses

Under initial expenses, budget categories might include these:

- Resource library for counselors and counselees

- Counseling training handouts/notes

- Counseling filing cabinet for secure storage of confidential counseling files

- Pastoral/trainer salary/stipend

- Secretarial/administrative support salary/stipend

Keep two things in mind in these categories. First, start slow to grow large and stay long. For example, you don't need the Library of Congress when you start. Based upon your needs assessment, purchase resources that are most pertinent to the needs of your congregation and community. Second, be creative. For example, ask for donations of quality biblical counseling resources. With secretarial support, many ministries can begin with volunteer staffing. Some churches ask their trainees to pay for the cost of producing counseling training notes.

Annual Counseling Budget

Related to your annual counseling ministry expenses, budget categories to consider may include these:

- Insurance increases due to counseling liability

- Paper and copying costs for counseling forms

- Expanding the resource library for counselors and counselees

- Pastoral/trainer salary/stipend

- Secretarial/administrative support salary/stipend

- Additional training for trainees, graduates, and trainers

- Advertising/marketing

- Attorney/consulting fees

- Website fees for online biblical counseling record keeping

Next Steps Budget

For larger counseling ministries, a few additional budget line items might include these:

- A dedicated phone line

- A Director of Counseling (part-time/full-time scheduler/organizer)

- Expanded advertising—mailings, business cards, brochures, website/blog

Counseling Ministry Income

In chapter 12, related to legal issues, I recommend that charging for counseling services is an unwise best practice for a *local church ministry*. However, there are a few other potential sources of counseling ministry income.

Some churches charge a cancellation fee. Some churches generate some income through donations to the counseling ministry. Other churches cover their resource expenses through selling resources at cost to counselees. However, most of the twenty-four best-practice churches covered their counseling budget through specific ministry line items in their overall annual church budget.

Communicate: Telling Your Ministry Story

With the word "communicate," I'm addressing what some would call advertising or marketing. I like to call it *ministry-based marketing*. You tell your ministry story by providing *free* ministry resources. A primary way to do this in today's world is through social media. You post blogs on counseling and Christian living topics. You provide links to free resources on your ministry social media pages.

Another primary way to share your story is word of mouth through counselees whose lives have been changed. I've never had to advertise my local church counseling or the counseling of a LEAD ministry. More than enough referrals came via word of mouth.

To communicating clearly and with excellence, you can create a ministry brochure (online and hard copy). Most of what can appear in a brochure comes directly from your MVP-C Statement. Add to that your ministry name and logo, testimonials, and contact information, and you have a ready-made ministry brochure.

LEADING MINISTRIES FROM GOOD TO GREAT: MENTORING AND SUPERVISING MINISTERS

Continuing our chronological journey, you've evaluated and graduated your biblical counselors. You've designated where they will serve and, in some cases, co-created their new ministry. Behind the scenes, you've automated the ministry policies and procedures and formulated the ministry budget. With everything in place, you've communicated to a congregation and community in need of biblical counseling.

Now your trainees have moved from graduates to ministers. They're flying solo for the first time, likely with trepidation. However, you remind them that they are not alone—Christ is always with them, you are there for them, and they are there for each other. There are two primary means of ongoing training to help scared soloists grow into confident and even more competent pilots: mentoring through continuing education, and supervision in individual and group formats. The Disciple-Making Champions below demonstrate that there are many creative ways to assure that graduates keep growing.

DISCIPLE-MAKING CHAMPIONS

Continuing Education and Ongoing Supervision

As part of the 4E Ministry Training Strategy Questionnaire, two dozen best-practice churches responded to the question, Once trainees become graduates, what ongoing training and continuing education do you offer? The following list collates typical responses.

- Four times per year we have a four-hour continuing education session.

- We offer three all-day in-services annually.

- We encourage our graduates to attend a biblical counseling conference annually.

- Graduates attend thirty hours of training annually.

- We have periodic seminars for our team, involving discussion of topics, case studies, and ongoing training.

- We require our graduates to read resource books.

- We offer specialized training classes on an as-needed basis.

- We offer training videos.

As part of the 4E Ministry Training Strategy Questionnaire, two dozen best-practice churches responded to the question, Once trainees become graduates, what modes of supervision do you offer? The following list collates typical responses.

- They meet with our Director of Biblical Counseling in individual supervision once per month.

- Once per month we sit in on their counseling and provide feedback after the session.

- We have group supervision that they attend bimonthly and share their cases with their trainers and their peers.

- We provide periodic supervision sessions and on-call assistance.

- Before graduation, they are supervised for fifty hours. After graduation, they receive supervision every other week.

- We meet once a month for two hours for team meetings to talk about cases.

- Graduates sit in on my counseling sessions.

- We developed a system of tiered peer supervision and accountability.

Mentoring Through Continuing Education

You can divide continuing education options into in-house or outsourced opportunities, ongoing or specialized opportunities, and reading/researching or listening/viewing opportunities. There are several advantages of in-house training. You can tailor your continuing education to the specific expressed and observed needs of your counselors; it's typically free for your counselors and it avoids travel time and expense. The disadvantage is that either you have to create the training experience or organize bringing someone in to provide the continuing education. Your in-house training can be periodic—meeting whenever a special need arises, or offering a periodic seminar. Or it can be ongoing—meeting at planned times and intervals.

Outsourced training tends to be much easier for the trainer (you) but can be more time-consuming and costly for the graduate counselor. However, it can expose your counselors to the best training in the world, and it allows them to hear different perspectives. With outside training, counselors can choose to attend (in-person or online) a general conference or a specialized seminar on a specific counseling issue.

In today's ever-changing world, the reading/researching and listening/viewing options are ever-growing. Your graduates can attend webinars, podcasts, livestreams, and more from the comfort of their home computer, listen to audiobooks, view recorded sessions of expert counselors, and much more.

Individual and Group Supervision

While continuing education can be obtained in a host of ways with great flexibility, I tend to be more structured with supervision. I've found tremendous value in monthly group supervision combined with monthly individual supervision.

The group supervision has several advantages. It allows continued development of the group cohesion experienced during your training phase. Graduates consistently express that ongoing group supervision is a cherished time of reconnecting. They also articulate how helpful it is to receive feedback from people who are committed to the same approach to counseling and who know each other well.

Typically we meet for at least two hours. We start with one individual sharing one of their counseling cases whether in individual counseling or small-group ministry. (Confidentiality is addressed either through written permission of the counselee, or by general discussions with no names or identifying comments.) Just as in the training labs, sometimes the focus is on case wisdom (how to apply truth to life), sometimes it is on counseling intervention, and sometimes it shifts to the life of the counselor. Even though only one or two individuals may share their cases during the meeting, everyone benefits from the joint discussion about lovingly applying biblical principles to counseling situations.

In individual supervision, we often listen to sections of recorded counseling (with written permission of the counselee). As was the case during the training phase and in-group supervision, the individual supervision might focus on content application, counseling competency and intervention, or on the life of the counselor.

In addition to group and individual supervision, it is necessary to maintain crisis availability. Counselors must have access to a trained supervisor 24/7. If you are the only supervisor in your church and you will be unavailable, then you need to make arrangements for someone from outside the church to be available. That sounds more drastic and time-consuming than it normally is. Emergencies, by their very name and nature, don't happen that often.

This raises the issue of the ratio of supervisor to counselors. You can understand why twelve-to-one is a maximum ratio. This also raises the issue of training other trainers—of raising up additional supervisors, which is our next area of focus.

LEAVING A LASTING LEGACY OF LOVING LEADERS: PASSING THE BATON OF MINISTRY

We need to practice what we preach regarding every member a disciple-maker. We do that by making it our goal to identify at least one person from every training sequence to whom we can pass the baton of ministry.

In my first church, my co-trainer was a high school guidance counselor. Since that time, he has become a church planter with a focus on equipping equippers. In my second church, my co-trainer was my administrative assistant. A dozen years later, I now have the privilege of consulting with her and her Associate Pastor as they launch a fresh round of biblical counseling training in their church. I understand now what the apostle John meant when he said, "I have no greater joy than to hear that my children are walking in the truth" (3 John 4).

I've found that there are five fundamentals to leaving a lasting legacy of loving leaders. We need to evaluate the ministry, scope out qualified leaders, offer on-the-job training, de-parent, and leave well.

Evaluate the Ministry

This chapter has emphasized evaluating your trainees as they become graduates. We also need to be humble learners willing to turn that process around by asking our trainees and graduates to evaluate our training (see Appendix 11.2, available free online at https://rpmministries.org/ebc-resources/, for a sample LEAD Biblical Counseling Ministry Evaluation Form). How our counselees evaluate us is certainly an important aspect of evaluating our overall equipping ministry. Yet who is better prepared to offer us feedback on our 4E equipping for 4C ministry than those we have been training? We want to be sure that what we pass on is as effective as possible. We want to lay a solid foundation for others to build on.

Scope Out Qualified Leaders

Like Paul in 2 Timothy 2:2, we scope out and equip those who are qualified to equip others. From the onset of the enlistment process, I'm always praying that God would give me wisdom to identify potential future trainers.

Once I've identified someone, I'm not shy about sharing my vision with them. Typically people are shocked, humbled, terrified, and honored when I say, "Would you be willing to pray about my training you to become a co-trainer?" Already motivated to be trained as a biblical counselor, you can imagine how this enlarged vision keeps the person focused throughout the training process.

Offer On-the-Job Training

I'm also not shy about telling the rest of the group that I've identified a group member whom I will be mentoring for future co-leadership. I mention that others in the group may sense a calling and giftedness for that role. I never want to exclude anyone God may call into a leadership role.

Anyone I train as a future co-trainer receives all the regular mentoring of other trainees. In addition, during our supervisory meetings, the first semester we discuss the 4C training process. I want to help this person begin looking at equipping through the eyes of a trainer.

Depending on the person, by the second semester of the first year or by the second year, the person is participating in some leadership roles. They lead sections of a lab, teach portions of a lecture, and offer supervision of another trainee. This on-the-job training is vital.

I never have the person move directly into the training role unless they are counseling others. I don't want people moving from being trained to counsel to training others to counsel without having counseled others. During the next round of training, this person becomes a co-trainer. Under my supervision, they share in all the training leadership roles.

De-Parenting

With co-trainers I always think about de-parenting. Or, as I put it, de-Kellemenizing. Yes, I have a 4E and a 4C structure. And, yes, I have a curriculum. However, it can be improved upon, and it should be taught and shared out of each person's giftedness, teaching style, and unique personality.

When co-trainers are teaching a lesson, I insist that they make it their own. They need to do their own biblical study of the topic. They must craft their own lesson outline, illustrations, and interactions. If they lead a small-group lab, they need to do it their way, not Kellemen's way. We are not creating clones. We want to model our best way of equipping so that co-trainers develop their best way of equipping.

Leaving Well

We all like to think that our ministry will continue forever. Yet we all know that is impossible. Our ministry description may change. Our mission or vision may change. God may call us to another place of service.

When any of those occur, we need to leave well. We have prepared the way for that by passing the baton of leadership throughout our training. Now we need to make that final handoff in a mature, God-honoring way.

Circumstances always vary, but whenever possible it's helpful to have a final meeting with all past trainees and graduates and all current trainees. Gather the entire team. Explain the reason for your departure from this ministry. Remind the team of the thorough training that their new leader has had. Exhort the team to love, honor, and respect their new leader the way they have you. Remind everyone that their ultimate leader is Christ. Pray for their new leader. Then share a goodbye time akin to Paul's farewell to the elders at Ephesus (Acts 20). This allows people to grieve the departure of one leader and begin to transfer ownership to a new leader.

COMMENCEMENT: PICTURES OF THE CHILDREN AND GRANDCHILDREN

This past December, my wife and I received a Christmas card from someone I trained in my first LEAD group—nearly three decades ago. The connection and bond is even closer because she and my wife were encouragement partners. She included a note in her card thanking us for our ministry in her life and saying that to this day, the training was life-changing. She went on to say that she and a pastor at her church are now co-leading a grief recovery group, and that she's using her training from our LEAD group.

As I did at the beginning of this chapter, I share this story for God's glory. It never ceases to amaze me how God empowers us to empower others. There's great joy in having children and grandchildren in the ministry. As Sister Ellen said in the introduction, "These are your grand-babies, Dr. Kellemen!"

It would be fun to stop writing right here. Grandbabies could be the bookends around this book. However, there's that elephant in the room yet to be considered—legal and ethical issues. It's not time just yet to end with fun because we need to address that elephant so that you are fully equipped. So, let's address the elephant one bite at a time, and then find another way to end with fun!

GROWING TOGETHER: QUESTIONS FOR REFLECTION, DISCUSSION, AND APPLICATION

1. As you think about the ongoing oversight (organizing the organism) of your biblical counseling ministry:

   a. What excites you about the process?

   b. What scares you about the process? How could the material in this chapter help you address those fears?

2. Regarding launching ministries built to last:

   a. Of evaluate, graduate, designate, create, automate, formulate, and communicate, which do you think you need to work on the most? Why?

   b. What one or two specific action steps do you need to start with in each area of evaluate, graduate, designate, create, automate, formulate, and communicate?

3. Regarding leading ministries from good to great:

   a. What continuing education opportunities do you believe are best for graduates of your biblical counseling ministry?

   b. What forms of group and individual supervision have you

experienced? What would you want to replicate from those experiences? What would you want to change?

4. Regarding leaving a lasting legacy of loving leaders:

   a. Of evaluating the ministry, scoping out qualified leaders, offering on-the-job-training, de-parenting, and leaving well, which one do you think is most important? Why?

   b. What could you do right now to begin the process of passing the baton?

Practicing Ethical and Legal Wisdom in Ministry

Caring Carefully

I n my consulting, I've found that it's easy for churches to cascade into extremes regarding biblical counseling and the law. One extreme causes churches to retreat in paranoia because of the fear of lawsuits. In response, they decline to launch church biblical counseling ministries and refer everyone to outside help. On the other extreme, churches ignore legal issues and place at risk their church, their biblical counseling ministry, and the people to whom they minister.

We overcome our extreme reactions to legal requirements (either fearing them or ignoring them) by understanding that they are a mere shadow of the far higher ethical standards of God's law. *We must obey the law of God and the law of the land in the fear of God and not the fear of man.*

THE LAW OF LOVE

Paul teaches us to submit ourselves to God-established authorities—the law of the land (Romans 13:1–7). Paul then immediately writes about the law of God—the law of love. "Let no debt remain outstanding, except the continuing debt to love one another, for whoever loves others has fulfilled the law" (verse 8). Paul explains that "whatever other command there may be, are summed up in this one command: 'Love your neighbor as yourself.' Love does no harm to a neighbor. Therefore love is the fulfillment of the law" (verses 9–10).

The precept "First, do no harm" is not simply a principle of medical ethics. It's a foundational principle of Christian life and ministry. Jesus reserves his most scathing judgment for ministers who abuse their power by abusing those to whom they minister. His list of woes to unethical, unloving shepherds in Matthew 23:1–39 should cure every ministry leader of a lax attitude toward ministry relational standards. Jesus warns of certain and severe judgment for anyone who mistreats the little child (Matthew 18:1–9) or fails to minister to the lost sheep (Matthew 18:10–14).

Jesus and Paul contrast the hireling and the true shepherd, the savage wolves and the good shepherds, the true apostle and the false (John 10:1–21; Acts 20:13–38; 2 Corinthians 10:1—12:21). Paul and Peter, in outlining the requirements of God's shepherds, highlight godly character and ethical conduct (1 Timothy 3:1–16; 1 Peter 5:1–5).

These specific law-of-love requirements flow from the most foundational requirement of God. "What does the LORD require of you? To act justly and to love mercy and to walk humbly with your God" (Micah 6:8). All ethical ministry behavior flows ultimately from the character of God. "Just as he who called you is holy, so be holy in all you do; for it is written: 'Be holy, because I am holy'" (1 Peter 1:15–16). This Godlike holiness has specific life, ministry, and relationship application. In the same text, Peter writes, "Now that you have purified yourselves by obeying the truth so that you have sincere love for each other, love one another deeply, from the heart" (verse 22).

I do not pen this chapter in a spirit of legalese. Practicing ethical and legal wisdom in ministry is nothing less than being Christlike in how we practice biblical counseling. It is nothing less than assuring that every possible safeguard is in place so that the hurting people we minister to are helped and not harmed. It is nothing less than overseeing that our biblical counseling ministry fulfills God's law of love. When we do that, fulfilling the law of the land, while still necessary, will be undemanding in comparison.

So as you read this final chapter, suppress the thought, *Ugh, not legal stuff!* Emphasize the thought, *I can't wait to learn more about how to oversee that our biblical counseling ministry cares carefully by loving biblically!*

PRACTICING WHAT WE PREACH

We need to practice what we preach about God's law of love and about the law of the land. Regarding God's law of love, be a good Berean Christian (Acts 17:11). Search the Scriptures to determine how God's law of love applies to your unique biblical counseling ministry in your specific church and community.

Regarding the law of the land, I need to practice what I preach with this preliminary disclosure statement.

> As the author of this chapter, I am *not* a legal expert. The reader should *not* consider this chapter legal counsel personally or for any specific church or ministry. I provide this chapter simply as a synopsis of my research of best practices designed to help readers become more aware of some basic ethical and legal considerations. I encourage readers to *take responsibility* for *remaining current*, as legal interpretations change over time. I encourage churches to *contract with an attorney* who is an *expert on the pertinent laws in their state*, as laws vary from state to state. I encourage churches to *maintain and provide malpractice and liability insurance* covering the church, pastors, trustees, elected leaders, and those trained in the biblical counseling ministry.

The nature of your training ministry (informal one-another ministry or formal biblical counseling) will play a significant role in how you address these issues. The information in this chapter is for the formal implementation of biblical counseling in the church.

PERTINENT LEGAL HISTORY AND THE LEGAL CLIMATE: THE LAW AND CHURCH COUNSELING

Before exploring specific wisdom principles, it's helpful to gain a lay of the land. What is the history (in the US) of the legal system and church counseling, and what is the legal climate relative to the church?

The Records Show

We can trace the issue of church counseling and the law back over four decades to the case of *Nally v. Grace Community Church of the Valley*.[1] On April 1, 1979, twenty-four-year-old Kenneth Nally committed suicide. Four years earlier, Ken had begun seeing a secular psychologist. In 1978, he began a discipleship relationship with one of the pastors at Grace Community Church.

The records show that in the two-month period between February 1979 and

---

1. *Nally v. Grace Community Church of the Valley*, 763 P.2d 948 (S. Ct. Cal. 1988). Information on this case is summarized from Steve Levicoff, *Christian Counseling and the Law* (Chicago: Moody, 1991) and from George Ohlschlager and Peter Mosgofian, *Law for the Christian Counselor* (Eugene, OR: Wipf and Stock, 2012).

his death, Ken saw at least four physicians, one psychiatrist, a psychologist, and a psychologist's assistant, and had several counseling sessions with pastors at Grace Community Church. Ken's parents, Walter and Maria Nally, could have sued anyone who had seen their son over the few months prior to his death, but they chose Grace Community Church.

They charged, among other things, wrongful death based upon "clergyman malpractice" and negligent counseling. They alleged that following a suicide attempt, the pastors "actively and affirmatively dissuaded [Ken] from seeking further psychological and/or psychiatric care."[2] Despite the records showing that the pastors encouraged Ken to keep his appointments with physicians and outside counseling professionals, the case went through the California court system twice before the Supreme Court of California exonerated the church in November 1988.

Levicoff explains, "The key question was whether the pastors, as spiritual counselors, had a duty to refer Ken Nally to professional secular counselors to help prevent his suicide. The Court of Appeal ruled that 'nontherapists [nonlicensed] counselors—*both religious and secular*—have a duty to refer suicidal persons to psychiatrists or psychotherapists qualified to prevent suicides.'"[3]

Levicoff continues, "In reversing the Court of Appeal, the state Supreme Court rejected the imposition of a broad 'duty to refer,' not only for the defendants, but for nontherapist counselors in general."[4] Addressing pastoral counselors specifically, the court stated:

> The Legislature has exempted the clergy from the licensure requirements applicable to marriage, family, child and domestic counselors and from the operation of statutes regulating psychologists. In so doing, the Legislature has recognized that access to the clergy should be free from state imposed counseling standards and that the secular state is not equipped to ascertain the competence of counseling when performed by those affiliated with religious organizations.[5]

Expanding their holding to nontherapist counselors in general, the court noted:

---

2. Levicoff, *Christian Counseling and the Law*, 18–19. *Nally v. Grace* at 952.

3. Ibid., 19, *Nally v. Grace* at 954, italics in the original.

4. Ibid.

5. Ibid., 20, at 959–960.

By their very definition, nontherapist counselors are not professional medical experts on suicide. Their activities are undertaken
pursuant to doctrines explicitly left unregulated by the state.[6]

Levicoff concludes, "The good news is that, in addition to religious counselors,
the decision protects peer counselors."[7]

The Nallys appealed the case to the United States Supreme Court, which
refused to hear the case, thus allowing the California Supreme Court opinion
to stand. Levicoff summarized his conclusions based upon this case and other
case law.

Legally, Christian counseling falls under the general term *spiritual*
or *religious* counseling and enters a realm that civil courts are neither
prepared nor permitted to adjudicate. In terms of the law, the primary difference between spiritual and secular counseling is in the
area of regulation. While secular counseling can be regulated by the
government or licensing board, spiritual counseling deals with religious beliefs, and the courts are precluded from making value judg-
ments as to the truth or falsehood of those beliefs.[8]

The Changing Legal Climate

Levicoff does not believe that Christians and churches should be naïve. He
explains that the American Bar Association sponsored a seminar called "Tort
and Religion." It was touted for "attorneys who want to be on the leading edge
of an explosive new area of law."[9] The purpose of the seminar was, in effect, to
train attorneys in how to sue churches.[10]

Jay Quine, a lawyer, pastor, and seminary professor bluntly opines, "Law
school professors are not friends. They have one goal: to make you a shrewd
lawyer. Lawyers are trained to think with one word: LAW! Law is competitive,
cut-throat, brutal. Lawyers are different. They have no qualms about suing your
church. The law is the law."[11]

---

6. Ibid., 958–959, fn. 7.

7. Levicoff, *Christian Counseling and the Law*, 20.

8. Ibid., 33-34.

9. Quoted in ibid., 23.

10. Ibid.

11. Jay Quine, "Legal Issues for Christian Workers and the Church." Quotes derived from lecture notes.

Perhaps you're thinking, *Bob, if your goal is to reassure me, then I'm not sure it's working.* My goal is *not* reassurance. My goal is wisdom. Wisdom requires that we face facts, that we not be naïve. Churches are not immune from lawsuits. They can be sued for a divot in the parking lot that causes Aunt Sally to fall and break her hip, but the answer is not to eliminate all parking lots. The answer is to take care of our parking lot *because we care about Aunt Sally.* There is nothing anyone or any organization can do to guarantee they will never be sued. However, there is much that we can do to practice ethical and legal wisdom that seeks to do no harm and do much good.

SCOPE OF CARE: COMMUNICATING HONESTLY AND ACCURATELY ABOUT YOUR MINISTRY

The first law-of-the-land and law-of-love issue that biblical counseling ministries must address relates to informed consent. Informed consent means that the caregiver has a duty to disclose fairly the scope and nature of the care provided and alternative modes of care so that the person seeking care can make an informed voluntary decision. Adequacy of disclosure is judged by what a reasonable person would want to know to make that informed decision.[12]

Practically speaking, this means that with our biblical counseling ministries we need to communicate honestly and accurately who we are, what we offer, and what we do *not* offer. We never hold out our graduates to be more than they are trained and qualified to be. In the event of a legal action, the standard our graduates will be held to in a court of law is that which we held them to in public.

In Appendix 11.1, you will find three forms (LEAD Biblical Counseling Ministry Welcome Form, LEAD Biblical Counseling Ministry Consent Form, and the LEAD Biblical Counseling Ministry Consent to Minister to a Minor Child) that express ways to communicate informed consent in local church biblical counseling. The second form states, in part:

> I have been informed that the spiritual care I will be receiving from _____ (Name of Biblical Counselor) at _____ (Name of Church), is Christian and biblical in nature. I have also been informed that _____ (Name of Biblical Counselor) is an encourager and discipler trained at

---

12. Ohlschlager and Mosgofian, *Law for the Christian Counselor,* 54.

_____ (Name of Church) as a biblical counselor and spiritual friend in the church's LEAD (Life Encourager And Discipler) Biblical Counseling Ministry. Under supervision from one of the LEAD trainers, _____ (Name of Biblical Counselor) offers to provide biblical encouragement and discipleship on personal and relational matters from a spiritual perspective guided by biblical principles. He/she is *not* trained, authorized, or licensed to provide professional counseling, psychological treatment, or psychological diagnosis. I understand that if and when I desire and request professional counseling, then I will be encouraged to seek such outside assistance. I give my consent to _____ (Name of Biblical Counselor) to discuss any and all of the information that I talk about in our meetings with his/her supervisor(s) in the LEAD Biblical Counseling Ministry.

Clearly Communicate Who You Are

From Appendix 11.1, you'll note several important points. First, the forms carefully label the type of care being offered. In the sample forms, "biblical counselor" is the primary label chosen and defined. It is supported by other terms such as "spiritual friend," "encourager," "discipler," "soul care," and "spiritual direction." Second, the forms repeatedly use terms like "ministry," "discipleship," and "local church" to highlight the nonlicensed, spiritual nature of the help offered.

Practitioners in best-practice churches debate whether or not to use, in any form, with any modifiers, the terms "counseling" or "counselor." Some people choose to avoid terms such "lay counselor," "Christian counselor," "biblical counselor," or "spiritual counselor" because of the possibility of someone mistaking this nonprofessional, nonlicensed counseling for professional licensed counseling. Instead, they choose other legitimate words and descriptions used in the Bible or in church history—words with less potential for causing confusion to the person seeking care. Others strongly desire to claim and even reclaim the mantle and label of "biblical counselor," seeing it as a legitimate scriptural description that the church should not allow the world to usurp. They then carefully explain what they mean and do not mean by their terms. See below for how twenty-four Disciple-Making Champions address this issue.

Whatever term you use, never label your graduates something they are not trained to do. Regardless of which term you choose, the vital issue is how you describe, define, and communicate your terms.

Clearly Communicate What You Offer and What You Do Not Offer

A central aspect of defining your label involves stating what goals you aim to address and what goals you do *not* aim to address. What is the scope and nature of the care you offer? The LEAD Biblical Counseling Ministry Welcome Form outlines specifically what our church means by "biblical counseling," using the biblical and church history categories of sustaining, healing, reconciling, and guiding.

The LEAD Biblical Counseling Ministry Consent Form (all those who receive care must read, discuss, and sign both forms) clearly distinguishes between what is offered and what is not offered, what the biblical counselor/spiritual friend is and is *not* qualified to do. LEAD biblical counselors offer to provide biblical encouragement and discipleship on personal and relational matters from a spiritual perspective guided by biblical principles. They are not trained, authorized, or licensed to provide professional counseling, psychological treatment, or psychological diagnosis.

To maintain this distinction, I recommend never charging fees for counseling services. Once a fee is mandated, then an implied professional relationship is established. At that point, both the state and the individual receiving counseling could likely perceive you to be offering professional counseling.

Chapter 11 noted that some churches charge a cancellation fee (with a clear statement of the nature of that fee), some accept donations toward the counseling ministry or the church, some ask people to cover the costs of texts or handouts, and some ask people to cover the cost of resources such as books. I have never participated in any of those practices. I have always covered the cost of the counseling ministry budget through line items in the church budget. When we had a church bookstore, transactions of counseling-related books took place separately from the counseling ministry. I have never charged a cancellation fee for missed appointments.

DISCIPLE-MAKING CHAMPIONS

What Do You Call Your Ministry?

As part of the 4E Ministry Training Strategy Questionnaire, two dozen best-practice churches responded to the question, What do you call what your graduates do? Is it "counseling," "biblical counseling," "lay counseling," or do you avoid the word "counseling"? If so, what do you call it? The following are the most common answers. The number after the answer indicates how many of the twenty-four best-practice churches use that term (some churches use more than one term).

- Biblical Counseling: 9

- Lay Biblical Counseling: 4

- Soul Care: 4

- Encouragement and Discipleship: 3

- Biblical Discipleship Counseling: 3

- Spiritual Friendship: 3

- Spiritual Direction: 2

- Biblical Pastoral Counseling: 2

- Gospel Conversations: 2

- Gospel Counseling: 2

QUALITY OF CARE: BUILDING SAFEGUARDS IN YOUR MINISTRY

We can compare scope of care and quality of care in a nontechnical, nonlegal sense.

- Scope of Care: Claim to do only what you are trained to do.

- Quality of Care: Do with integrity and propriety what you claim to do.

In terms of legal theory, quality of care relates to negligence and/or malpractice. Both Levicoff and Ohlschlager see overlap in negligence and malpractice; even the definitions they provide are similar. Malpractice is an act or omission by a professional practitioner in the treatment of a patient or client that is inconsistent with the reasonable care or skill usually demonstrated by ordinary, prudent practitioners of the same profession, similarly situated.[13] Negligence can be defined as an act or omission to act that was unreasonable in light of an established duty of care, which was breached, resulting in harm of another.[14] There are four elements of a negligence suit:

- *Duty of Care:* The caregiver's responsibility to ensure the safety and welfare of the person receiving care

- *Breach of Duty:* The caregiver either does something he/she should not do (for example, sexual involvement with a counselee), or does not do something he/she should have done (for example, failure to refer when necessary or failure to inform a third party in danger of harm from the counselee)

- *Injury:* Harm done to a person's physical or mental well-being, reputation, pride, rights, and privileges (lawsuits in this area may include issues related to church discipline and public disclosure of information)

- *Proximate Cause:* The counselor's breach of duty of care was the proximate (or direct) cause of the injury[15]

While these matters can seem technical and even intimidating, they involve practical and necessary safeguards. Seven pertinent issues summarize the quality-of-care matters that every biblical counseling ministry should address are these: propriety, humility, referral, confidentiality, church discipline, documentation, and supervision.

Propriety in Biblical Counseling Ministry

We've all heard horror stories of sexual involvement between a counselor and a counselee. Obviously, the motivation for safeguarding this area must be much greater than simply avoiding a lawsuit. Propriety should be motivated by our desire to honor God and to minister in holy, healthy, and helpful ways to hurting, vulnerable people. Safeguards include the following:

---

13. Ibid., 17.

14. Quine, "Legal Issues for Christian Workers and the Church," 2.

15. Levicoff, *Christian Counseling and the Law*, 84–85.

- Perform background checks on all trainees. This is increasingly a common, necessary, and expected practice in all church ministries. It should be standard as part of the enlistment process for a biblical counseling trainee.

- Do not allow in-person counseling sessions off premises (video conference counseling raises its own set of issues).

- Require all in-person counseling sessions to meet in a building when others are around.

- Require that in-person counseling sessions meet in rooms that have doors with windows. While this can be problematic in some buildings, it is worth the cost.

- Discourage mixed-gender sessions without a third person present.[16]

- Whenever possible, have a trainee, co-counselor, staff member, or advocate included in the counseling.

Humility in Biblical Counseling

God's Word commands us not to think more highly of ourselves than we ought, but rather, to think of ourselves with sober judgment according to our gifting and training (Romans 12:3; 15:14). We all have limits and limitations. Thus, we should never allow any of our graduates (or ourselves) to counsel beyond their competence, ability, or training. A detailed intake policy and procedure (see Appendix 11.1) provides a safeguard so the person needing care is assigned to a person qualified to care for that individual with that specific issue.

We should not give counselees cross-disciplinary advice (advice related to any profession for which we are not trained such as law, medicine, and psychiatry). Regarding medications or physical issues, defer and refer to qualified medical personnel. It is a wise best practice to maintain a consulting relationship with trusted medical professionals. Those who lead the biblical counseling ministry need to have access to other pastors, counselors, and educators with whom they can confer and consult.

Seeking certification from national biblical counseling ministries for your counselors or for your counseling ministry can be another sign of humility. It

---

16. We should not assume that eliminating mixed-gender counseling removes all possibility of sexual temptation or inappropriate behavior. Same-sex counselor/counselee attraction and seduction also must be guarded against.

communicates that you are part of a group larger than yourself, it typically provides opportunities for outside continuing education, and it often offers collegial relationships and supervisory connections.

Referral and Biblical Counseling Ministry

Referral is one specific way that we demonstrate humility in biblical counseling. No one is equipped to minister to everyone. No training program has the time to equip trainees for every possible issue. Your informed consent form should list the areas on which your ministry will focus. Counseling issues outside those areas should be referred to others with pertinent expertise. It's imperative that your ministry identify professional resources to refer people to when issues arise beyond the competency of your team.

Related to referral are the issues of wrongful termination, abandonment, and follow-up care. The duty of care operates continually until the counseling relationship is validly terminated. If the counselee desires continued counseling but the counselor believes that further counseling would no longer be effective, the counselor is responsible to recommend (and document) an appropriate referral.

Ideally, the decision to end counseling would be mutual. If the decision is made because the initial issues that brought the person to counseling have been satisfactorily addressed, then the counselor should complete a Commencement Summary (see Appendix 11.1). The final counseling session should address a summary of the initial goals, a summary of the growth resulting from the meetings, insight concerning any unresolved areas, suggestions for further growth (including appropriate follow-up care), and the reasons for commencement. The counselee should complete a Biblical Counseling Evaluation Form (see Appendix 11.1). Counselees should know that if an issue returns or new issues develop, they are invited to contact your offices again. Often it is helpful at commencement to schedule another appointment three months later (or a mutually determined time) for a check-in/check-up.

Confidentiality in Biblical Counseling Ministry

Like each of the quality-of-care issues, confidentiality has legal meanings as well as biblical/ethical implications. In the legal realm, most states do not recognize a confidentiality privilege for lay Christian counselors who are not pastors. Privileged communication is codified in the law and means that a minister acting in his professional capacity as a spiritual advisor cannot be forced to reveal the content of confidential communications to any outside party, including a court of law. Confidentiality, on the other hand, is an ethical decision not to reveal what is learned in the context of a professional relationship, and it does not have legal protection.[17]

Our focus is on the ethical and relational nature of confidentiality in biblical counseling and on a counselee's expectation of confidential communication. Each biblical counseling ministry must develop clear organizational policies. These policies need to be in writing, explained to the counselee at the start of counseling, and signed. Embedded within The LEAD Biblical Counseling Ministry Welcome Form (see Appendix 11.1) is the following statement:

> Confidentiality is an important aspect of the spiritual friendship relationship, and we will carefully guard the information you entrust to us. All communications between you and our LEAD Spiritual Friendship offices will be held in strict confidence, unless you (or a parent in the case of a minor) give authorization to release this information. The exceptions to this would be 1) if a person expresses intent to harm himself/herself or someone else; 2) if there is evidence or reasonable suspicion of abuse against a minor child, elder person, or dependent adult; 3) if a subpoena or other court order is received directing the disclosure of information; 4) if/when LEAD Spiritual Friends consult with their supervision; or 5) if a person persistently refuses to renounce a particular sin (habitual unrepentant rebellion against the Word of God) and it becomes necessary to seek the assistance of others in the church to encourage repentance, restoration, and reconciliation (see Matthew 18:15–20 and our Church Discipline Policy). Please be assured that our biblical counselors strongly prefer not to disclose personal information to others, and they will make every effort to help you find ways to resolve a problem as privately as possible.

Some people assume that discussing and signing a policy like this would have a chilling effect on a person's willingness to share personally. However, every legitimate counseling organization and ministry will have such a statement, so counselees will not find this out of the ordinary. By discussing this openly at the outset, you will put counselees at ease.

---

17. Levicoff, *Christian Counseling and the Law*, 71–73.

Church Discipline and Biblical Counseling Ministry

As noted in the confidentiality statement, church discipline is one of the exceptions to confidentiality. The potential legal ramifications include invasion of privacy, defamation of character, publication of private facts, and infliction of emotional distress.[18] God's Word contains guidelines designed to restore errant believers by bringing them to repentance and reconciliation with Christ and the body of Christ (within or outside the context of a formal biblical counseling ministry).

Within the context of biblical counseling, counselees frequently bring to counseling their struggles to overcome besetting sins. Struggling against sin is not a cause for increased levels of church discipline intervention. However, persistent refusal to renounce a particular sin (habitual unrepentant rebellion against the Word of God) can lead to the initiation of a church restoration/discipline process.

Churches should create a written Church Discipline Policy (see Appendix 12.1, available free online at https://rpmministries.org/ebc-resources/). It should be discussed with and signed by every new member, and it should be read at least once a year at an official church meeting. The policy should identify the biblical principles and practices, the spiritual motivations and goals, and the step-by-step process to which every member agrees to adhere.

As of this writing, case law seems to support a church's right to discipline members who have agreed to such discipline as part of the membership process. However, when members under discipline remove themselves from membership, at least some case law suggests that this withdraws the person's consent to participate in a spiritual relationship. Therefore, disciplinary actions no longer have First Amendment protection.[19] Some would suggest that you only discipline members.[20] Others would suggest that the Church Discipline Policy explain that resignation from membership after the initiation of church discipline does not void the church's responsibility to carry on the church discipline process.[21]

If a counselee evidences continued unrepentant rebellion, it is essential that the church restoration/discipline policy be followed carefully. Each step of the

---

18. Ibid., 105-115.

19. Ibid., 110.

20. Quine, "Legal Issues for Christian Workers and the Church," 5.

21. Levicoff, *Christian Counseling and the Law*, 114.

process should be documented. If the process continues to the step of public discipline, the discipline announcement should be discreetly shared at a members-only meeting.

Documentation and Biblical Counseling

Chapter 11 addresses many of the issues related to appropriate documentation. Documentation serves both to organize the organism and to assist in caring carefully. In case scope-of-care or quality-of-care issues arise, it would be extremely helpful for you to carefully document your *training*. Maintain a basic outline of your 4E/4C structure, have available copies of your training materials, and keep copies of your completed evaluations of trainees (see Appendix 10.1).

You should also document each counseling relationship with basic case notes (see the Biblical Counseling Record Sheet in Appendix 11.1). Case notes should include the name of the person seen, the date, the session number, a review of the previous session, goals for the current session, an in-session summary, a list of post-session homework, and the next meeting date and time. On the back of this form include a treatment plan that matches your training model (the sample contained in Appendix 11.1 uses the map/model of sustaining, healing, reconciling, guiding, relational, rational, volition, and emotional). In this way, all record keeping stays consistent with the training received. In case notes, assure that your graduates do not use psychological labels and diagnostic categories. Typically they lack training for this. Additionally, the use of such labels could be perceived as movement away from spiritual care to psychological and even licensed counseling.

Keep these records on-site in a secure location. There is no clear, uniform standard for how long to keep such records. Best-practice ministries tend to keep them for at least three years, after which they are destroyed.

There are also no clear standards regarding who keeps the records if the lead trainer departs the ministry or moves to another church. If the baton has been passed well, as discussed in chapter 11, then I recommend that the notes pass to the next lead trainer. If, on the other hand, the ministry for some reason disbands when the lead trainer leaves, then the departing trainer could maintain the notes for three years before destroying them.

Supervision and Biblical Counseling

All graduates must be supervised by qualified individuals. As part of supervision, the supervisor should discuss all counseling evaluation forms completed at commencement (termination), and these evaluations should be maintained. The supervisor should also document and keep records of all continuing education.

COUNT THE COST:
PRUDENCE AND COMMITMENT

I'm not naïve. This is not an easy subject. However, I don't like to pretend. We have to address these elephants in the room. They deal with the law of the land, to which God commands us to submit, and they deal with the law of love, which God commands us to obey.

God calls us to be prudent in regard to our responsibilities to abide by and respect the law. And he calls us to be loving and above reproach as we minister to people. We are to be shrewd and wise as snakes and innocent and harmless as doves (Matthew 10:16).

There's nothing we can do to prevent someone from suing us. We can only provide the best practices possible to defend our actions before the legal system, and more importantly, before our God. Nothing can, or should, prevent us from ministering to the body of Christ. Yes, we need to count the cost (Luke 14:28–33). And yes, we need to serve God even when there will be a cost—as there always will. We can never allow the fear of man to stop us from serving God.

COMMENCEMENT: CHANGING LIVES
WITH CHRIST'S CHANGELESS TRUTH

Because this book has been a collegial process with two-dozen best-practice churches participating, it seems only fitting to conclude/commence not only with my words but also theirs. Ponder and apply their final words of counsel.

DISCIPLE-MAKING CHAMPIONS

Final Words of Counsel

My final question to these Disciple-Making Champions in the 4E Ministry Training Strategy Questionnaire was, What advice would you like to offer others who are about to launch a biblical counseling training ministry? The following five categories summarize themes I heard repeatedly:

- *Be God-Dependent:* "Pray, pray, and then pray some more. The Spirit of God will bring about your ministry launch as you submit to him."

- *Model It:* "Begin by engaging your fellow believers in the personal ministry of the Word. Then grow your ministry as you equip others to do what you're already doing as a biblical counselor."

- *Humbly Keep Growing:* "Seek God's Word so you can be biblical in your approach. Ask others for advice and helpful input. Then watch the Holy Spirit transform lives."

- *Seek Quality, Not Quantity:* "Focus on a few key men and women in the early going. Pour your training into them, getting them firmly rooted in the gospel, the Word, and a Christ-centered counseling paradigm."

- *Do It:* "Start small. Do not wait until you have everything figured out. To borrow the old Peace Corps motto: 'It's the hardest job you'll ever love.' My advice is...do it!"

My prayer is that this book *persuades you* to launch and lead 4E training ministries. It can be done. Others have, so can you. You can do this!

My prayer also is that this book *encourages you as it equips* you. Here's my paraphrase to *you* of Paul's words from Romans 15:14:

> I myself am convinced, my active participant-readers, that as you apply these best practices in your ministry context, that you yourselves are competent to launch and lead a formal biblical counseling ministry in your church as you keep depending upon God to strengthen you to envision, enlist, equip, and empower a team of one-another ministers and biblical counselors.

Do you want to change lives? Do you want to change lives like an Ed Sullivan? Do you want to leave a legacy of loving leaders? Do you want to birth some spiritual grandbabies? Then change lives with Christ's changeless truth by equipping God's people to speak and live gospel truth in love.

GROWING TOGETHER: QUESTIONS FOR REFLECTION, DISCUSSION, AND APPLICATION

1. When you think about legal and ethical issues, which extreme do you tend toward—fearing them or ignoring them? Why?

2. Before getting too caught up in the details of this chapter, ask yourself how you could apply the big picture of this chapter: *Obey the law of God and the law of the land in the fear of God and not the fear of man.*

3. How does it change your perspective, attitude, and mindset about legal and ethical issues when you realize that they...

   a. Are just a mere shadow of the deeper requirements of God's law of love?

   b. Flow ultimately from the very character of our holy God?

4. What specific biblical counseling ministry applications do you need to make relative to scope of care and communicating honestly and accurately about your ministry?

5. What specific biblical counseling ministry applications do you need to make relative to each of the seven quality of care matters:

propriety, humility, referral, confidentiality, church discipline, documentation, and supervision?

6. Will you "just do it"? No, that's not what I want to ask with my final
   question. Here's my final question for *you*. How, when, and with
   whom will you start 4E biblical counseling equipping?

Practical Equipping Resources

All appendix materials are available *for free online* as Word documents. You can find the home page for all the Appendices documents online at https://rpmministries.org/ebc-resources/.

I've talked throughout this book about the value of you making this material your own—fitting your church's MVP-C to match your church and community. By having access to the materials online in Word documents, you have the best of both worlds. You don't have to reinvent the wheel. You have these templates in formats that allow you easily to adjust them to fit your setting and your preferred wording.

Below is a list of the individual appendices mentioned throughout this book. The number of each appendix indicates which chapter it is from. The following link will give you access to and free use of all the documents: https://rpmministries.org/ebc-resources/

1. Appendix 2.1: Congregational SWORD Heart Exam

2. Appendix 3.1: A Churchwide MVP-C Statement

3. Appendix 3.2: A Biblical Counseling Ministry-Specific MVP-C Statement

4. Appendix 3.3: An Elder Ministry Team MVP-C Statement

5. Appendix 4.1: A Personal Ministry MVP-C Statement

6. Appendix 4.2: A Sample Discussion Guide: Discovering Our Biblical Counseling Mission

Works Cited and Consulted

Adams, Jay E. *The Christian Counselor's Manual*. Grand Rapids, MI: Zondervan, 1973.

———. *Competent to Counsel*. Phillipsburg, NJ: P&R, 1970.

———. *A Theology of Christian Counseling: More Than Redemption*. Grand Rapids, MI: Zondervan, 1979.

Aden, L. "Comfort/Sustaining," in *The Dictionary of Pastoral Care and Counseling*. General editor Rodney J. Hunter. Nashville: Abingdon Press, 1990, 193–95.

Baker, Amy, editor. *Caring for the Souls of Children: A Biblical Counselor's Manual*. Greensboro, NC: New Growth Press, 2020.

Begley, Sharon. "A World of Their Own." *Newsweek* (May 7, 2000): 52–56.

Behm, J. *"noeo,"* in *The Theological Dictionary of the New Testament*. Abridged by G. Bromiley. Grand Rapids, MI: Eerdmans, 1992, 636–646.

———. *"parakletos,"* in *The Theological Dictionary of the New Testament*. Abridged by G. Bromiley. Grand Rapids, MI: Eerdmans, 1992, 782–784.

Berman, J. S., and N. C. Norton. "Does Professional Training Make a Therapist More Effective?" *Psychology Bulletin* 98, no. 2 (1985): 401–407.

Brown, Francis, S. Driver, and C. Briggs. *The New Brown, Driver, and Briggs Hebrew and English Lexicon of the Old Testament*. Lafayette, IN: Associated Publishers, 1981.

Bullis, Ronald. *Sacred Calling, Secular Accountability: Law and Ethics in Complementary and Spiritual Counseling*. Philadelphia: Brunner-Routledge, 2001.

Burck, J. R. "Reconciliation," in *The Dictionary of Pastoral Care and Counseling*. General editor Rodney J. Hunter. Nashville: Abingdon Press, 1990, 1047–1048.

Cheong, Robert K. *Restore: Changing How We Live + Love*. Greensboro, NC: New Growth Press, 2020.

Clebsch, William A., and Charles R. Jaekle. *Pastoral Care in Historical Perspective*. New York: Harper, 1964.

Durlak, J. "Comparative Effectiveness of Paraprofessional and Professional Helpers." *Psychological Bulletin* 86, no. 1 (1979): 80–92.

Earle, Ralph. *Word Meanings in the New Testament.* Peabody, MA: Hendricksen, 2000.

Emlet, Michael R. *Cross Talk: Where Life & Scripture Meet.* Greensboro, NC: New Growth Press, 2009.

———. *Saints, Sufferers, and Sinners: Loving Others as God Loves Us.* Greensboro, NC: New Growth Press, 2021.

Eyrich, Howard, and William Hines. *Curing the Heart: A Model for Biblical Counseling.* Fearn, Tain, Scotland: Christian Focus, 2010.

Faith Biblical Counseling. "Starting a Counseling Ministry." Seminar notes presented at Faith Church, Lafayette, IN, 2009.

Graham, L. K. "Healing," in *The Dictionary of Pastoral Care and Counseling.* General editor Rodney J. Hunter. Nashville: Abingdon Press, 1990, 497–501.

Grudem, Wayne. *Systematic Theology: An Introduction to Biblical Doctrine.* Revised Edition. Grand Rapids, MI: Zondervan, 2021.

Hattie, J. A., H. J. Rogers, and C. F. Sharpley. "Comparative Effectiveness of Professional and Paraprofessional Helpers." *Psychological Bulletin* 95, no. 3 (1984): 534–541.

Henderson, John. *Equipped to Counsel: A Training Program in Biblical Counseling—Leader Notebook.* Mustang, OK: Dare 2 Dream Books, 2008.

Herman, Keith. "Reassessing Predictors of Therapist Competence." *Journal of Counseling and Development* 72 (September/October 1993): 29–32.

Huntford, Roland. *Shackleton.* London: Hodder & Stoughton, 1985.

Kellemen, Bob. *Consider Your Counsel: Addressing Ten Mistakes in Our Biblical Counseling.* Greensboro, NC: New Growth Press, 2021.

Kellemen, Bob. *Counseling Under the Cross: How Martin Luther Applied the Gospel to Daily Life.* Greensboro, NC: New Growth Press, 2017.

Kellemen, Bob. *God's Healing for Life's Losses: How to Find Hope When You're Hurting.* Winona Lake, IN: BMH, 2010.

Kellemen, Bob. *Gospel-Centered Counseling: How Christ Changes Lives.* Grand Rapids, MI: Zondervan, 2014.

Kellemen, Bob. *Gospel-Centered Family Counseling: An Equipping Guide for Pastors and Counselors.* Grand Rapids, MI: Baker, 2020.

Kellemen, Bob. *Gospel-Centered Marriage Counseling: An Equipping Guide for Pastors and Counselors.* Grand Rapids, MI: Baker, 2020.

Kellemen, Bob. *Gospel Conversations: How to Care Like Christ.* Grand Rapids, MI: Zondervan, 2015.

Kellemen, Bob. *Grief: Walking with Jesus.* Phillipsburg, NJ: P&R, 2018.

Kellemen, Bob, and Jeff Forrey, editors. *Scripture and Counseling: God's Word for Life in a Broken World.* Grand Rapids, MI: Zondervan, 2014.

Kellemen, Bob, and Karole A. Edwards. *Beyond the Suffering: Embracing the Legacy of African American Soul Care and Spiritual Direction.* Grand Rapids, MI: Baker, 2007.

Kellemen, Bob, and Kevin Carson, editors. *Biblical Counseling and the Church: God's Care Through God's People.* Grand Rapids, MI: Zondervan, 2015.

Kellemen, Bob, and Steve Viars, general editors. *Christ-Centered Biblical Counseling: Changing Lives with God's Changeless Truth.* Revised Edition. Eugene, OR: Harvest House, 2021.

Keller, Timothy. *Ministries of Mercy*, 2nd Edition. Phillipsburg, NJ: P&R, 1997.

———. "Puritan Resources for Pastoral Counseling." *Journal of Pastoral Practice* 9, no. 3 (1988): 11–44.

Kittel, Gerhard, and Gerhard Friedrich. *Theological Dictionary of the New Testament.* Abridged by G. Bromiley. Grand Rapids, MI: Eerdmans, 1992.

Lake, Frank. *Clinical Theology.* London: Darton, Longman & Todd, 1966.

Lambert, Heath. *A Theology of Biblical Counseling: The Doctrinal Foundations of Counseling Ministry.* Grand Rapids, MI: Baker, 2016.

Lane, Timothy S., and Paul David Tripp. *How People Change.* Greensboro, NC: New Growth Press, 2008.

Lelek, Jeremy. *Biblical Counseling Basics: Roots, Beliefs, and Future.* Greensboro, NC: New Growth Press, 2018.

Levicoff, Steve. *Christian Counseling and the Law.* Chicago: Moody Press, 1991.

Marshall, Colin, and Tony Payne. *The Trellis and the Vine: The Ministry Mind-Shift That Changes Everything.* Kingsford, Australia: Matthias Media, 2009.

PDR Network, editors. *The Physician's Desk Reference.* Whippany, NJ: PDR Network, 2017.

Meiburg, A. "Care of Souls," in *The Dictionary of Pastoral Care and Counseling.* Editor Rodney J. Hunter. Nashville: Abingdon Press, 1990, 122.

Mills, L. "Pastoral Care: History," in *The Dictionary of Pastoral Care and Counseling.* General editor Rodney J. Hunter. Nashville: Abingdon Press, 1990, 836–44.

Nicewander, Sue. *Building a Church Counseling Ministry: Without Killing the Pastor.* Carlisle, PA: Day One, 2012.

Ohlschlager, George W., and Peter T. Mosgofian. *Law for the Christian Counselor: A Guidebook for Clinicians and Pastors.* Dallas: Word, 1992.

Packer, J. I. *Knowing God.* Wheaton, IL: InterVarsity, 1993.

Pierre, Jeremy. *The Dynamic Heart in Daily Life: Connecting Christ to Human Experience.* Greensboro, NC: New Growth Press, 2016.

Pierre, Jeremy, and Deepak Reju. *The Pastor and Counseling: The Basics of Shepherding Members in Need.* Wheaton, IL: Crossway, 2015.

Porter, Robert E., editor. *The Merck Manual of Diagnosis and Therapy.* 20th Edition. Chicago: Merck, 2018.

Powlison, David. *How Does Sanctification Work?* Wheaton, IL: Crossway, 2017.

———. *Seeing with New Eyes: Counseling and the Human Condition Through the Lens of Scripture.* Phillipsburg, NJ: P&R, 2003.

———. *Speaking Truth in Love: Counsel in Community.* Winston-Salem, NC: Punch Press, 2005.

Quine, Jay. "Court Involvement in Church Discipline," Parts 1 and 2. *Bibliotheca Sacra* (January-March 1992).

———. "Legal Issues for Christian Workers and the Church." Seminar notes presented at Lancaster Bible College, Lancaster, PA, 1998.

———. "Legal Issues Related to Confidentiality and Pastoral Counseling." *Bibliotheca Sacra* (January-March 1997).

Richards, Lawrence O., and Gary J. Bredfeldt. *Creative Bible Teaching.* Revised and Expanded Edition. Chicago: Moody Press, 1998.

Robertson, A. T. *Word Pictures in the New Testament.* Concise Edition. Nashville: Holman, 2000.

Sande, Ken. *The Peacemaker: A Biblical Guide to Resolving Personal Conflict.* Revised and Expanded Edition. Grand Rapids, MI: Baker, 2004.

Scott, Stuart, and Heath Lambert, editors. *Counseling the Hard Cases: True Stories Illustrating the Sufficiency of God's Resources in Scripture.* Nashville: B&H Academic, 2015.

Tan, Siang-Yang. *Lay Counseling: Equipping Christians for a Helping Ministry.* Grand Rapids, MI: Zondervan, 1991.

Tan, Siang-Yang, and Yiu-Meng Toh. "The Effectiveness of Church-Based Lay Counselors: A Controlled Outcome Study." *Journal of Psychology and Christianity* 16, no. 3 (1997): 260–267.

Tautges, Paul. *Counsel One Another: A Theology of Personal Discipleship.* Leominster, Great Britain: Day One, 2009.

———. *Counsel Your Flock: Fulfilling Your Role as a Teaching Shepherd.* Leominster, Great Britain: Day One, 2009.

Tripp, Paul David. *Instruments in the Redeemer's Hands.* Phillipsburg, NJ: P&R, 2002.

Viars, Stephen. *Loving Your Community: Proven Practices for Community-Based Outreach Ministry.* Grand Rapids, MI: Baker, 2020.

Warren, Rick. *The Purpose-Driven Church: Every Church Is Big in God's Eyes.* Grand Rapids, MI: Zondervan, 1995.

Welch, Edward T. *Caring for One Another: 8 Ways to Cultivate Meaningful Relationships.* Wheaton, IL: Crossway, 2018.

———. *Side by Side: Walking with Others in Wisdom and Love.* Wheaton, IL: Crossway, 2015.

Whitney, Donald S. *Spiritual Disciplines for the Christian Life.* Colorado Springs: NavPress, 2014.

ABOUT THE AUTHOR

Bob Kellemen, ThM, PhD is the Dean of Students and Professor of Biblical Counseling at Faith Bible Seminary in Lafayette, Indiana. Bob is also the founder and CEO of RPM Ministries, through which he speaks, writes, and consults on biblical counseling and Christian living. Dr. Kellemen served as the founding Executive Director of the Biblical Counseling Coalition. For seventeen years, he was the founding Chairman of and Professor in the MA in Christian Counseling and Discipleship department at Capital Bible Seminary in Lanham, Maryland. Bob has pastored four churches and equipped biblical counselors in all four. Bob and his wife, Shirley, have been married for more than forty years; they have two adult children, Josh and Marie, one daughter-in-law, and three granddaughters. Dr. Kellemen is the author of twenty-three books, including *Gospel-Centered Counseling*, *Gospel Conversations*, *Gospel-Centered Marriage Counseling*, and *Gospel-Centered Family Counseling*.

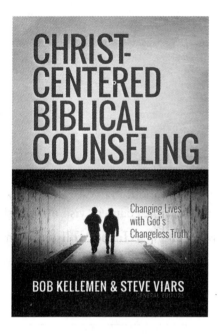

Christ-Centered Biblical Counseling is a comprehensive resource that will help you understand how to minister from God's truth to change lives. With the cumulative wisdom of almost 40 contributors with exceptional credentials and experience, you'll discover a valuable model for counseling that explains...

The Why of Biblical Counseling

- *Why* the Bible is sufficient and relevant for addressing every issue we face
- *Why* biblical counseling is so effective in helping people face life's struggles in Christ's strength

The How of Biblical Counseling

- *How* you can lead struggling, hurting people to the hope and strength available only in Christ
- *How* to counsel in a way that is Christ-centered and God-glorifying

Every chapter provides a wonderful blend of theological wisdom and practical expertise, and is written to be accessible to everyone who wishes to extend Christ's love to others— pastors, church leaders, counseling practitioners, instructors, lay people, and students.

To learn more about Harvest House books and
to read sample chapters, visit our website:

www.HarvestHousePublishers.com

HARVEST HOUSE PUBLISHERS
EUGENE, OREGON